Falling in love with CA Bar Exam

A layperson also plays an important role

By Hellas Leung, Esq

Contents

Preface

This book is for everyone who plans to, who is thinking of, or hesitating about, as well as all U.S. students who are currently going to the law schools and whoever who preparing to take the bar exam in California. For logic, skills of writing analysis, formulating arguments and defenses, as well as drawing conclusions would be universal for all law school students. (But the book mainly focuses on the law students in the United States.) Or if you just barely passed the law school exams or graduated a decade ago but have been busy taking care of your children and would like to strengthen your basic skills in writing essays before you sign up for another bar exam, this book would be desirable for you.

In addition, for people who have lawyer friends or have family members just beginning their law school adventures, this book would also help them to understand the mindset and mentality of future lawyers, as well as the languages, the words, the terms and the adverbs lawyers always use. Or if you think you do not understand the stresses your loved ones are going through, you can also read the book to get a sip of his or her pain.

There are so many outlines and sample essays on the market, but merely reciting all of them may not help you pass the bar if you still do not know what is wrong with your own writing. This book would be the solution for repeated failures or constant low scores for law school essays.

There are four big sections in the book: (1) words for laypeople who live around the law students or attorneys, or who are the friends or the family members of the law students; (2) skills for all law school students in the U.S.; (3) essay writing skills for CA bar exam takers and repeaters; (4) skills for handling CA Performance Test (PT).

Section 1

For laypeople around the law students or attorneys

1) The laypeople also play an important role

This book is called "Falling in Love with CA Bar Exam." Why would I reserve one chapter, and also the very first chapter to the laypeople? That is because lawyers and also future lawyers are facing many laypeople in their daily lives, including strangers they meet on the street and their loved ones who never go to law school. Before they pass the bar exam, the laypeople could be a source of support or extra stress. How they act or respond matters to law students who are still struggling for success.

Asking about the exam result is actually creating stress for exam-takers

Before I passed the bar, my mother always asked me about the exam results. I told her many times not to ask me this question anymore. She would definitely know the positive result if I passed. I must put the good news on my Facebook page immediately. I would not be able to resist the temptation of making the public announcement of my late-coming achievement. Nevertheless, she did not listen to me. She kept asking the same question over and over again to fulfill her own curiosity. In fact, the question could be the second harm created to any failing exam takers.

When you fall in love with someone, people around you will become external forces that somehow affect you and your lover. That would be the same as struggling to pass the bar exam. When we are fighting a battle that could last longer than a decade, it would be hard for us to ignore everyone around us unless we live alone inside a castle in the mountains, far away from any businesses and residential areas. Therefore, I reserve the first chapter for the laypeople around the future lawyers. You are the source of our mental support. Please do not create more stress for the bar exam takers. We have enough stress from the bar exam itself. What we need from you is encouragement. If you do not know how to express your support verbally, please remain silent.

Before we pass, we are like falling into infinity or having eternal doom. If you do not understand why we suffer and what we are suffering from, please read this book to feel the stresses we have been going through for years.

2) The path to success is rough and bumpy

Many people like to complain about how expensive the attorney fees are, but they fail to acknowledge that the path for us to success is rough and bumpy. Before a law student passes the bar, the stresses they have gone through are deemed cycles of torture.

A layperson may try a mock bar exam herself.

If you want to feel the stress of our exam sessions, you can simply write three essays on different topics (could be about anything you are interested in or familiar with) for three hours without a break, and each essay has to be at least six pages long. Even though the topic is something you are good at, you will be exhausted after three hours; and then, in the afternoon, please continue to write two more essays on any topics of the same length, plus reading at least ten pages of information of any issue and writing your standpoint on the issue, with the facts you find from the big stack of information to back up your argument.

Then you can also do 200 MBEs questions on another day. You do not have to know the rules or make the correct choices. Simply read it and make a choice from the perspective of a person without legal training. You would have to finish reading the 100 questions and four choices available for each question in three hours. Then, you would get a rough sense of our stresses.

Expressing emotional support to a future lawyer

If you have a family member struggling with the bar exam, please say something positive and pleasant to him or her. If you do not know how to convey your messages of support, mere silence, handing him or her a cup of coffee, or tapping his or her back would also be helpful, or simply hanging out or taking a walk with him or her, and chatting with him or her about anything other than the exam. Expressing emotional support to a future lawyer does not require any legal knowledge.

3) Bar exam repeaters may have to isolate themselves Before they pass

"Bar exam syndrome"

Bar exam repeaters feel so helpless and lonely when they are questioned by their family members about their failures. Their loved ones need to be considerate of their feelings, even though laypeople may not understand the difficulties of exam takers. The takers are almost driven crazy by the exam. No, it is not correct. In fact, some of us could become crazy already after multiple failures, since stresses do not just come from our heads, but also from the bosses and colleagues of our full-time jobs who are complaining about our constant time-off requests, which happen twice a year. The cells of craziness are accumulated inside our bodies in every one of our organs, including our intestines, our stomachs, our hearts, and our brains. Therefore, when we are stressed out, we may have stomach pain or cannot digest well. We look normal to the regular public most of the time, but once we hear the word "bar," even if we are talking about the bar for liquor or chocolate bars as snacks, we would think about how intimidating the bar exam is. This is called "bar exam syndrome." However, the good news is that once you have passed the bar exam and sworn in to be a licensed attorney, all the symptoms mentioned above will go away.

Every failure made me feel like falling into reincarnation.

Every time I failed, I felt like I fell into reincarnation again because I had to study everything all over again. Every failure is one "death" for me: wasting so much money and sacrificing so much time but getting no achievement and nothing else but frustration. Then, I would have to go back to reincarnation.

Please do not use the words "stupid," "lazy," or "dumb" to describe law school graduates who have not passed the bar exam yet. Many repeaters have received very high scores for their essays. Passing the bar would require the takers to perform well in each of the four exam sessions. Any discomfort from our bodies could jeopardize our performances on the exams, such as headache, stomach pain or menstruation.

Not asking or questioning would help.

When we are counting down to the announcement of the exam result, all bar exam takers would feel nervous and stressful. If we fail the exam, we would not want people around us to ask too much or talk too much because it is not going to help.

Almost every time I checked my bar exam result, I hid myself somewhere. Whatever it was, good news or bad news, I did not want anyone around me to criticize or question my ability. I may need personal space to drop my tears or review my scores in every part of the exam. I would like to enjoy happiness for the high scores and find out why and how to improve the portion for low scores.

Getting rid of distractions

Creating a quiet study environment for yourself - Studying inside a motel room

When I prepared for my bar exam, a huge amount of money was spent on hotel or motel rooms in different cities in Northern California. The one farthest could be about a 1.5-hour ride from my home. It was a study trip for me, which was a combination of essay writing and a mental break from my work and my husband. I worked five days a week, but I also needed to study on the weekend, with the desire to rest and relax. I wrote at least one or two essays when I was staying in the hotel room and also walked around the hotel area after I checked out. Then, I also went to buy groceries before I headed back home.

The cheapest motel room was still costly. Most of my salary earned in those two years of bar preparation was spent on motel rooms. You might say you could stay home studying. Yes. That is true. But my husband always interrupted me in the middle when I was writing my essay. He thought he just asked me one or two simple questions, so it should not matter, but I wanted to fully focus on the world of the scenario created by the fact patterns of essays. I would feel grumpy if someone bothered me. In fact, before I grasped the skill of analyzing, anything could distract me. But after I have passed the bar, I think I can handle the distraction much better because I am clear about what I need to write in each paragraph.

Besides hotel rooms, my income was also spent on tutoring and buying different preparation courses. In other words, I was unable to save any money in those years of preparation. Sometimes, I even had to tap my husband's income to pay for this and that. If I continue to fail, I think that would be devastating for both of us. We both have to cry because of the loss of time and money. Fortunately, and probably because I fully focused on study and practice, the time period of struggling for bar exam success finally ended. There would be no more "eternal doom" for me!

My advice is: Please try to stay away from your family members, siblings or lovers if they do not provide any or the appropriate type of mental support; or mentally, they appear to support you, but physically, they create noises or mental stresses. The qualities of our own emotional states are important, so we have to get rid of anyone around us jeopardizing our emotional state, or we have to affirmatively stay away from them.

Going to the library

Going to the library would be another choice. I did not go to the library very often when I prepared for the bar just because of the requirement to wear masks: During the pandemic, the library required people to wear masks all the time when they stayed inside the library, and I felt so uncomfortable about that. If they have rescinded such a requirement now, writing essays in the library would be a good idea.

4) Please be nice on our long journey to success

Who are ideal companions?

If you are planning to have a long road trip, like driving from San Francisco to Los Angeles, who would you like to invite to be your companions?

To be practically useful and helpful, companions with driver's licenses would be the best because all of you can take turns driving; if all of your family members or friends cannot drive for some reason, either they are too young or their licenses get suspended, who would you invite then?

I would like to invite someone who has a lot of jokes in his head then I would be able to enjoy my ride, which is going to last for six to eight hours. I would also invite someone who tends to be supportive if I get lost, not those moaning when you cannot find the way out. That would be very disgusting to have someone keep complaining next to you when he or she cannot help at all.

A law student needs someone supportive on her journey to success

That would be the same as whom we need in our long journeys of becoming attorneys. We need someone to be able to share our pain and difficulties, and who is also humorous and supportive.

Who are you if you do not pass the bar?

From the date I signed up for law school till the date I took the attorney's oath, it took about nine years. If I pass both the baby bar and the general bar on my first attempt, this long wait would be shortened. But for probably half of the bar exam takers, it could take a decade before they succeed. Some of them may even struggle from their middle ages till retirement ages.

Let us review the long journey of our struggle: After we have signed up for the law school, we would first identified to be law school students; after we have finished the law school curriculum, we would then be identified to be law school graduates. But two or three years after our graduation, how would we identify ourselves or how would we be identified by others if we still have not passed the bar yet? A glorified term can be future lawyers or attorneys-to-be; Or if you are working for a law firm, you would be called a legal assistant or a paralegal, But if you are working for a grocery store or driving for a ride-sharing company to make a living, or delivering for Uber Eats, it would be clear that you are nothing if you do not pass the bar exam.

Why would you spend a huge amount of time and money?

You already set the goal to be a licensed attorney when you signed up for the J.D. program.

If you just want to be a paralegal, you do not need to take MPRE or go through the moral character exam. Your investment of time and effort can be spent elsewhere, achieving other positive outcomes, or you can spend the same amount of money enjoying a luxurious vacation in Europe.

Multiple failures are like bones getting stuck inside your throat

Just because of the huge investments we have already made, our psychological state before passing the bar is very close to depression, especially after multiple failures. It is just like you have swallowed a big piece of bone into your throat, but it does not go down to your digestion system, and you cannot throw it up, either. You cannot voice out your frustration. You can tap on the table, or step hard on the floor with your legs to tell others that you are suffering, but I am not sure whether others are interested in finding out what is wrong with you.

If you are able to cry, your mental condition would be more optimistic because you can find a way to release your frustration; but if you fidget with the failure and cannot flush the frustration out from your body with teardrops, or through sweating, the problem could be worse.

That is why I said the laypeople around future lawyers also play an important role: whether you will find one more successful attorney around you in future, or a person with lunacy or insanity, your words and attitudes could make a huge difference. Please do not treat all our peers with cynicism.

5) Is it difficult to get along with a lawyer friend?

Are you interested in trying to see things from the perspective of a lawyer?

Disagreement with lawyer friends?

Do you have a lawyer friend or spouse, or sibling or any lawyer family members…?What do you feel about them?

You might find it difficult to communicate with the lawyer friends, a lawyer spouse or lawyer family members when the ways they speak, think or perceive the world are so different from the ways you do.

Lawyers are trained to make decisions in a mechanical and rational manner

When you express your thoughts to your lawyer friends, and believe that something is apparently right or wrong, they may not agree with you. You might think that they just like to argue, but I do not think they would like to do this when they have already walked out of their law offices or the courtrooms. They are not interested in arguing with you at all after office hours. You might find that they are difficult to get along with, but in fact, they are just trained to have a different thinking mechanism.

Attorneys analyze and make decisions in mechanical and rational manners, rather than doing that on impulse. Also, they are supposed to have higher emotional intelligence.

Example: Hit and run

If you witness an incident of hit-and-run with a lawyer friend, his or her focus is more likely to be recording the license plate number of the driver, or checking if surveillance cameras are installed nearby, while everyone is stunned or screaming. His or her professionalism would enable him or her to collect or contribute required information to help the investigation. When everyone gossips about an incident, an attorney could be clam enough to collect required information and make logical inference. An attorney is certain that "hearsay" and the eyewitnesses' opinions about the incident does not matter, but the objective facts and information.

However, when an attorney is also a witness, he or she may not represent any of the parties involved.

6) Is your lawyer friend talking to you in the manner similar to questioning the criminals?

When your lawyer friend asks you a few questions for clarification, you may feel uncomfortable that she seems to treat you like a criminal. But in fact, she just needs more concrete information for her to fully understand what happened, and you can avoid her further questioning by first making your descriptions clear enough.

When you talk to a lawyer friend……

(a) Please avoid providing your own subjective conclusions

First of all, avoid telling the lawyer friend your own conclusion. That is because your conclusion may not be the same as the lawyers 'conclusion, and the way you conclude is very likely to be different from how a lawyer would conclude.

Please stick with objective facts. The adjectives you insert into your description are not going to help your lawyer friend to understand what happened.

Example: "Being cheated" could just mean "unsatisfactory" to some people

Subjective conclusion:

A man claims that he is "being cheated" by his attorney.

Objective fact:

But what he actually means could be:

He does not get everything he wants from the settlement agreement, but his attorney believes that is the most favorable terms or outcome for him under current laws.

(b) Filter out all glamorous adjectives and learn the pure facts

Glamorous adjectives are only the "coating" of boring facts. Those adjectives would make the dull facts look more appealing than they actually are, and those adjectives would also be barriers stopping you from realizing and understanding the raw facts.

*Please state objective facts rather than your own subjective perception.

Example: The glamor has nothing to do with the singer

The following is the conversation among D, E, and F.

D: "Wow. It was exciting, glamorous and elegant. I was thrilled."

E: "What happened?"

D: "The most popular male singer showed up at the grand opening ceremony of the romantic restaurant."

F: "He is a 17-year-old boy who just quit the school and became a singer. He was popular among teenage girls as well as young ladies, and he was invited to the grand opening ceremony for the French restaurant. It was a big investment for the restaurant owner."

E: "But the glamor has nothing to do with the songs or the singing technique of the young singer. Right?"

F: "I think so. An amateur singer at karaoke may sing better than he does."

D: "But the opening ceremony was an unusual occasion to me."

Explanation:

When D talked about how he felt the event, he used many adjectives: "exciting, glamorous and elegant," but such a description indicates nothing to E or F because that was only D's personal opinion: D describes the singer to be "the most popular male singer," but F describes him to be "a 17-year-old boy who just quit the school and became a singer."

Moreover, the perceptions of D, E and F are also different: D thinks that the opening ceremony for the French restaurant is a big event, and F thinks that the restaurant is a big investment by the owner, but E thinks that the glamour has nothing to do with the talent of the singer. In other words, the association of the big ceremony with the singer would not make the singer's singing standard higher than his real standard.

(c) Do not add your own judgment or speculation

Secondly, please do not add your own guess, judgment, speculation or prediction to your description. That is because what you imagine or guess is based on your own family history, education, personal experiences, personality, etc, and all factors mentioned above have nothing to do with the nature of the incident.

Example: Oops! She forgets today is Halloween!

A middle-aged woman said, "The man is so abnormal, insane and silly that he wears a horrible mask to scare me. He is an adult, not a kid anymore."

But the fact could be: Today is Halloween and the mask is the man's costume. She thinks he is crazy because she completely forgets today is Halloween.

Conclusion:

In a nutshell, your reaction to the particular incident is not going to help categorizing or determining the severity of the incident.

(d) State the acts in sequence instead of connecting them with conjunctions indicating the inter-relationship of the acts

Describe the series of acts in terms of time sequence rather than using conjunctions such as "because." That is because act A happened right before act B does not mean B happens because of A.

Example: Anthony resigned from the job after he found that his boss did not trust him

Descriptions with "cause" and "outcome"

A layperson may say: "Anthony left his job because he was found stealing money."

Facts:

The boss accused Anthony of stealing his money without any evidences. Anthony then resigned from his job because his boss did not trust him.

Descriptions in sequence:

"Before Anthony resigned from his job, his boss thought that Anthony might have stolen his money but there were no evidences. Anthony did not want to work for a boss who did not trust him."

Thus, Anthony's resignation was due to the ungrounded accusation of stealing money, but has nothing to do with the likelihood of stealing money by Anthony.

(e) Handle second-hand information with reservation

Fifthly, second-hand information is unreliable because the interpretation of any acts could be biased, outdated, fabricated, or deviated from the truth because of different reasons, including the ability to recall and narrate with the appropriate vocabulary. Do not completely trust the person's words when someone tells you this and that. Stick to what you saw and heard, not what someone narrated to you.

Example: Kyle's income at the Korean restaurant

Gabriella, Nicole, Phoebe and Querida are sitting and chatting in the cafeteria.

Gabriella: "Kyle said he earned $40 only for the eight-hour work at the Korean restaurant in San Francisco, California, according to his mother."

Nicole: "So he earns merely $5 per hour? That is too low."

Phoebe: "Kyle's aunt said Kyle also has a basic hourly pay of $16."

Querida: "That is not bad, then."

Nicole: "When did you see Kyle?"

Gabriella: "I did not see him for two years. "

Phoebe: "I just heard everything from his aunt."

Rachel and Stella just come in and then sit down with them together.

Rachel: "His aunt died three months ago."

Nicole: "What you heard may not be the latest then."

Querida: "We may all have dinner at the Korean restaurant tonight to see Kyle for more updated information."

Stella: "The Korean restaurant permanently closed about two months ago."

Gabriella: "Perhaps I can call Kyle tonight after dinner."

Teresa just walks by.

Teresa: "Kyle moved to New York last week. New York State is three hours ahead of California. Just call him tomorrow."

<u>Explanation:</u>

When you do not have first-hand information, almost nothing from others can be trusted. Even though the person is honest, he or she may not have the full picture or the complete truth, or what is known already turns outdated.

Herc, what G and P know is second-hand information. Some information is outdated because G did not see Kyle for two years. His aunt, the information source, already passed away three months ago, meaning the information was not updated for three months.

Furthermore, the Korean restaurant they talked about was already permanently closed, and Kyle also moved from California to New York.

7) When you talk to a lawyer friend, specifications are required to avoid misunderstanding

In order not to be questioned or challenged later, we always have to specify what we want or need. When you talk to a lawyer or a future lawyer, he or she would like to get specific information in order to fully understand what you mean.

Example: What kind of water you would like to have?

Here is the scenario in a restaurant:

Waiter: "What would you like to have, sir?"

Customer: "I need some time to read the menu. May I have water first?"

Waiter: "Do you prefer running water or bottled water?"

Customer: "Bottled water, please."

Waiter: "Do you want sparkling water, spring water or distilled water?"

Customer: "Sparkling water, please."

Waiter: "Do you prefer sparkling water at room temperature or from the refrigerator?"

Customer: "At room temperature, please. Do you have more questions? I am really thirsty. "

Waiter: "No more, sir. I know exactly what you want. The bottled sparkling water at room temperature will come in a moment."

Explanation:

If the customer is a regular customer, the first time he answered would be: "I would like to have bottled sparkling water at room temperature." Then, it would save a lot of time, as well as back-and-forth questions and answers.

Assumption vs Specifications

Being requested to provide very specific instructions could be difficult for some people, especially for people who are uncertain about the exact situation. The lawyer friend or a friend of a lawyer-like personality may guide you to be more specific.

Wrong assumptions would lead to misunderstandings

Without specific details, people would tend to make default assumptions according to their own preferences or backgrounds of different demographics.

Example: Preparing food for a party

Bobby wants to hold a party for twenty people. Bobby asks her two teenage friends, Cherry and Danny, to prepare food. Cherry is supposed to buy food, and Danny is supposed to buy beverages.

Cherry gets chocolate icebreakers, chips, cookies, and mango pudding; Danny buys coke, iced tea, mocha and orange juice; Bobby also prepares a kettle for hot water.

Eventually, Bobby brings twenty seniors to the party. They can almost eat or drink nothing purchased by Cherry and Danny.

Bobby made twenty cups of hot water in total for all the seniors.

Without specifications, Cherry and Danny have assumed that the twenty people are of the same age as they are.

Conclusion

It is hard for the coordinators to prepare for a party without specifications.

Misunderstanding can be avoided at the upfront

Example: Preparing dinner for vegetarians

The wife receives a phone call from her husband in the morning. The husband, who is a clerk in the trade company, tells his wife that his two supervisors will go to their house for dinner tonight. The wife spends five hours buying ingredients, preparing meat, marinating them with seasonings, and cooking. Shrimps, lobsters, steaks, pork stews, and roasted chicken are served with steamed rice at the dinner. However, the two supervisors do not eat anything on the table but steamed rice only. They tell the wife of the clerk that they are, in fact, vegetarians.

Conclusion:

If the two supervisors are clear and specific to the husband upfront, and the husband tells his wife in the morning, much effort can be saved by the wife of the clerk.

8) Laws are just rules

A world of various rules

We are living in a world of various rules. In order to survive, we have to accommodate different rules: if you want to travel to a country that requires a visa, you have to apply for the visa in order to enter the country; if you want to apply for a job requesting a copy of your school transcript, you have to fill out the forms to request a copy of the transcript from your school and also pay for the copy of the transcript.

Facts have to be presented in a way to fits the rule

Laws are just the rules for the order and safety of society, and lawyers are just people trained to practice laws. They are not as perverted or unattainable as people might imagine them to be.

Many people wrongfully think that lawyers like to use perverted logic or twist the facts unethically. But in fact, the lawyers just know how to organize the facts accordingly to fit the rules set by others on many occasions. Presenting the facts in a way favorable to oneself is not inherently wrong or unethical.

Example: Job interview advertisement

Job position 1: Phone operator at Men's Club:

"We are hiring people with sweet voices."

The rule here: The voices of the candidates have to be sweet.

Your task as a candidate: To show that you have a sweet voice. (In order to get hired)

Job position 2: Receptionist at Larry's Law Firm

"We are hiring people who can deal with our clients in a professional manner."

The rule here: The manner of dealing with people has to be professional.

Your task as a candidate: To show that you have professionalism. (In order to get hired)

Job position 3: Counselor for international students at San Francisco Private College

Advertisement:

"We are hiring people who have rich experiences dealing with people from different countries or cultures."

The rule here: Applicants need to have rich experiences dealing with people from different countries or cultures.

Your task as a candidate: To show that you come from a melting pot of various cultures and diversities and know how to help them solve problems. (In order to get hired)

Conclusion:

Emphasizing your own strengths in order to show the prospective employer that you are a "good fit" for the job for the purpose of getting hired is not unethical. That is the way to win the game.

9) A lawyer is not a magician

Sometimes, people think that the lawyers are able to turn the impossibility into a possibility. In fact, they are just trained to be more sensitive to trivial facts and are able to explain the uncertainty with logic or raise doubt. They are more capable than untrained people to spot the parts which are unreasonable, or illogical and the existence of other more plausible possibilities.

Do not make unrealistic expectations

Please do not make unrealistic expectations of an attorney.

If you lost a case and the deadline for appeal has passed, attorneys are very unlikely to be able to help you. Or if a senior would like to make an elder abuse claim in financial matters, but when the alleged fraud happened, he was only 55 years old, then there would be no "elder abuse" claim, even if he is currently a senior. This is not something an attorney can change.

The trick is the analysis

The lawyers do not only know the rules, but also have skills in analyzing.

Do not be misled by the firmly entrenched first impression

Example: A person with a home vs. a Homeless person

When you are walking on a street, a lady in a hat, with a damaged sleeveless blouse exposing two big arms with much fat, and in a dirty pant, wearing peep toe shoes, comes to you suddenly. She told you: "I am pretty. I have dressed up. I look better than you do."

You stare at her from her head to her toes. Your lips move upwards with ridicule. You are not persuaded by what she told you.

You look at yourself in a big mirror. You are wearing a business dress suit, with black leggings. You think that the words "pretty" and "dress up" would only apply to you, not her.

Then the lady stands next to you. Two of you are looking at the mirror on the wall together.

The lady: "From a certain distance, you look elegant. You are in a business dress suit." You feel flattered when you hear that. "But please take a closer look."

Then you find that there is a hole in your black leggings. You do not even know when it was torn. You also find that your leather shoes are dusty. Besides, the metal part of your belt is rusty.

The lady: "I believe you have a home."

You nod your head.

The lady: "That means you have a wardrobe, and you have an iron; You might also have a washer and a dryer. "

You nod your head again.

The lady: "But your shirt has wrinkles; Your skirt has some dots, which could be dirt; Your hair is not combed properly; Some of your hair sticks out."

Then you look in the mirror. What she just said is correct.

The lady: "I sleep on the street with a tent every night. I hang my clothes on a robe with two ends fastened on two big trees. I am wearing a pink blouse and it is the most pretty blouse I have. There is a hole at the back, but it looks perfect on the front. My pants are dirty at the bottom only, but that is the best I can do without a washer. I comb my hair this morning and I also put on this new hat."

You look at her again.

"I look better than you do," she said.

You drop your head and walk away.

Explanation:

Regardless of who actually looks more pretty, do you get the point? When the homeless lady first told you her conclusion, you are not persuaded and you might think that is so ridiculous. It would be impossible for a homeless person to look better than you do.

However, after she explains and you take all circumstances into consideration, you might agree with her: You sleep on the bed, but she sleeps on the street; you use the washer and dryer but she just hangs her clothes on the rope; you failed to comb your hair properly, but she combed well, and she is also wearing a new hat. While you have more resources than she does, you are wearing a pair of leggings with holes, a pair of leather shoes with dust and a belt with rust.

Certainly, you can argue that you have a full-time job and she does not, so she has more time to take care of the trivial tasks while you are being overwhelmed by your stressful job.

However, the point here is not what to wear or how you look. It is about the magical power of persuasive explanation and analysis. Do not be misled by the firmly entrenched first impression. You have to look into details and consider all circumstances.

10) Do not lie to a lawyer and expect her that she would be fooled

Hiding from or lying to a lawyer

Many clients like to tell partial stories to the attorneys and keep the most important part or the secrets to themselves, but at the same time, they expect the attorneys to represent them and fight for what they want. Clients do not tell the whole truth, probably because they merely want the attorney for a particular purpose, so they do not think the attorneys would need to know everything. Also, there might be some things involving their own privacy, involving their secrets or their shameful acts, so they try to hide or deny.

Sorting out facts should be the task of an attorney

Whatever the reasons are, clients have already made their decisions on what facts are relevant and what facts are irrelevant by filtering the information, which could be a legal decision regarding strategies. In other words, the clients also take away the task from the lawyers. By hiding partial truth, clients are also deprived of the chance to sort out facts or select particular favorable facts to help the clients from the lawyers.

Inconsistencies or unreasonableness may reveal the truth

However, if you lie to a lawyer, or lie in your teeth with no compunction, do not expect they would be cheated by you, without any doubt, even though they may not expressly point that out to you. From the perspective of attorneys, it is not difficult to spot the inconsistencies or unreasonableness of what attorneys are told. Being sensitive to the unknown facts, which could make a big difference in the outcome of a case, is exactly the skill all attorneys are trained to have from the law school education or the bar exam. Please do not try to undermine the value of the legal education the attorneys have. The attorneys may or may not follow up with the inconsistencies, depending on how relevant it is to the main issue of the case.

Nevertheless, even if the attorneys choose not to follow up with the clients or avoid directly asking the clients, do not think that they would not know you are trying to hide. There is so much information and data online now. Unless you hide your secret under your own bed, it would not be difficult for your attorneys to find that out in their own ways.

Example: Running away from the car crash scene

Take a traffic incident as a hypothetical example: One may tell his attorney that he ran away from the scene and left his car on the scene just because he was scared and he does not speak English. However, as an attorney, she must call the CHP for reports to understand where his car was located when his car was found, and also the positions of other cars involved in the incident. The details of the report may corroborate what the client said but may also refute or be contrary to his description.

Since he ran away, there would be no way for anyone to verify later that he took drugs or alcohol on the day of the incident. But other information discovered may lead his attorney to disbelieve him and not even want to take his case.

Due to the attorney-client privilege, no real examples can be given here.

11) Laypeople's logic vs. Lawyer's logic

Leaving doubt on others 'words

When a friend tells you something sincerely, would you completely believe it? Assuming he is telling the truth from the bottom of his heart, I would still have doubt about his words due to the subjectiveness and hopefulness of everyone: People tend to choose to believe in what they hope to be true, regardless of the likelihood of occurrences.

Example: Wrong perception of love or friendship

Subjective thoughts could be wrong

Subjective thoughts usually play a big part in love relationships, but the perception could be wrong. When someone single in marital status tells me he thinks that a girl is "falling in love with him" or wants him to be her boyfriend, I would directly ask him based on what facts he would draw such a conclusion. In my opinion, sometimes a man just subjectively or unilaterally wants a particular lady to be his girlfriend, so whatever the girl says or does, he would interpret the words or the act as an implication of "falling in love with him."

Love also requires "logic"

Even though love relationships have many irrational aspects, logic is still required from the perspective of others to prove its existence. It is just like we need wedding ceremonies or marriage certificates to objectively verify the intention of someone to get married to another. If you just talk about your desire or your plan but never take real action, I would have reservations about your "love."

Merely reading facial expressions may not be a good indicator of people's responses from a legal perspective

"Reading eyebrows, eyes and forehead."

Reading facial micro-expressions of people would help you reveal their emotions, including anger, disgust, fear, happiness, sadness and surprise. This is also the "people skills" we need in order to survive in the workplace. In Chinese, reading people's facial expressions to realize their thoughts or preferences is known as "reading eyebrows, eyes, and forehead." Its actual meaning is not literal but the totality of facial expressions and behaviors.

"Facial expressions are not unambiguous"

However, reading facial expressions may not be a good indicator of people's intentions from a legal perspective because they are not unambiguous. There is big room for the opposing side to argue that is not exactly what they mean.

Example: Smiling in a contract negotiation

For example, when Party A and Party B discuss a contract, party A smiles. Does smiling mean accepting the terms? The laypeople may say yes, but the slight movement of the lips is not equivalent to consent in the legal standard.

On a social occasion, in order to blend in oneself with the rest of the group, most people would try not to disagree with almost anything people talk about unless the context is really offensive. Thus, the lack of disagreement or argument is not equivalent to genuine agreement.

Nodding does not necessarily mean consent

Reactions such as nodding could mean consent or merely expressing that "I heard that" without any implication of agreement or disagreement. Or I believe you just talk about something unrelated to me, and there was no need for me to agree or disagree, but for courtesy, I just nod my head to show that I am actually listening.

Conclusion

If you need instructions or get consent from an attorney, you'd better get a verbal expression or in black-and-white to avoid misunderstanding.

12) Argument is a kind of "logic clash"

Everyone has logic

Everyone has logic in his or her mind, regardless of one's age or education level, though you may not agree with their logic. For example, a boy may think that having ice cream is the most important to him. If you drop his ice cream, it means you ruin his day; a salesperson may think that making the maximum sales is the most important, so he would treat the customers well and please them, regardless of how disgusting those faces are; a taxi driver may think driving for a longer time and longer distance would allow him to earn more, so he may choose to drive a longer route to a particular destination. These are their own logic, and it is highly likely that a lot of people would not agree.

Generation gaps are somehow related to logics

People in different generations may have difficulties agreeing on an issue, partly because they are from different generations. People from different generations tend to have different dream lives, dream jobs, and dream spouses.

In my parents' or grandparents' generations, people "must" marry and "must" have children. Without a spouse or children, others would look at you with much sympathy. They almost want to label you as "disabled." But this logic does not make sense for the current young people. They simply want to live happily. They like to enjoy themselves as individuals rather than taking the whole family's wishes, expectations, and glorifications as lifelong burdens.

"Enabled" vs. "Disabled"

But in my generation, marriage is not the only option for lifestyle, and may not even be more desirable than leading a single life. As a single person, you can make your own decisions on almost everything, but when you are married, your decisions would somehow affect your spouse, so you must get his or her consent before you take any action. Hence, being single, in fact, "enables" you to act according to your own preferences, as opposed to the label "disabled" imposed on you by the last generation.

The lack of freedom or autonomy after marriage could be offset by joy and warmth if you have great fun in your marriage life; if not, why bother to seek a spouse? (I am not single. But I would not set a goal to marry just for marriage. That should be something happening naturally, and I should not and would not make the process like job-hunting.)

In my grandparents' generations, once a female has grown up, marrying and bearing children would be the default lifestyle, and if you deviate from it, you almost have to explain "why" to your family to a satisfactory level. If you do not have your own lovers, the old people would like to arrange "blind dates" for you. The deep-rooted rule in their minds is having a family and having the next generation would be the best lifestyle, but my own rule is enjoying myself, or enjoying every day, or pursuing my own achievement would be the best lifestyle. The old people think that having children means that you will have someone to rely on physically, mentally and financially when you grow old. But is it going to be true? Is it guaranteed? If having someone to rely on is your sole purpose of bearing children, then most likely, you would be disappointed.

Live beyond the frames of traditions

In a cyber generation with so many products or services of new technologies, such as self-driving cars, I cannot accept people's overly traditional views. The traditions could act as frames of reference for us to build our futures, but we do not have to be confined by the frames, or we can even go beyond the frames.

Certainly, it is almost impossible to change the concepts of other people. Thus, the best way to avoid arguments or to handle the generation gaps would be to avoid logic clashes, meaning not to talk about topics that would certainly cause conflicts. Just talk about where to eat, what to eat, the security guards of your residential areas, or the policies enforced by the government. The government departments or officials are always the common enemies of the general public, or at least a group of people because the government is aimed to serve the general public, and definitely, their policies would not be pleasant to everyone.

Shift the blame to someone outside of your family

In a nutshell, the solution to the argument would be simply shifting the focus from individuals within families to individuals outside of the families or even to the government departments when you foresee or encounter a logic clash in your family. At least you would have temporary and brief peace of mind at home.

Insistence on one's own logic

An argument or dispute is a kind of "logic clash" to me when each side insists that what he or she thinks is correct. The differences in logic can be due to each other's personality, value judgment, deeply-rooted concepts, beliefs and notions. If you interpret an argument as a clash of logic, you would understand that you would not be able to change one's own logic overnight. Merely increasing your voice or showing how powerful or robust you are in an argument would not be able to utterly resolve the problem; however, if you are able to develop a solution that would be consistent with both sides' logic, that could successfully resolve the dispute.

A battle of logics

Litigation is also a battle of logic unless one side is totally unreasonable. Both sides would present their arguments with documents and evidence. The judge would favor the side whose logic is more sensible. If your logic is simply based on your personal preferences, but the rest of the world would not accept it, then you are more likely to lose the battle. In other words, if the standard of right and wrong is based on objective standards, you have to use a logic that would be widely accepted; if the standard is based on subjective thought, then you can pull out your weird logic to showcase your distinctive personal thoughts, in order to justify your own behaviors.

13) Be the king or the queen of the logic

What is logic?

Logic is the reasoning conducted or assessed for us to explain or connect the events or incidents.

Nevertheless, we do not always act or speak strictly according to logic.

Logic game/ jokes can be fun

Please provide logically correct answers to the following questions, regardless of other circumstances of the reality:

Let's read the following six logic jokes.

(1) An act possible only after marriage

Q: "What act must we wait till after marriage to do?"

A: "Divorce."

Explanation: If you are just dating or cohabiting with your lover but never marry, then you do not even have the chance to apply for divorce. Getting married is the prerequisite to getting divorced.

(2) Looking for a boyfriend who can drive

A retired and single woman wants to travel around the nation but she does not drive.

"I would like to get a boyfriend who is able to drive. Where can I find it?"

A little boy just walks by and promptly answers her question: "The parking lots."

Explanation: People who pick their cars up from the parking lots must be able to drive, even though they may not own the cars.

(3) Using my own money to satisfy your own preference?

A: "I just bought a new car. It is Lexus IS 250."

B: "But Mercedes Benz is much better. I like it more."

A: "Why would I spend my own money to buy something you like? To satisfy your desire?"

B: "You are right. The most ridiculous part is your own money as opposed to my own preference."

Explanation: Many people like to forcefully exert their own preferences on other people's choices without realizing how ridiculous it would be to expect other people to act to fulfill their own desires.

(4) "Do not enter"

Simon gets ready to leave his workplace at the end of his shift. He sees a sign "Do not enter" on the pole of the street, but he drives forward into the street.

A traffic patrol officer stops Simon and then gives him a driving ticket. Simon asks why, and the patrol officer points to the sign: "Do not enter."

"Yes. I saw it," Simon said. "But I was not entering. Instead, I was exiting because I was trying to leave my office. You do not have a sign: 'Do not exit. ' I did not violate the rule."

Explanation:

In my opinion, the sign "Do not enter" needs to be revised to "Do not drive forward," which would apply to all drivers trying to go in or go out.

(5) Can you shorten your life?

This is a dialogue between an optimistic man (O) and a pessimistic man (P):

P: "The economy is not doing well. Many people are unemployed, and many stores close permanently."

O: "It will recover after a while."

P: "I am sure it would not fully recover for the rest of my life."

O: "Can you shorten your life then?"

Explanation: This is just a joke about logic, not promoting suicide. The pessimist man says he has ascertained that the economy would not fully recover within his life, then the optimistic man responds that the solution could come up earlier if his life ends earlier. He simply focuses on finding a solution as soon as possible.

(6) Do not drink water when you eat spicy food?

This is a dialogue among the father (F), the mother (M) and their five-year-old daughter (D):

F: "I would like to try spicy food tonight."

D: "Spicy! Spicy! Spicy!"

M: "I do not like spicy food."

F: "You can choose to have "mild spicy" when you place the order."

M: "It still irritates my throat, though. Also, it would make my stomach full and my belly swelling."

F: "Why?"

M: "For every bite of spicy food I have, I would drink water once. Drinking too much water in a meal would make me feel too full."

D: "Do not drink water then. Just eat! Spicy! Spicy! Spicy!"

Explanation:

Eating spicy food would always be paired with drinking water or other liquids. Hence, when we have spicy food, our stomachs have to deal with both spicy food and a large amount of water intake. The mother predicts that she will drink a lot of water then her belly will grow bigger. But when the child fully focuses on her mother's concern, which is frequent water intake leading to a swelling belly, the child suggests she simply not drink any water.

Logically, it sounds like the problem gets resolved. Her belly would not grow too big without water. However, it would cause another problem. Her throat would be irritated due to the lack of water after swallowing spicy food. In reality, almost everyone has to drink water and would drink even more than usual when they have spicy food. Apparently, the daughter fails to consider the actual needs of human beings when she makes the suggestion.

Please read the dialogue again: The mother did not explain that she needs to drink water to comfort her throat after having spicy food. She merely said that drinking water would make her feel too full. Thus, from a logical perspective, her daughter's suggestion is not wrong.

Conclusion

<u>Restrictions should be made clear at the upfront</u>

When people bring up a problem and their concerns, they should also point out the restrictions, meaning the proposed solutions would have to take the restrictions into consideration. Do not assume other people must know a particular fact. Here, drinking water in a meal with spicy food sounds like common sense, but the five-year-old daughter fails to realize that. In more complicated situations, not everyone is aware of its limitations or boundaries. In order to come up with a helpful solution, restrictions should be made clear upfront.

Section 2

For prospective law students or all law students in U.S.

1) Potential: Are you a good fit to the law school?

Many students drop out in the first year of law school: Some think the material is too difficult to understand, and some think it is too boring, or the homework and reading assignments are too demanding.

Who has the potential to go to the law school?

In order to succeed in law schools, what characteristics or capabilities do you need to have?

No need to be a bookworm

There can be a variety of possibilities. But you do not need to be a bookworm, or a person with myopia, or wearing a pair of eyeglasses with very thick lenses; and you do not need to be a person who looks very dull or weak, even though you might need to study for eight to twelve hours a day.

Need to be able to handle massive readings and writings

Instead, you have to enjoy writing and reading for sure, or at least you are able to "tolerate" massive readings and writings. That is because in law school curriculums, the reading assignments are more than 100 pages every week, and one or two essays need to be submitted within the same week. The professors would expect you to complete both reading and writing assignments, even though you have a full-time job.

You have to be fully devoted

You have to be open-minded and humble when your writings are being criticized or to be thick-skinned enough when you need to look for help in essays or MBEs. You have to be persistent to work hard towards your goal, regardless of any difficulties. Studying law is not like a hobby for leisure like gardening, or playing guitar. You need to be fully devoted into learning, reading and writing, and ready to give up time for entertainment.

Going to law school is challenging

If you always got high scores from the exams of elementary school, high school, and university, or found that studying was no longer challenging to you when you pursued your bachelor's degree, or you are in fact, very arrogant and believe that you are the best of the best, going to the law school would be a desirable and intense training for you in your life journey.

People with high emotional intelligence would have advantages

Riding an emotional roller coaster

Taking but failing the bar exam is just like riding an emotional roller coaster, which is devastating:

You take time off to prepare for it and take it, put all your time and money resources into it and, make yourself hopeful and wait for the exam results day after day. Eventually, you fail it. All your investments on that particular exam are gone. You made so many sacrifices, but you get nothing. The failure is just like someone gives a slap on your face. It is insulting, but you do not have to kill yourself just because of this. You could get drunk for a few days, hammered, but you must recover from the heavy blow and go back to study.

Do not let your frustration control your path!

If you know how to handle your emotions well, you are more likely to succeed, not just in the legal profession, but in every aspect of your life. Do not let your frustration control your path. That means do not change your destination due to the frustration, but change the ways to reach your destination. You can detour to reach the same place. Frustration is just like the viruses of cold: They might control your body for a few days, but you will recover within one week.

The worst way to handle your emotions would be blaming the State Bar instead. The system set up by the State Bar is not perfect but the obligation of passing the exam is still on the exam takers. We have to improve our abilities to go far beyond the cut score in order not to fail with high scores.

Really want to be an attorney?

You have to be sure you really want to be an attorney. If you just want to make big money or to be successful, being an attorney is not the only option. The path to become an attorney could take away ten years from your life. If being an attorney is just one of your options and you simply like its glory, you could like another career more. Please think seriously before you start investing time, money and effort.

Spending precious resources

Going to the law school and taking exams cost a lot of money. If you are a person at the grassroots level, you need to make sure you invest your money in the right place; if money is no object to you, maybe that does not matter! However, time and energy are still limited resources for everyone, taking the limited amount of time one would have in his or her lifetime into consideration.

Feel proud of the legal profession

You need to be proud of being an attorney. If you do not think the title Esq. is a glorified title, you may give up your dream fast when you are frustrated. But if your dream is to be Esq., you must be able to find ways to overcome all barriers. It is just like when people wait in line for something they like to buy, such as a new Apple iPhone, a new favor of cheesecake, or an on-sale electronic appliance, they would keep waiting with foldable chairs, tents, blankets, even though they feel hungry, tired, and sleepy. But if the store is only giving out free recycle bags and you do not care about them, you will give up waiting once you feel tired.

Ignorance of unnecessary comments

You have to be able to ignore those who spread discouraging words to you, whether they are attorneys or not. Their comments mean nothing to you. They just enjoy being critics when they find you to be a fun topic to talk about.

Able to maintain a steady income

You have to be able to maintain a steady source of income or need to have some savings you are willing to spend or have to be able to get student loans. The tuition, textbooks, reference books, tutoring services, exam fees, and hotel accommodations for the general bar or the baby bar exam all cost money, and the dollar amount is not small to a regular person at the grassroots level. That means even though you are born with great potential to be an attorney, you still have to be able and willing to take odd jobs to create income before you swear in to be an attorney. But if you are born into a wealthy family, then money would not be a concern for you.

Having patience

You have to be patient to wait for the ultimate reward. It would take a long time before you would graduate from law school and pass the bar exam. If you are the kind of person who likes to make money in the morning and spend all of it in the afternoon, then pursuing the dream of attorney may not be a good fit for you. If you need to take the bar multiple times before you pass, studying for a decade without reward would be just like working for a sweatshop for you. You would not receive your rewarding "paycheck" until ten years later.

Did you ever lead a revolution?

Did you ever propose changes to the existing systems, such as a school policy, the employee manual, or the bills, before they were made into law? Did you ever participate in any demonstrations against fee hikes, law changes against undocumented immigrants, or protests urging a “ceasefire” for wars? Or at least signing up to recall a public official?

If you have ever led a revolution of any type or have done the above acts, you appear to have the courage to speak up for yourself or others when things do not seem to be right. I would say you have the potential to be a lawyer. Definitely, you still have a lot to learn before you take the attorney's oath. However, skills can be improved but personalities cannot be changed. If you do not get used to blindly following or listening to the authorities, you could be a good fit to work for the legal profession.

What types of personalities would not fit the legal profession?

"Blind obedience" would not fit

"Blind obedience" is complying with whatever is told to do by a leader, regardless of whether he or she believes what is told is morally or practically correct. If you are an obedient person and never ask why, you would probably be a good fit for the team of police force firefighters rather than an attorney.

Courage to challenge the authorities is required

A future attorney is supposed to possess the traits of not following the majority because the majority could be wrong. You need to have the courage to challenge the big groups, or organizations, or departments of authority. If your parents ever blame you that you are not an obedient child, and you like to advocate for yourself, then probably you also have the potential to be an attorney.

"Don't be carried along by the tide"

I think I am a good fit to the law school because I never like to follow others to do something which I believe is incorrect. There is a Chinese idiom, "Don't be carried along by the tide, " meaning we should not blindly follow others when we do not agree or that does not sound right.

Please do not make decisions for me

Many of my classmates, colleagues or friends would choose to comply with the request of the majority even when they feel uncomfortable. When I was a teenager, some of my classmates signed up to join the singing contest held by the school and forced us to sacrifice our lunch time to practice singing.

But they never asked me for my opinion before they signed up for the contest on behalf of the class. I never said I wanted to join the contest. How could they make a decision on my schedule without asking me? I dislike any acquaintances with controlling personalities.

Celebrations at workplaces

When I worked for a certain organization, many people had different happy events in their lives, such as weddings, baby showers, birthdays, or housewarmings. But not every co-worker was personally close to me, and some were even repugnant to me. If I was close to them, I would certainly buy gifts for them or celebrate with them.

Asking for money contributions sounds like a command

Some of my disgusting coworkers got used to choosing an expensive gift by themselves and merely asked me to contribute my money to the bill without asking me whether I wanted to participate or what gift I would like to buy for the person having happy things. The way they handled it sounded like it was mandatory. Someone even came to my desk and said, "$20, please." It is a command rather than a suggestion.

This arrangement was very disgusting, and many of my colleagues were disgruntled about it. But they did not dare to say anything because those controlling colleagues had the authority to control your work schedule and even recommend you to take desirable or undesirable assignments; most importantly, they were able to sway my manager's decision to adjust my salary level.

For other people who did not expect me to say "no" to their requests for money contributions, they did whatever they could to make me look bad when I chose not to pay for a gift which I never gave consent to buy. I do not think defending my own precious resources is wrong. How can you expect me to sacrifice my family members just because you have a new family member? I would rather spend money on a meal with my own family members. Your wishes cannot be fulfilled at the expense of my family.

Someone else's exertion of her value judgment onto my own value judgment is disgusting.

Everyone spends money on something they think is important or attractive. When you try to take my money away from my wallet, you are actually telling me the important things to you are in fact, more important than those important things to me, which is insulting. In general, I dislike those colleagues who exert their own value judgments onto my value judgment.

Is it an office robbery?

Money is a precious resource which can be used to fulfil our plans or wishes, and we all have different financial burdens in our families. Based on what foundations those colleagues would think that I have to sacrifice my own plan just because of their spouses, their babies or their new houses? Selfish thoughts of those colleagues go beyond words but also acts. They actually take money from others who do not dare to say "no." I would call it an office robbery, while robbery means theft with intimidation. They intimidate other colleagues with the consequences of their work schedules or work performance evaluation.

Are you able to handle stresses?

These are my personal stories. My point is: If you dare to speak up for yourself or others, you seem to be a good fit for the law school. If your concept of correctness or incorrectness is determined by the number of people following that, then you could be a good fit for public relations, communications, or social work. When you stand up for yourself to fight for your own rights, you definitely would have to face a lot of stress. Are you ready for such stresses?

Share with family and friends

Test your own understanding

Even if nobody around you studies law, you can still try to share interesting or complicated concepts with your friends or spouse. Here is the advantage of sharing: If you are able to explain to them in your own words, without referring to the books, that would mean you fully understand the concepts. Then in the real exam, if you forget the wording of the rules, try to recall the conversation with your friends or spouse, or how they reacted, what questions they asked, and how you clarified their misunderstandings. That conversation would definitely help your memory to last longer because that is going to be a real scenario in your mind, while those legal doctrines are just a whole bunch of alphabets on paper. Without real experiences in litigation, those words are just forcefully squeezed into your head. The cells in your head are more likely to be resistant to these cold and inhospitable concepts.

Understanding legal concepts may not require any legal knowledge

Some legal concepts can be relatively easy for us to explain to people who know nothing about legal terminology. For example, the acts of any business partners would hold all partners liable; Property acquired before the marriage would not be shared with your spouse at divorce unless transmutation takes place; A trust would not fail due to the lack of trustee because the court can appoint one; if a testator promises to give you a specific gift in his will but the gift is gone for whatever reasons before his death, then you would get nothing, and do not expect any compensation because of the eliminated gift.

Try to explain legal concepts in plain language

In other words, try to explain legal concepts in plain language. For something you truly understand, it would not be difficult. You can keep the legal terms for yourself, such as "respondent superior", and just state the central idea of the doctrines to your family and friends: "An employer can be held accountable for negligence for the wrongdoings committed by his or her employee within the scope of employment." That was what I did in my first and second years of law school: sharing the legal concepts I learnt with my husband, my mother, my sister, and my friends.

Create a fun conversation and discussion about the rules

We always remember a joke or an interesting incident well, but not a whole bunch of boring data. Hence, we can try turning the boring data into an interesting incident by discussing those rules with your humorous friends or family members. Most likely, they would make some comments on what you share with them. They might find the rules ridiculous or stupid, and that conversation would help you remember the rules. In a nutshell, try to make it fun to remember all the rules.

Embellish the boring data with comments and generalizations

You can reinforce your memory by adding some interesting or humorous descriptions to the cold and deadpan rules. For example, any gifts given by your spouse during the marriage are still deemed community property unless the gifts are of a personal nature, and not of substantial value. That means if your husband buys you a big diamond ring during your marriage, it could be too early for you to feel happy about it. You might end up having only half of it if your relationship adversely changes, But if a wife buys her husband a beard trimmer, it is highly likely he would possess 100 percent of it, and she would not try to get it back when the relationship turns sour. In other words, receiving something cheap from your spouse during your marriage is more solid and real than receiving something luxurious.

I would also tell my husband not to buy me any expensive gifts because "I do not want to be a storage locker for you to hold the item and then return half of it to you when you are tired of me."

2) Emotional struggle: Changing your mentality to a lawyer's mentality

Villian vs. Victim

In the first year of my law school, my ways of thinking and reasoning were not adjusted to the lawyers 'mindset and mentality yet, but they all need to be fixed in order for me to pass the baby bar: The exam questions test how we respond to a situation with a wicked person and a victim; a good-faith act and a bad-faith act. The exam questions always include scenarios in which a good person loses but a bad person wins. In order to pass the baby bar, I must put aside my sympathy to rationally handle the situation.

Your task is not to tell the professor how hard you study

When you start going to law school, you need to get rid of your old ways of writing: Merely writing all the rules you learn from the lectures and the books. You would get a passing score as long as you are able to write out some important rules in a regular class. But I am so sorry to tell you that this method is not going to work in law school.

Addressing the controversy and resolving the issue is the key

When you answer an essay question in law school, you cannot just write out some rules somehow relevant to the topic of the essay. You have to accurately identify the exact issues, discuss them with the rules, and apply the rules to the facts given; then also talk about the plausible opposing arguments and explain which side is more likely to win with legal reasonings.

Instruction: Do not randomly interpret two acts as the cause and the outcome

The laypeople always randomly interpret two acts as the cause and the outcome even when they know almost nothing about the background of the incident, the characters and other information. As a future lawyer, please do not randomly interpret two acts as the cause and the outcome without sufficient supporting facts.

Example: Lost money inside the boutique

"Lara, a sales associate at a boutique, claims that she lost $45 in dollar bills inside the boutique, and she may have dropped them somewhere without realizing it. She worked close to the display window for at least 10 minutes. About 40 minutes after Lara's discovery of losing $45, a female customer, Fiona pays for a dress in $45 cash."

Laypeople's perspective: The customer must have found the $45 somewhere inside the store and then used the bills to buy the dress she likes.

Attorneys' perspective:

A few more aspects need to be considered before reaching a conclusion.

Bills combination

How were the bills combined of the cash lost by Lara? Were they two $20 bills plus one $5 bill? Or four $10 bills plus five $1 bills? Or are all $1 bills? Were there any marks written by pen on the bills, or did Lara make some markings on the bills? Does Lara remember the number of at least one bill?

If the bill combination of the cash lost by Lara were exactly the same as that used by the female customer, there is a higher likelihood that the female customer may have taken the money, but it is still unconfirmed. That is because even if both people's combinations consist of two $20 bills and one $5 bill, they are still not something unique. It is also possible that after someone finds the cash, he can go to the bank to deposit the cash into his own account and then withdraw the same amount immediately, then, the combination of the dollar bills would immediately change without trace.

Time – Fiona paid the dress 40 minutes after Lara discovered she lost $45

Fiona paid the dress 40 minutes after Lara discovered the loss, but this "40 minutes" just means Lara dropped her money for "at least" 40 minutes, but the actual length of time she dropped her money could be hours. That is because she may not discover her loss until a few hours after she dropped the money. The relevancy of time lag would be: The longer time the money gets lost, the more variations or possibilities could appear after her money gets lost. Whoever finds the money may have grabbed it and have gone far away from the boutique, then it would become meaningless for Lara to focus on people still around her physically.

Location - display window

If Lara believes she dropped the cash close to the display window, and the female customer also walked close to the display window, it slightly increases the likelihood of the customer grabbing Lara's money, but the two acts may not be related. That is because Lara simply believes she dropped the cash there, but this is speculative. She could have dropped inside the area of “employee only,” then the female customer would not be a "suspect" because she is not allowed to go into the area. Furthermore, it is very ordinary for a female customer to walk close to the display window, and this act is indicative of almost nothing.

Surveillance Video/ Videos taken by other customers

However, if there is a surveillance video showing that Lara actually dropped the $45 cash close to the display window, and the female customer actually took it and grabbed the dress, and then paid for it with the cash picked up from the floor, there would not be any doubt on the certainty of the female customer spending Lara's cash.

Or if there is a video filmed by a regular customer showing that the female customer actually picked up the cash dropped by Lara somewhere, it would be more likely that the female customer, in fact, used Lara's money.

However, if the video clips are segmented or edited, and then put together, then it may not show the whole picture. The reality could be: The female customer picked up the cash dropped by Lara, and then walked to Lara and returned it to her. Lara put the money into the pocket of her pant, but the pocket was shallow, and the cash dropped again to the floor, and someone else got the cash. Then, the female customer paid the dress with the cash from her own wallet.

In conclusion, when two acts have one common item or element (both involving $45 cash here), it does not mean both must be related to each other. You could have doubt or suspicion, but you cannot rule out all other possibilities.

Accuracy of the claim

Here, facts show that Lara "claims that she lost $45." There are at least two possibilities: She claims that, but she, in fact, makes a mistake, or she is lying. If the fact "losing $45" itself is untrue, there is no point for further discussion.

<u>*There are always other possibilities</u>

<u>Lying</u>

When you find out someone is a liar to you, what would be your conclusion? Or interpretation?

<u>Example: Alibi</u>

Ulla said she had an alibi for the time the murder of Saffron happened, but the police detective found out her alibi was fabricated.

Question:

Does it mean Ulla was the murderer?

Inference: It does not mean Ulla killed Saffron, but she must have something to hide. For example, she was spending time with someone's husband in a hotel room; she was burglarizing a luxurious house with her friends, etc.

<u>Example: What did you do at the weekend?</u>

On Monday, when we see our colleagues in the office, we would like to ask how their weekends were. People may tell you the truth, or make up something.

What would be your interpretation?

He or she is not an honest person? I would not say so.

Explanation:

People might think that they are not close to you, so they would not want to disclose details in their private lives.

Example: The sound coming out from Unit G

According to the lease, two people are living at the Unit G with a cat, including Yeshua(Y) and Xolani(X). This morning, the security guard talked to Yeshua, and Yeshua told the guard that he would travel to Europe this afternoon. In the evening, the property manager heard some sound coming out from Unit G.

What are the possibilities for the sound when Yeshua is supposed to be gone?

Xolani does not travel with Y;

Both X and Y are traveling. The sound is made by the cat;

A burglar broke into the unit;

X and Y hand a key to their families or friends to check on their unit while they are away;

There are unauthorized occupants living inside Unit G;

X and Y did not turn off the television before they left.

There are many possibilities for the facts given.

Applying to essays

Do not be too conclusive. Always consider other possibilities.

What you see may not be the whole picture

When we witness part of an incident, please do not "automatically" fill in the blanks with your own imagination. What you imagine is always made without any grounds or support from that particular incident, and that would be merely a by-product of your own personality, value judgment and how you perceive the world after you have been surviving for decades.

Example: A boy falling on the ground in front of the bumper of a car

When you see a boy falling on the ground in front of the bumper of a car in traffic, the first perception to many people would be the boy getting hit by the car; but if you look around for more details, you will find other possibilities: If you see a scooter on another side, it is also possible that the boy falls himself when he rides on the scooter; Or the boy may never have a real fall, but simply pretends to get hit by the car in order to ask for money compensation from the driver.

Advice:

Please observe the surroundings in detail to get a panoramic view and think broadly.

3) Elements: Breaking one single act into a few parts

Lawyers tend to break one single act into a few elements to see if the act has fulfilled all the elements required in an offense or accusation.

Example: Kicking inside a train compartment?

This is a scenario inside a train compartment full of people, luggage boxes and animals. A, B, C, D, and E are individuals inside the train, and they do not know each other.

A: "Oh! You kicked me."

B: "No, I did not. "

A: "You did. Some material on your clothing is attached to my knee."

B: "Yes. This is from my clothing. But I was squeezed by others to touch your knee."

C: "Kicking means you have a target to attack, and you have to lift your leg and hit her with your shoes. But his legs are not lifted, and in fact, there is no room for him to lift his legs. Everyone is being squeezed. "

B: "Yes. Even if your two feet do not rest on the floor, your body will not fall down because people's shoulders are close enough to hold your body in the air."

D: "Also, his shoes do not touch your knee but his pant does. It is pant-to-pant touching. No kicking has ever taken place. "

E: "And no one ever targets anyone. "

B: "We are all passive, and we have no choice except to get off the train."

Explanation:

In the above example, C has defined what is kicking. Assuming this definition is correct, A has to prove a few elements to back up her accusation:

(1) having a target to attack, (2) lifting one's leg, and (3) hitting the target with shoes.

Based on the above definition, if someone lifts his leg to stretch it when he is inside the train and accidentally hits another person, then the act is not deemed kicking; or if the person wants to lift his leg to attack a particular man but miss the kick, and eventually slips into the body of the target, then the act is not deemed kicking either. (It is transferred intent in torts but not here.)

Considering every element

Example: Sexual harassment

Sexual harassment is a type of harassment involving the use of explicit or implicit sexual overtones, including unwelcome and inappropriate promises of rewards in exchange for sexual favors.

Keyword: "Unwelcome"

One of the keywords here is the word "unwelcome."

"Unwelcome" means people do not want them or do not like them.

If the alleged victim smiles at the defendant, participates in the conversation, or even contributes more jokes to the conversation, the element "unwelcome" would be defeated because the victim appears to love the words or enjoy flirting.

The importance of conjunctions "and" & "or"

Example: Filling out the forms

"In order to meet our staff for help, you have to fill out the red form and the green form."

That means: Both forms are required in order to seek help.

Example: Confirmation of identities

In order to confirm your identity, please provide your driver‘s license or your passport.

That means Either one is fine, not both.

Example: Threatened lawsuit by the landlord

"In order not to be sued by the landlord, both Johnny and Timothy have to move out by Saturday, and all of their stuff have to be gone."

That means: The Landlord aims to get rid of Johnny and Timothy and all their belongings.

Options:

If they are all gone by Saturday, the problem will be resolved;

Otherwise, the landlord would start the lawsuit.

4) IRAC would be your new friend from now on

IRAC would be your new friend once you have started your law school education, and they would be your closest friend throughout your legal career.

When I first started law school, I did not fully and smartly use IRACs to fulfill the purposes in essays. At that time, I treated IRAC as a frame or the exercise of "Fill in the blanks," so I had to squeeze something out of my head to fulfill the blanks in the issue, rule, analysis and conclusion. It was just like when I had to fill out an application for a job: What information to disclose depended on how the forms were designed. My thoughts were, in fact, segmented and broken when I tried to answer the questions in the form. However, one of the purposes of the form could be to stimulate us to provide necessary information to the employers. Imagine if the employers give you five pieces of white paper and ask you to write anything you like to introduce yourself, many people might get lost.

If you handled IRAC like me when I first started law school, you are not using IRAC as a tool to help you resolve the problem, but instead, you are being confined by IRAC, like being tied up. If an IRAC is deemed a handcuff for you, you really need to spend more time understanding how to use IRAC to fulfill your purposes in legal writing.

Each IRAC has its unique role

Figure out which facts go to which arguments with what rules before you start typing

Before you start typing or writing, you have to first clarify which facts go to which arguments: Some facts only belong to argument #1, then you should not include that particular fact in argument #2.

Example: Three problems pointed out by your supervisor

Imagine if your supervisor at work thinks that you have the following three problems:

Your manner in answering the phone is not professional enough; (2) you have too much personal stuff on your desk; and (3)you have too many lunch bags in the refrigerator, including one for main dishes, one for beverages, and one for snacks, which takes away the space for other colleagues.

Then she may suggest you buy your own mini refrigerator and put it under your desk, Putting unnecessary stuff in your desk drawer or locker; and finding someone who is experienced to train you how to answer the phone in a professional manner.

However, when she refers you which brand is good for a small refrigerator, she would not criticize how you talk on the phone; while the person trains you to speak more professionally on the phone, he would not mention your excessive stuff on the desk; and the staff who assigns you a locker for your personal stuff would not talk about the fact that you take up too much space in the refrigerator.

Applying to essays

Each essay has to resolve a legal problem or issue, and each IRAC in the essay would be able to find something helpful to the final solution. Even though one of the issues is the biggest, it does not mean the issue has to be constantly repeated in every IRAC.

Each IRAC would be one step closer to solving the ultimate problem

In the above example, the supervisor mentions that you have three problems, and the main purpose is to resolve these three problems so you can retain your job position. But when she tries to solve the three problems for you, she does not have to keep repeating that you may lose your job or get fired if you do not speak professionally on the phone, if you put too much personal stuff on your desk, or if you take up other colleagues' spaces in the refrigerator. We all know if we fail to meet the expectations of our employers or have discipline problems, we could be terminated, but that would be the final conclusion if some of the problems remain unresolved. We know the ultimate purpose for us to fix the problems is to maintain our job position and our income. But when you try to improve your phone manners, organize your desk or buy your own refrigerator to store your lunch, beverages and snacks, you do not need to keep saying "I do not want to get fired."

Your task is to work on the problems identified by your supervisor. Eventually, if you are able to solve two out of three problems, your job is relatively safe, but if you are unable to solve any of them, then you may receive a warning letter from the employer, and your job would be threatened. But that would be the final conclusion made by your employer rather than the conclusion of each problem.

Topics in your book may not work as headings in your IRAC

There are many topics in the law books, but topics in different chapters of a book may not work as meaningful headings for IRACs.

Example: Battle of Form

"Battle of the form" is one of the chapters I studied in my memory.

But if you use "battle of form" as the heading of an IRAC and then conclude "there is battle of form," the conclusion does not serve any purpose to the ultimate conclusion of your essay.

Imagine if I start a heading known as "legal disputc," then I conclude: Thus, there is a legal dispute. Then how is it going to benefit the solution to the main problem?

Solution:

You can simply say "UCC 2-207" in the heading.

UCC 2-207

When there is an additional term made by a certain party, and the dispute is whether that term has become part of the contract, you may have a heading "Mirror image rule vs UCC 2-207."

Sample Writing: Mirror image rule vs UCC 2-207

If the common law applies, the mirror image rule would be used; but if UCC applies, UCC 2-207 would apply to the additional term.

Here, the products at issue are pairs of scissors, which are tangible commodities, so UCC applies instead of the common law. UCC Article 2 has changed the mirror image rule. Hence, UCC 2-207 would be in place……

Thus, the additional term would become part of the contract.

Or

Here, the contract is about the construction of the backyard, which is a kind of service. As such, the common law applies, and the mirror image rule would be used. The mirror image rule states that the terms of the offer must be exactly the same as the terms of the acceptance. When the terms of the acceptance are slightly different, including…..there would be no valid acceptance.

Thus, the additional term would not become part of the contract.

<u>What is not worth an IRAC?</u>

An IRAC is used to analyze an issue. Hence, if some terms can be defined by a few words, and those terms are not controversial in the essay, they do not deserve extra IRACs.

For example. in a contract essay, if the product is a combination of goods and services, you might need an IRAC talking about whether the contract is deemed a contract of goods or services, meaning which part is predominant, or whether the UCC or the common law governs.

However, if the products in the contract are merely cups, pens, or books, they would not deserve your effort to use another IRAC to make an analysis of something which do not need analysis at all to draw a conclusion that the cups, pens, and books are goods, so the UCC governs. You should know that and define that at the very beginning of the contract essay, and put all of them in the IRAC named "which law governs." Or you can simply insert a few words for the definition of goods when you have the IRAC "Governing law."

(You do not need another IRAC talking about whether the cups and pens are services. That would be redundant and ridiculous and make yourself look stupid unless you find reasonable reasons to justify that. For example, one party thinks that the contract is about the designing service of cups rather than selling cups.)

In a nutshell, you do not need a whole IRAC to demonstrate that you know the definition of a certain term. Just insert the definition into an IRAC talking about a controversial issue. That is also a wise use of time.

Practice IRAC in daily lives

Do a daily or weekly log of something which can be analyzed with IRACs. It could be anything, for example, the train authority plans to increase the fare for train; your HOA requires all residents to accommodate to a policy change.

Example: What mode of transportation

Four of us would go to watch a game tonight at the stadium.

Question:

What mode of transportation should we use in order to get to the stadium in this evening? Bus, train, Uber or driving by ourselves?

Instructions:

You have to do at least four IRACs:

The rule portion for each option would be talking about the price for each passenger, the total price for the whole party, and the time needed for each mode of transportation, which are similar to the elements of a rule.

Bus

The bus fare costs $2.5 for each person. There is a 20-minute walk from the bus stop we would get off at to the destination "stadium."

If we take the bus, the total amount we are going to spend would be $2.5 x 4, which would be $10 for one way and $20 for two ways. However, when there is a big game, many people go to the stadium at almost the same time, so the bus must be crowded. Moreover, there is a 20-minute walk from the bus stop to the stadium, which would be burdensome when we need to carry cans of soda, food and the banners.

Thus, taking the bus would be inconvenient if we have heavy stuffs to carry.

Driving

Driving to the stadium costs $30 gas on round trip and $14 for parking, which is a flat fee, without the option of driving in and out. There would be a walk for at least 10 minutes from the parking lot to the main entrance, depending on the location of the parking space we are going to find.

If we drive to the stadium, our total cost would be $44 for the round trip, more than double of the expenses on the two-way bus fares for four people. Everyone would spend $11 on average. It would be little easier for us to carry stuffs to the stadium when compared to taking bus, but after we have parked the car, there is still a long walk to the stadium.

Thus, without better options, driving may be more desirable when heavy stuffs have to be carried to the stadium.

Uber

Taking Uber usually costs $15 to the stadium for one way, and $30 for round trip; but when there is a game, or if it rains, the charge could go up to $40 to $60, which means $80 to $120 for round trip.

If we take Uber, there would be no parking issue, and the Uber can stop almost right in front of the stadium. However, the rate of Uber is uncertain.

When the demand for Uber is high, thc rate could be doubled or more. Moreover, the weather is also a factor driving up the price, which is out of our control. If it rains, a one-way trip could cost more than $50, plus a long wait for the ride due to heavy traffic.

Regardless of the weather, many people would be gathering around the exit and the entrance at the end of the game, it would be difficult for the Uber driver to drive close to the stadium; and it would also be difficult for us to spot the Uber driver when many cars are stopped close to the entrance. If almost everyone calls Uber at the same time, too many cars may double park outside the stadium, causing problems in traffic, or the enforcement team may issue driving tickets to the Uber drivers for illegal parking. The penalty for the tickets issued would not be deemed part of our commute cost, but that would be concerns for Uber drivers to reject the rides if they think they might get into trouble.

Thus, taking Uber seems to be more convenient, but we would be subject to a big risk of uncontrollable prices, difficulties of spotting the Uber driver, and the chance of rides being cancelled.

<u>Train</u>

Taking train would avoid the heavy traffic on the freeway, and the train station is just right next to the stadium with the shortest walking distance. The train fare is $3 per person.

If we take train, four people would cost $12 for one way and $24 for the round train, which is little more expensive than taking bus, but cheaper than driving because there is no parking cost. If we carry food and cans of soda, they would still be heavy for us, but there is not much walking because the train station is just right next to the stadium. However, there may be some discomfort inside the train because the train is likely to be crowded when there is a big game.

In fact, when there is a big game, it is hard to avoid crowds anyway. In terms of inconveniences, it would be the least inconvenient to take the train because there would be no parking issue, and the walking distance would be the least for us.

Thus, taking train seems to cause the least trouble for us to attend the game held at the stadium tonight.

Ultimate conclusion

Based on the foregoing reasons, taking train to the stadium would be the best option for us in terms of the amount of expenses and inconveniences caused.

IRAC exercises with your friends or family members in our daily lives

Example: Mandatory service charge

Rule

"A 20 percent mandatory service charge would be added to every bill in any restaurants, regardless of the number of guests."

Discussion

Please fully discuss the above rule with your friends or family members, and talk about whether this rule should be imposed on all restaurants in your area. That would train your skill and ability to thoroughly discuss something from different perspectives, and also the ability to rebut the opposing arguments.

Facts

The facts to use can be what you observe in the particular restaurant or other restaurants or in other aspects of your daily lives.

Analysis of anything in anytime in your daily lives

In our daily lives, we encounter a lot of different issues every day, such as traffic congestion, the lack of parking space, the increase of bridge toll, the increase of interest rates, inflation, too many vacant store spaces, unemployment, shoplifting, homelessness, etc. We can analyze at least one issue a day or a week to practice the use of IRAC. If you are able to smartly use this methodology to rationally and mechanically resolve your problems or finish an analysis of complicated issues, you would love IRAC.

5) Diagnosis: Correct identification of the issue/problem

In an IRAC, the "issue" is the first thing, so accurately identifying the issue or the main problem would be the first step and could be the most important. The issue would determine what rule you need to recall and what elements would be used. If you misidentify the issue, the whole analysis, explanation and conclusion would go towards the wrong direction.

Please read the following dialogue between Alexander (A), Benjamin (B) and Charles (C). It shows that misidentification of an issue would lead to an untrue standpoint, a wrong analysis, and an unreliable conclusion. The "supporters" could, in fact disfavor the idea.

Example: A story of "no work"

A: I am going to have a "day off" tomorrow.

B: "Day off" again? That is good.

C: Alexander's job is really nice. He always has time off. I want to apply for the same job position in his company.

A: But I would earn less money by having a "day off."

B: Why?

A: I am asked to take a "day off" just because of insufficient work available in the company.

B: Then it is not a "day off," but a reduction of work hours.

C: Yeah. This is similar to a layoff or partial unemployment because the employees are passive. They are told to stop working. Alexander has no choice at all.

B: Alexander's job is not promising because the income for every employee would be unsteady. It would be a problem for people who have to pay for mortgages, vehicle installments, or tuitions for children. Alexander should look for another job.

C: I am glad I did not apply for the job yet! My current job guarantees me 40 work hours per week.

Explanation:

Here, Alexander wrongfully interprets his "reduction of work hours" as a "day off." From the perspective of Benjamin and Charles, a "day off" is getting paid with no need to report to duty. But when Benjamin and Charles learn that Alexander does not get paid if Alexander does not work, and he is, in fact forced to stop working because of insufficient work, both Benjamin and Charles change the way they describe the situation, as well as their analyses and conclusions.

Summary:

Issue: A reduction of work hours again happens to Alexander.

Analysis: This is similar to a layoff or unemployment. Alexander has no choice at all. Alexander's job is not promising.

Conclusion: Alexander should look for another job.

6) Rule

"Elements are the ingredients!"

Example: Ingredients determine the identity of the beverage

Coffee

= caffeine + tannin + fixed oil + carbohydrates + proteins

Mocha

=Coffee+milk+cocoa powder

Latte

= espresso + steamed milk + a thin layer of frothed milk on top

Elements of acts determine the offenses

Question:

What is the difference between robbery and theft in California?

Let's see the definitions of each:

Theft= The taking of another person's personal property with the intent of depriving that person of the use of their property.

Robbery=The unlawful taking of property from the person of another through the use of threat or force.

Answer:

The primary difference between robbery and theft is that theft doesn't involve any interpersonal interaction.

Please pay attention to the exact wording of the elements when applying the rules

One word is sufficient to increase the chance of prevailing or losing an argument. Even though you believe a certain party has done something wrong, he or she may not necessarily lose. That is because you can always turn the tables by spotting the key element of a rule.

Example: Happy Pineapple and Mango Restaurant

Here is a scenario at the Happy Pineapple and Mango Restaurant:

There is a rule: "Every birthday person would be given a free mango pudding."

Dickson (D) claims that today is his birthday. But when the assistant manager checks his ID, it does not show that today is his birthday.

D: "Today is my birthday in the Chinese Lunar Calendar."

Assistant Manager: "I am sorry, sir. I have no idea of what the Lunar Calendar is. Our standard procedure is to verify the date of birth with one's government-issued identity cards or passports."

Elaine (E): "Today is my birthday, and I can show you my passport."

The assistant manager checks E's passport.

Assistant Manager: "Yes, that is correct. Happy Birthday!"

E: "I already ate a pineapple pudding. Can you deduct the $8 dollars charges for the pudding from my bill?"

Assistant Manager: "No. It has to be mango pudding."

E: "But all your mango puddings were already sold out one hour ago."

Assistant Manager: "I am so sorry, sir. That is not your fault, but this is not the rule either. The free dessert must be mango pudding, which is on promotion."

E: "You are so inflexible."

Assistant Manager: "Again, I am sorry, sir. Only managers are allowed to make changes to the rules. But I am just an assistant manager."

Fiona (F): "Hey, Assistant Manager, I am smart. I know that the mango pudding may be sold out, so I already grabbed one by myself two hours ago. It must be free, then. I do not have to pay for it. Correct?"

Assistant Manager: "I am sorry, sir. You have to pay $8 for it. The rule specifies that 'Every birthday person would be given a free mango pudding.'

But you are never 'given' one. You grabbed it by yourself. You just told me. That is not how the rule says."

What are the hidden rules?

The standard of "birthday" is the date of birth shown on one's government-issued identity card or passport.

Only mango pudding applies, not puddings of other favors.

Only managers are allowed to make changes to the rules.

Every birthday person would be "given" a free mango pudding by the staff. The customer is not allowed to grab it by themselves. If they get the pudding by themselves, the pudding would not be free.

Take-away from the above situation: An impression from the rule could be unreliable

When we analyze, we cannot solely rely on the impression in our mind; instead, we have to focus on every single word. The impression would only reflect an approximate idea, which could leave out many details, which would deviate from the expected scenario.

In the above example, the customer thinks that:

The birthday person = would get a free pudding of any favor

But in fact, free pudding is limited to mango favor only, and the customer is not allowed to grab one but has to be "given" one.

Deviations in definitions may screw up the situation

Different people may have different interpretations and expectations of the same term or word.

Example: What is "Romance"?

Here is a conversation between a girlfriend(GF) and a boyfriend (BF):

GF: "I would like to have a dinner with "romance" on Valentine's Day."

BF: "No problem. I will try my best."

"Romance" means a feeling of excitement and mystery to BF.

BF has done some research online. On Valentine's Day, BF goes to the indoor Go Kart racing and the house of horror with GF. However, GF feels disappointed and unhappy.

GF: "I would like to wear an elegant dress, and then have a luxurious dinner with you, and also receive beautiful flowers from you."

Question:

What caused the problem of misunderstanding and disappointing arrangements?

Answer:

BF and GF have different elements of "romance" in their heads.

BF's definition of romance: Excitement and mystery

GF's definition of romance: Elegance, luxury and with flowers

According to BF's own definition, he has fulfilled his duty of creating romance for GF; but according to GF's definition, no romance ever happened.

Applying to essays

Please write out the elements clearly the upfront and analyze the facts according to the elements in the list. Do not change the course of analysis unless you would also change the elements in the rule section.

Your rule or my rule?

Calling the rules during a dispute

During a dispute, we would call some rules to support our standpoints to make us sound right.

Serving the justice or being served?

The rules we quote would make us appear to be serving the justice. In fact, the one who uses the rules could be served by justice, meaning the label "justice" is helping the person to fulfill his or her own purpose.

Rules are tools for the users

Are there any preferences for us when we choose the rules?

There are so many rules in the world: On the face, the rules are designed to restrict everyone, but in fact, the rules are always used to serve the purpose of the users. Believe it or not, that is the reality.

The rules are always being used as tools to attack others and defend ourselves. People use the rules to resolve problems, making them favorable to you or your client to your advantage.

When the rulcs are disfavor able to you, you might argue that the rules would not apply here because…

Example: Noises insides the coffee shop

An old man is reading the book on one side and three teenagers are talking loudly on another side. A few baristas are diligently working at the counter while a few customers are quietly enjoying their coffee.

Old man: "Can you please lower the volume of your conversation?"

The teenagers are astonished.

Old man: "I am studying."

Teenager A: "There is a library down the street, Sir."

Old man: "I need you to keep quiet."

Teenager B: "Excuse me, sir. This is a coffee shop, not a library. We are allowed to talk in a coffee shop."

Old man: "You have to be considerate of others."

Another female customer who is talking on the phone interrupts. She told the old man to lower his volume.

Young lady: "You are also very loud, sir. Please be considerate of a person talking on the phone."

Other customers start walking away from the people involved in the argument to avoid trouble.

Then, Barista A walks from the counter to the position where the old man, young lady and those teenagers can see.

Barista A: "Can you all please leave our coffee shop?"

Old man: "Whom are you talking about?"

Barista: "All of you, including the gentleman who is reading the book, the teenagers who are chatting, and the young lady who is talking on the phone. Please walk out of the door now!"

Young lady: "Why?"

Barista: "That is because all your interactions threaten the safety of our regular customers. They felt uncomfortable to witness all of you arguing loudly. They left because of all of you."

Unique rules for defending one's own interest

In this scenario, what rule does each individual use to protect his or her own interest?

Teenager A: Studying should take place in the library.

Teenager B: Chatting should be allowed in a coffee shop

Old man: Loud noises should not be allowed to distract him from reading.

Young lady: Loud noises should not be allowed to disturb her from talking on the phone.

Barista: Whoever scares or threatens the safety of other customers, and makes their customers go away would not be allowed to stay inside the coffee shop.

This example shows that people do not really care about the correctness of every rule but whether the particular rule can put them in a more favorable position.

Applying to essays

This is what we need to do in writing arguments in an essay:

There are so many rules on a certain subject, and each rule has many exceptions. Which rule to emphasize depends on your need or your situation.

Example: The tenant has no heater in his house unit

This is a dialogue between a tenant(T) and her landlord(L):

T: “Hi, Landlord, it is so cold this week.”

L: “Yes. It is winter.”

T: “But there is no heater at my house unit. I was shivering last night.”

L: “You can buy one yourself.”

T: “The law requires every rental unit to have a heater.”

L: "When I was a tenant, my landlord never gave me a heater.”

What is the controlling rule?

The above conversation shows that the rule in the landlord's mind is not the law set by the government but her own personal experiences instead: Her previous landlord did not give her a heater, so she would not give a heater to her current tenant. However, this logic does not work in the legal system. We cannot change a rule just because other people treated me the same way in the past. In reality, we have to follow the rules in our jurisdiction. Nobody can set her own rules based on her own preferences.

Incomplete picture would lead to unfair comments

Many people like to label others with their own judgment

Many people like to label and comment on others with their own subjective judgment without the desire to fully understand what actually happened. They like to generalize what they see and put events with similar features in the same category.

Example: Sleeping on a couch in daytime

Beatrice is sleeping on the couch at 2 p.m. Yaniel just walks by and sees Beatrice through the window. "Beatrice is lazy," Yaniel said. Later, whenever Yaniel talks about Beatrice, he calls her "lazy Beatrice."

Here, Yaniel describes Beatrice to be lazy just because Beatrice still slept at 2 p.m. on that particular day. The rule for Daniel could be: Everyone should wake up at 7 am and go to bed at 11pm. As such, anyone sleeping in the afternoon would be deemed "lazy" to Yaniel.

However, Yaniel does not know the whole story behind sleeping at 2 p.m.: Beatrice spent two months preparing for the bar exam. In the past week, she slept less than four hours a day. The day before Yaniel met her, Beatrice just finished her two-day bar exam. She was exhausted.

Thus, in order to accurately reflect the truth, the correct description by Yaniel should be: "Beatrice was so exhausted after the bar exam that she fell asleep on the couch at 2p.m."

"Truth Murderers" use their weird logic as invisible weapons to defeat people

A weapon does not have to be physically sharp and huge. A conclusive adjective itself, without giving the chance for a person to explain the whole truth, is a horrible weapon; Criticizing people with one's own hidden subjective logics, without exploring the whole truth, can be an invisible weapon.

Example: Going to a job interview in a bloody shirt

A man named Manfred applies for the job position of social worker who has to help low-income households and vulnerable people.When he sits in front of the panel of three people on the job interview, three interviewers spot some blood stains on his shirt.

But none of them asked Manfred why, and Manfred just focuses on talking about his rich experiences of helping different people for different organizations in the past.

After Manfred left, three interviewers put a big cross on each copy of his resume. One of them wrote: "Manfred is an untidy man. He does not care about his appearance and also, he does not respect the job interview opportunity."

Eventually, Manfred is not hired. The three interviewers do not care about the story behind the blood stains.

Explanations:

There are many possibilities for the blood stain. That could be the outcome of helping an injured person. But the narrow-minded interviewers just regarded the "blood stains" as dirt, and interpreted his bloody shirt to be disrespectful of the job interview opportunity.

What could have changed the outcome?

If one of the interviewers asked Manfred why his shirt has blood stains, they may find out Manfred just saved a boy who was injured on his way to the job interview. In fact, Manfred could be found a "good fit" to the job position of social worker, who needs to "help the low-income households and vulnerable people."

One's subjectiveness could hurt others

Judge you with one's senseless rule

Many people like to judge others with their senseless rules:

Example: My legs hurt

This is a scenario between two sales associates, Elaine (E) and Fanny (F), in a store selling women's purses.

E: "I am tired. My legs hurt. I would like to take a break."

F: "No. You have to wait 30 more minutes before another break."

E: "No. I cannot stand anymore. I need to take a seat."

F: "No. You are only 40 years old. Grace is 55 years old. She never complains about any pain."

Do you find any problems in F's logic?

Legs pain can be caused by a combination of different reasons, while age could be one of the factors. But it does not mean younger people would not have any leg pain while older people do not mention that. According to Fanny's rule, everyone would die in a sequence of ages: older people must die before younger people. But that has not been the case. We all know that. A baby or a child can die of different reasons.

"People not complaining about their pain" is not equivalent to "they do not have any pain. " It depends on a variety of factors: older people may try to hide their health problems from their employers in order not to be targeted if they plan to layoff. Or some people's personality is more introverted so they do not like to disclose their problems to others.

Forceful exertion of one's subjective perception

Many people like to draw a conclusion or make a judgment on others or matters without any qualifications, so their conclusions do not have any value of reference, solely to make themselves feel good for criticizing other people. I would describe it as one's subjective perception being forcefully exerted on others.

Example: Tutoring for bar exam takers

Someone talked to me like this after I passed the bar exam.

"You just passed the bar exam. If I were you, I would not tutor other bar exam takers due to no experience. "

The speaker is not confident to be a tutor even if she has passed the bar. (The reality could be: This person does not have a chance to start tutoring until five years after passing the bar, or this person never goes to law school, and has no idea of what capability means by passing the bar. Whatever it is, this person tries to downplay my ability as a tutor; but based on what foundation, she thinks that she is qualified to judge my ability? It is unclear.)

Do I have to explain to her? No. Am I a good tutor? My students would make their own judgments. I do not need this person of unknown background to judge me. In my opinion, recently passing the bar is my advantage because everything is still fresh in my mind.

Moreover, for people who have ten-year experiences of tutoring, or who own schools of private tutoring, did they ever have their first days of tutoring work? If they stop tutoring on their first days due to no experience, how can they accumulate ten years of experience?

Distorted rules may not have any values of reference

Many rules are so subjective that they do not have any values of reference. I would call them "distorted rules." You do not need to get angry, but you have to be clear that why they have no value, and then just stick to the more sensible rules.

Applying to essays

When we write essays, we use rules we learn from the school or the book, but the characters in the essay question may have their own rules, or some students may also have their own versions of the rules. Please be sure to use the legitimate rules acceptable to the bar graders.

Example: Does smiling mean consent?

Scenario:

"Billy and Jimmy talk about a possible agreement of buying and selling a kind of toy product. Billy smiles when he reads the terms but does not sign. Jimmy then bought the equipment, getting ready to produce the toy products he thinks Billy would pay for."

In your analysis, you have to state the rules for consent in the contract and then talk about the rules for Jimmy: smiling means consent. You have to negate the validity of "consent" defined by Jimmy and explain why it is invalid.

When the essay question involves distorted rules like the above one, you must clearly state the correct rule and not be swayed by the distorted rule.

7) Facts handling: Getting rid of distractions

Stay focused on your goal

When a student first starts law school, a massive amount of information would be intimidating. A law student always worries about missing information, so she would think she needs to include this and that and cannot get rid of this and that. Eventually, they get lost in the huge amount of information.

Some information looks important because of the nature of the incident, such as deaths, serious illnesses, and criminal charges, but when we refer to the goal of our task, they may not even bc relevant to discuss or do not need in-depth discussion.

Example: Termination by the employer after requesting a family leave

“Elizabeth, an employee for a retail store, is fired one week after she requested a family leave of ten weeks to take care of her gravely ill mother. Her mother is diagnosed with colon cancer and needs to receive a treatment called ABCDEFG technique approved by advanced medical technology association, which, especially works on the cells of the patient. That could help killing the cells with cancer. There would be a lot of side effects, so Elizabeth would like to stay with her mother. The unusual blood type, unusual heart problem and a medical history of bone caner of her mother may also complicate the situation.

If the new treatment works, the life of her mother could be extended for three to five more years.

But the Christmas and New Year holidays are coming. The retail store has a big promotion projection called "Santa Claus is shopping with you." In order to support this project, each department would need more staff than usual.

Stella, the immediate supervisor, hesitated when the verbal request was first made; but after Stella talked to the Human Resources Manager, Stella just asked Elizabeth to provide required supporting documents without saying yes or no.

One day before she is fired, a customer complains about Elizabeth, and the complaint is the third one Elizabeth receives in her five-year employment. The company policy states that an employee could be fired after three complaints in 24 months. The customer made the complaint was the former girlfriend of Elizabeth's husband.

Elizabeth plans to sue the employer, and you are an attorney representing the employer. Please research the rules about family leaves, termination, retaliation and write an objective memorandum analyzing the likelihood for Elizabeth to win her case. If Elizabeth has a good chance to win, the employer would be willing to settle the case earlier."

When you analyze, focus on the relevant rules and IRAC each of them.

Dazzling names would be a distraction

Do not let fascinating descriptions distract you when they are something about the subject but irrelevant to the main issue.

Avoid distractions:

Colon cancer;

ABCDEFG treatment technique;

The unusual blood type, unusual heart problem and a medical history of bone caner of her mother;

Big promotion projection called "Santa Claus is shopping with you";

The customer made the complaint was the former girlfriend of Elizabeth's husband.

The medical history of her mother is something severe, and the medical treatment is useful to possibly extend the life of her mother. But this is relevant and important to her mother's health only, not the lawsuit.

The big promotion project called "Santa Claus is shopping with you" sounds fun, and it is relevant to the need of labor force to the employer. It can explain why the immediate supervisor hesitated when she was informed verbally about the upcoming family leave, but the name of the promotion is not important, even though it sounds fun to have Santa Claus to shop with you. What the promotion means to your analysis is: the employer needs more people to work for it.

To be a qualified matchmaker

Example: Matrimonial advertisements /dating apps

Be a qualified matchmaker:

Read the rules, find the match, then develop and emphasize the facts

Lady 1: "I would like a wealthy man."

Your task: find one man with valuable assets;

A person with high income May or May not work because of expenses in commute, house, entertainment.

Lady 2: "I would like a highly educated man."

Your task: find one with a master or PH degree. Money does not matter

Lady 3: "I would like to find a good-looking man."

Your task: this is relatively difficult because good looking is very subjective. You may find a few men look similar to popular singers, actors, and YouTubers. That should match the rules requirement of the majority of women.

Emphasizing the favorable points and downplaying the unfavorable points

But what the ladies say are their top priorities only. The ladies may have other requirements for their ideal spouses.

Although the lady 2 says she wants a highly educated man, it does not mean she can accept a homeless PH. D; Lady 1 would not want a wealthy man with a tendency to violence. Other traits of the dream men have to be at least neutral if they are not outstanding in other aspects.

How would you introduce these three men to lady 1,2,3?

A wealthy 60-year-old man while lady 1 is 30 years old. The man has a fancy restaurant chain, two big mansions and five million dollars savings. He never married and has no children.

A PH D who has no stable job. He is a part-time delivery man and rents a small bedroom in an apartment. There are two other roommates in the same unit. Lady 2 is a teacher with a stable income.

A young and attractive man who is working at an auto body shop, but he was in jail for three months because of fighting with a customer. He lives with his mother. Lady 3 is an orphan. She is 20 years old.

As a matchmaker, your job is to try to match them to become a couple by emphasizing the merits of the man and downplaying his defects.

For example, lady 3 wants a good-looking man, and the man is young and attractive. Lady 3 is an orphan so she may want to build up her own family earlier in her life. Living with the parent of the man could be a way to make up for what she did not have for the first 20 years of her life. Although the man went to jail for three months, he just got charged for probably a misdemeanor. It was not something immoral. Young people may have difficulty controlling their emotions. That is not a big deal. After he gets married, he may become more mature.

You can think about how to introduce the Man 1 to Lady 1, and the Man 2 to lady 2.

Applying to essays

When we write essays, we also have to use the facts given like a matchmaker: downplaying the unfavorable points and emphasizing the favorable points.

Inferences from facts: Foundational knowledge may be required

When you make inferences from facts, you may be required to have some foundational knowledge.

The prerequisite of answering a question:

Before you answer a certain question, you first need to collect enough data. Otherwise, you would have no way to answer the question in a sensible manner.

Example: Buying cigarettes

Kendall: "Do you have enough money with you buying the cigarettes for Mason?"

Leon: "What???"

Explanation:

Here, even though Leon answers "Yes" honestly, the reality may not be yes. In order to be able to answer this question, Leon has to know how much one pack of cigarettes costs, what brand Mason wants, how many packs Mason wants in total.

Assuming Leon is a non-smoker and never buys cigarettes, he may not even know the price of one single pack of cigarettes. Assuming one pack of A brand costs $15, and B brand costs $18, and Leon has $16, then he would have "enough" money for A brand but not B brand.

Hence, in order to be able to provide an answer looking simple, many unknowns needed to be resolved beforehand.

Example: Pledging to help

Or you have your best friend named Ophelia. You told Ophelia whenever she has difficulties, you must help her: "For whatever difficulties you may have in future, I would help."

Assuming you are telling the truth from the bottom of your heart, you should at least modify the words you use: "For whatever difficulties you may have in future, I would try to help."

That is because you are not omniscient. You can only try to help her, but not necessarily able to help her.

Inferences can go different ways

The following is the dialogue between Stephanie (S) and Yasmine (Y), when you and Stephanie encounter Yasmine in a coffee shop:

S: "Next Saturday I will attend the wedding party of Rebecca."

Y: “Rebecca is going to marry again? That will be the third time in ten years.”

S: “Yes. Her first husband was a manager of a citywide trade company; her second husband was the manager of Northern California District of a nationwide company; and her third husband is going to be the CEO of an international high technology company.”

Y: “Wow! Good for her. She is smart and aggressive. She makes progress in her life every three years.”

S: “How about her high school boyfriend?”

Y: “Do you mean Richard? He has divorced twice.”

S: "I heard about that from some former classmates. He separated from his first wife when he lost his full-time job, and he divorced again two years ago when he could not afford the mortgage of his house.”

Y: “He has a new girlfriend now. She is the supervisor of Richard.”

S: “His supervisor must have more income than Richard does.”

Y: “Hope his third marriage will not fail again because of his financial difficulties.”

S: “Not necessarily about money. We all know Richard’s personality. Mere dignity matters.”

Y: “I think his mindset may have adjusted after two divorces.”

What would be your inferences?

Both Rebecca and Richard have divorced twice but S and Y have different inferences from their divorces. Certainly, the value of marriage cannot be measured in terms of money. Regardless of the moral standards or rightfulness, S and Y think that the two divorces of Rebecca mean success, but the two divorces of Richard are devastating. They make their judgment based on the amount of income or the job position one has.

You can also make your inference by how S and Y draw a conclusion and what facts support the adjectives they chose for you.

You may not agree with their value judgement, and you do not have to. But if you want to add your own thoughts and criticize, there are still many unknowns for S and Y. If I add a few more facts to the above scenario, your inference would be different, too:

The first husband and the second husband of Rebecca died within two years of the marriage.

The first wife and the second wife of Richard were both born into wealthy families, and the parents of his two ex-wives dislike Richard.

The current girlfriend of Richard is an orphan.

Many possibilities could be inferred from one fact

"When you come home, you heard sound of water from the bathroom. You assume your spouse is taking a shower in the bathroom because no one else lives with you. Then, you walk to the dining table. You see a big bowl with three pieces of shrimp. You touch the bowl and the bowl itself is not hot."

Question:

Did your spouse have dinner yet?

Answer:

Yes/No

Explanation:

Both are possible.

Yes. It is possible that your spouse just finished dinner, and the three pieces of shrimp are the food remaining in the bowl.

No. It is also possible that your spouse just checked if there is any leftover in the refrigerator and just found three pieces of shrimp left in a big bowl.

Other possibilities you can think of:

He or she already had dinner with friends but focused on chatting during the meal. Thus, he or she is not full. He or she wants to have more food.

Other helpful facts

Before your spouse finishes the shower, what facts would be able to help you determine whether he or she already finished his or her dinner and he or she has not had dinner yet?

*The food stored in the refrigerator this morning:

If you remember there are ten pieces of shrimp plus some noodles in the big bowl, then it is highly likely that your spouse has already finished his or her dinner.

*Whether there are other food in the refrigerator:

If you also remember there are some pork stews and spaghetti inside the refrigerator, and those pork stews and spaghetti are gone, then it is likely that your spouse has already had dinner.

*Whether your spouse is allergic to shrimp

If your spouse is allergic to shrimp, and there are only three pieces of shrimp in the bowl and no other food, then it is very likely that your spouse does not have dinner yet.

*Whether there are other used plates or bowls left inside the sink

If you see other used plates in the sink, then he might eat other food or he bought some food-to-go from the restaurant and ate at home.

Sensitivity to the facts vs. creativity to the inference

Sensitivity to the facts given would help you explore different possibilities, and you have to be creative, too. Take the above fact pattern as an example: You just heard the sound of water from the bathroom, so the person taking a shower may not be your spouse. It could be a suspect who just robbed your neighbor and wanted to take a shower before he escaped, but he does not expect you to come home that early!

8) Argument

A legal argument states the legal reasoning for the lawsuits from the perspective of the plaintiff, and the defendant may also argue about the elements of the torts or assert that the elements of criminal offenses are not fulfilled.

Scope of argument

When you argue, your focus should be whether the elements of the rule or the offense are fulfilled.

You are arguing whether your acts met the elements required to prove in that particular offense; but you are not arguing about the sentencing. That would not happen until your verdict is available. So if you are guilty of robbery and sentenced to three-year jail time, what you would argue in an appeal is that your acts did not fulfill the elements required in robbery, instead of staying in jail for three years would be too long, at least not in the exam. So far the exam essays do not require us to consider sentencing.

If the school says a student made an inappropriate speech and would suspend him for one semester, your argument would be: he has the right to free speech, not the length of suspension.

What is a hollow argument?

A hollow-man argument is a fallacious argument that involves inventing a weak fictitious position. People who use hollow-man arguments use vague and non-specific language without stating the identity of the opponent.

A hollow argument can be something you come up with in an exam under a time restriction. You feel that you need to show both sides, but you have no strong and concrete arguments in your mind, so you make something up, assuming some people may argue that way. But there is no real sensible argument on that point.

In order to avoid hollow arguments, you really have to think about the reasons for the opposing side. Even though you may hate the people who disagree with you, they are not entirely stupid. They must have their own concerns.

Do not make yourself feel glorified by thinking that the opposing side must know nothing. They are likely to understand your standpoint, but they might focus on another aspect or prioritize another aspect, and that is what make them having a different standpoint.

Getting rid of "nonsense" in your own arguments

In order to successfully get rid of "nonsense" in your own arguments, please start by learning from other people's nonsense.

We always hear a lot of nonsense in our daily lives.

Please collect all "nonsenses" you hear everyday and explain to yourselves why they are deemed nonsenses to you.

If you are able to figure out the reason rationally, please remind yourselves not to do the same thing in your own essays.

Collection of nonsenses in daily lives

Example: Denial of SSI

Let me share some nonsenses I heard recently:

A woman's application of SSI (Supplemental Security Income) was denied, and she said it should not be denied because she is not a person selling drugs or did any evil acts.

This is nonsense to me because the criteria for approving SSI is not whether you did bad acts or sell drugs. It is about how much income and assets you have and also if you have provided sufficient documentation to prove whether you have or you do not have certain income or assets. Thus, her verbal statement is nonsense because what she said does not directly respond to the rules of approving SSI. It is just her own thought believing that as long as she is a good person, she should be eligible for receiving SSI.

Hence, when someone explodes "nonsense" in your face in future, just ignore it. It does not make sense. It is not even worth your time to become angry or frustrated.

In writing essays, do not put similar nonsenses on the paper. Think about the rules and the facts given before you formulate your arguments.

Formulating your arguments

Example: Defend for DUI

A DUI checkpoint was set by the police from 9pm Friday to 5 am Saturday. At about 3 a.m. Denver was arrested and charged for "driving under the influence of alcohol." When he was pulled over, the police officer smelt alcohol from his breath. Then Denver was asked to do the one-leg test: It requires the tested person to stand on one leg of his choice raise another leg up in front of them approximately 6 inches off the ground while keeping both legs straight. But he swayed and used his arms to help while he tried to balance.

Also, his blood alcohol concentration exceeded the legal limit.

Defenses?

Are there any valid defenses for DUI? DUI is unlikely to be allowed in any emergencies, solely inferred from common sense. If a pregnant woman is going to have her baby born, the law would not allow a drunk driver to give her a ride to the hospital because it is going to create more danger than help her out. But if a terrorist put a huge number of explosives inside a car and planned to bomb the city, and you jump into the car to try to drive the car into the ocean in order to prevent from causing massive death, maybe it would be deemed an exception.

But I am not sure. It is just hypothetical.

Arguments?

In the above example, what would be your most compelling argument?

Denver was charged with "driving under the influence of alcohol." In my opinion, the most helpful argument would be Denver was not driving. Drinking alcohol itself is not illegal, but only driving under the influence of alcohol. Facts show that Denver was pulled over by the police officer, but it was unclear that whether Denver was sitting on the driver's seat or the passenger's seat; if there was another person present.

Another option would be to show that Denver was not "under the influence of alcohol." The above information shows that this argument would be unlikely to work because of the strong evidence of the fact that he had alcohol: the smell of his breath, the one-leg test, and the blood alcohol concentration limit. But in the exam, at least you can try to argue the first two facts of the evidence are subjective: The police officer doing the checkpoint for DUI had been smelling drivers for the whole night before Denver was pulled over. They might not be able to tell who had and who had not alcohol merely by smelling. This perception of human being is not reliable.

The one-leg test is also unreliable to show that Denver had alcohol because he could have bad balance all the time. Unless Denver had done a similar test before and did much better than the test on Saturday early morning. Then, the differences may be indicative of influence of alcohol.

The data from the blood alcohol concentration could be the most objective evidence. The counsel for the defense may try to attack the accuracy of the test since all tests have deviation. If the range of deviation is huge, then the test could be deemed unreliable.

Regardless of whether the above arguments would help Denver to be acquitted of the charge, the arguments are based on the evidence available and made rationally.

What would be offtrack arguments?

Examples of out-of-the-range arguments would be:

Even though the blood alcohol concentration limit of Denver has exceeded the legal limit, it would not affect the safety of driving for Denver because he gets used to drink alcohol. The same amount of alcohol consumption would have an impact on a regular person but not Denver.

The above argument would be offtrack. Even though what you claim is true, it would not be a valid legal argument.

This argument would not work for sure. The laws do not care about your drinking capacity for alcohol or whether you still remember where you live after you drink.

9) Defenses

A defense is an act of protecting one's own interests

A defense is an act of protecting one's own interests when one gets accused of any criminal offenses or torts.

The word "defense" (D) is not included in the acronym IRAC, but in fact, we need to include defenses when we write in IRAC. D can be included in the analysis part. Without D, your conclusion would not be accurate because you have assumed the opposing side would remain silent for the whole trial.

Example: Trespass to land

The defenses are a private necessity and public necessity. When there is an emergency, people can enter and stay on another property for their safety for a reasonable amount of time.

Private necessity:

For example, when there is a storm, a man can stay inside someone else's kiosk to protect his own safety, probably till the end of storm. If there are damages, the man has to pay for them.

Public necessity:

If there is going to be a foreseeable crash, the school bus driver can swerve onto someone's driveway to avoid the crash.

Both private necessity and public necessity are valid defenses because the law allows such exceptions.

What are invalid defenses?

Defenses need to be included in an essay, but they have to be valid.

Defenses are not chicanery

Defenses are not chicanery or chop logic, so chicanery or chop logic are deemed invalid defenses.

<u>You cannot say:</u>

“The man is so skinny that when he enters someone‘s land without permission, he occupies merely less than one square feet.”

“The man stayed there without permission for two hours only, so it is not a big deal."

“The driveway is always empty. Leaving it unoccupied is a waste of resources, so trespass to the driveway is a positive act rather than a negative one.”

“The school bus driver swerved the bus onto the driveway, and the grandma of the driveway owner was so happy to meet the ten children inside the school bus.”

<u>Explanation:</u>

In other words, you cannot exert your own thoughts onto a situation governed by existing laws by downplaying the harm or claiming that the entrance without consent is, in fact a more effective way of utilizing the resources.

<u>Let’s think</u>

Imagine what would happen if chicanery can be taken as defenses.

<u>Example: Robbing you for money would be more beneficial to the economy?</u>

A man robbed you because he claims that he is going to spend the 10,000 to stimulate the economy, which is going to benefit the economy and create more job opportunities, while keeping the money in your drawer would not create this beneficial impact.

The robber's defense sounds very logical and beneficial from the perspective of the labor force, but it would be horrible if the court would take this defense.

<u>A coin has two sides - Defenses may not be the "direct opposites"</u>

A coin has the front side, known as the heads; and the back side, known as the tails. In fact, the front and the back are opposite to each other, and the heads are the direct opposite of the tails.

However, the defenses may not be the direct opposites of the bad act included in the accusation.

<u>Example: The robber handed the victim medicine and water</u>

"Manfred is being accused of robbing the man named Viggo. Manfred carried a gun, and he got Viggo's wallet. Before Manfred started running away, Viggo felt sick for his chronic health problem. However, Viggo's medicine dropped on the floor. Then Manfred picked up the bottle of medicine for Viggo and also passed Viggo a small bottle of water before he fled. Manfred was arrested a week later."

Today, you are hired as his attorney.

Question:

What would be the best defense for him?

Let's think

Would it be helpful to emphasize the fact that Manfred helped Viggo pick up the bottle of medicine from the floor and gave him water, showing that Manfred is not cold-blooded or heartless?

Explanation:

A good-faith act is not going to offset an illegal act.

Answer:

Picking up the medicine for Viggo and handing him water are unlikely to be valid defenses when Manfred is accused of robbing Viggo because the subsequent good-faith act is not going to negate the previous illegal act of alleged "robbery."

Explanation:

Please pay attention to the wording

"...... Manfred carried a gun, and he got Viggo's wallet......"

Here, Manfred did not hold Viggo at gunpoint. Manfred simply "carried a gun," and he also got the wallet of Viggo. But how did Manfred get the wallet? It is unclear.

The definition of robbery is "larceny by threat or force." No facts show that "threat or force" was ever used. "Manfred carried a gun" can be an independent act from the act of getting Viggo's wallet. That is because carrying a gum can be the daily habit of Manfred, and it is also possible that Viggo misunderstood Manfred's intention and gave Manfred his own wallet. If that was the case, getting Viggo's wallet would not constitute a "threat or force" when Manfred simply accepted the wallet passed to him. Even though Viggo might feel threatened, Manfred did not affirmatively create the threat.

Conclusion

The best defense for Manfred would be no threat or force was ever used, and Viggo allowed Manfred to take his wallet because……

As such, there was no robbery.

Reminder

Be sure you are able to manipulate the two-side coin in the exam or in the court trial in future. But please do not get trapped when you try to figure out the valid defenses.

Defenses are not "pulling someone into the water"

Chinese people have an idiom known as "pulling someone into the water," meaning when you do something wrong, you will try to drag someone else onto your side in order to shift or share the blame.

Example: The manager came later to work than you did

You are being blamed for coming late to work today. You were two hours late to the office. Then you defend yourself by saying that the manager was three hours later. What you did was "pull the manager into the water" with you.

Let's think

Is it going to help your situation by "pulling the manager into the water" with you?

Let's think

When you are drowned in the sea, does it help if you pull one more person into the water?

Answer

No to both (1) and (2).

Solution

What you need is a piece of wood to make yourself able to float on the water. Having one more person drown with you is not going to rescue you from the danger.

Let's think

What is the purpose of the piece of wood?

Answer:

The piece of wood is to save your life. If there is no wood, try to find something which can help you float on the water. (A valid defense would be able to protect you from being blamed, sued or prosecuted.)

Let's think

Where can you find the piece of wood?

Answer:

The piece of wood is in your head:

How can you turn the accusation of "coming late to work" into not being late to work? (Based on facts; not lying)

Explanation:

People only saw you camc latc to the office, but if you already started working before you showed up in the office, then you would not be deemed "late to work."

You were two hours late. Think about what you did in those two hours: Did you return any emails somehow related to work? Did you complete any work for your boss? For example, picking up a suit from the dry-cleaning store for your boss to attend the work party tomorrow night. Or you did nothing today, but last week, you left two hours later than the scheduled time. That means you were just trying to offset the extra work hours last week in order to avoid overtime payment.

As such, you are not deemed to come late to work.

<u>Example: Defense of another person going to be harmed</u>

You are being prosecuted for causing harm to someone's body, known as G, and the reason was another person, known as H, was going to be harmed by G.

Your defense

Then, your defense would be "defense of another person." If you did not attack G at that moment, H would be harmed. This point would be your piece of wood.

Not your defense

Your defense would not be: Other bad people have harmed more victims than you did, which is "pulling other people into the water;" or you cannot say: G has harmed more people, so he deserved to be harmed.

If you say so, you are just holding your own court and making your own verdict.

Torts - Sharing liability

For torts, if you are able to show others 'faults, the ratio of your liability would be adjusted, but others 'faults would not constitute a valid defense.

Example: Trespass to land caused by the dropping of the metal numbers of address attached to the exterior wall of the apartment

For example, you entered someone's property without realizing that it is another one's property. That is because the number sign on the wall of that person's house is too small, or one number made of metal drops to the ground, wrongfully leading you to think that is the house of your friend. It is the homeowner's fault for not have fastened the metal number well, but your act of trespass is completed.

Example: Grabbing an identical bag

If someone puts an identical bag next to your bag on your own desk, and then you grab the wrong bag, that act would constitute conversion. You may say, "when you see my bag is identical to my bag, why do you still put your bag close to mine to cause the avoidable mistake?" You can grumble about that, but this act would not constitute a valid defense if all the elements of conversion were fulfilled. You are still liable to conversion.

Ambiguity in acts can be used as defenses

A rule may include vagueness, and an act may also have ambiguity for people to take advantage of when they try to explain or defend for themselves.

Example: Reporting to the Management at Romantic Apartment Complex

This is a rule set by the Romantic Apartment Complex:

"Only people listed on the lease are allowed to live at the unit. Any changes in the household size must be reported to the management team within 10 days of the changes occurring."

Let's think

When you are being accused of "failing to report," which terms or words would allow you to have wiggle room to argue or modify?

"Any changes in the household size" - Do pets count? If a household has adopted two dogs, is it deemed a change in the household size? (Pets are unlikely to count in reality; however, in essays, we can argue both ways and then conclude that they are unlikely to be counted. Pets are usually governed by the policy about pets.)

"Must be reported"-

The keys words here are "must" and "report." The word "must" means it is an obligation, and you have no choice, as opposed to the word "may" or "can." As such, you have to do so.

The word "report" leaves more wiggle room for you to explain:

Reporting can be formal or informal; it can be verbal or written; it can be by words or by gesture.

For example, Helen invites her friend Christy to live with her for one year when she starts studying in the U.S. as a foreign student. When Helen walks into the lobby with Christy carrying two big luggage boxes, Paul, the supervisor of the security guard, is talking on the phone. Helen points her finger to Christy and her luggage in front of Paul. The act of pointing can be deemed an informal way of reporting.

Question:

Is it a valid means of reporting?

Answer:

No one knows because the rule fails to specify it. But the tenant can argue and defend herself.

“Management team”- The management team can be the property manager or the clerical staff hired by the real property management company.

<u>Let’s think</u>

How about the security guard? How about a janitor hired by the property management company?

Explanation:

Probably, they are not deemed management. The management team should be those having authority to make decisions. A security guard who is responsible for patrolling or reporting when something unordinary happens, checking the ID cards of the visitors, they are unlikely to be deemed part of the "management team."

Defenses in essays

But in essays, you can still argue and then conclude that the argument is unlikely to prevail.

"Failing to report to the management team"

The valid defenses for you when you are accused of "failing to report to the management team" would depend on how businesses organize and direct their workflow, operations and employees to meet the goals of the company.

Here, Helen already reported the change in her household size to the supervisor of the security guard teams, who are responsible for arranging the schedule of the security guards and directing the work of the guard to fulfill the goal of safe and secure property of the property management company. When the supervisor of the guard received notification by the gesture from Helen, the act can be arguably deemed a valid manner of reporting, even though it is an informal way, as opposed to writing.

10 days

Ten is merely a number and ten days is the maximum length of time set by the apartment complex for the tenants to report household size changes, but how to count ten days is not specified.

Let's think

What is a day by definition? A calendar day or a business day? Does the weekend count? Does the Labor Day count? Does the four-day Thanksgiving holiday weekend count as one day, or two or three or four days? All variables mentioned above would make differences on the impact of the rule.

Question:

Which terms or words would have almost no wiggle room?

Answer:

"Only people listed on the lease" - The names on the lease were fixed when tenants moved into the apartment complex. If the lease includes four people, then it would be hard for anyone to argue there should be five or six. If the family has a newborn baby, the baby's name can be added but the legitimacy of tenants has yet to be confirmed by the procedure of adding the names. (In reality, having babies should not be a problem because discrimination against tenants because of children is a violation) In other words, even if the new tenant can be added and is qualified to be added, he or she is still not a legitimate tenant until his or her name is added to the lease.

Here, even if the existence of Christy is deemed notified by Helen, Christy would not become a valid occupant until her name is added onto the lease.

Reminder:

We have to be sensitive to those words without specifications. That is because there are so many possibilities encompassed.

10) Conclusion

Avoid ungrounded conclusions

No emotions for legal analysis

We make a lot of ungrounded conclusions, verbally or nonverbally, in our lifetimes, especially when we become emotional; But when we do a legal analysis, we have to get rid of all emotions and deal with the analysis rationally.

Type out all hidden words to help the conclusion make sense

We get used to having many ungrounded conclusions in our lives because when we utter the words in our daily lives, we may also have other words in our mind which are not expressed outwards; but in an essay, you have to type out all those hidden words to help the conclusion make sense.

Example: Breaking up on Valentine's Day

Here is a dialogue at 11 pm on Valentine's Day between Girlfriend(G) and Boyfriend(B), who spend their first Valentine's Day together.

G: "I have made up my mind. I need to break up with you. We should separate."

B: "Why? We just spent the whole day together today. We had a good time. What was wrong?"

G: "No. You did not take my Valentine's Day seriously."

B: “What? We had a movie in the afternoon and a delicious dinner at the hotel in the evening.”

G: “Yes. But you just randomly bought two tickets today for the movie. The story was about adventure in a desert. I would like to watch a romantic movie on Valentine’s Day.”

B: “Another movie about the love story was already sold out before we went to the cinema.”

G: “That is my point. You should have reserved two tickets at least one week in advance.”

B: “I think watching a movie was merely to kill time before dinner. Nevertheless, we had a luxurious dinner at a five-star hotel. It was fantastic!”

G: “But we sat at the bar only, not the booth at the window.”

B: “Those booths were all occupied.”

G: “Of course. Today is Valentine’s Day. You should have made a reservation on those booths at least two months in advance.”

B: “But I also bought you a bunch of flowers.”

G: “The bunch of flower was just sold inside the restaurant. You did not order a dozen of my favorite flowers to me from the flower store. You did not make any preparation for our first Valentine’s Day. You did not take today seriously.”

B: “I agree with you.”

G: "You agree that you are wrong. Is it correct? OK. Then I might give you one more chance."

B: "No, thanks. I agree that we should break up. Valentine's Day means a day of rest and fun to me but it means a lot of preparation works to you. I am so sorry. I do not want any overtime work besides my real job. Goodbye!"

Explanations:

Breaking up after celebration?

When the girlfriend first states her conclusion, which is her decision to break up, the boyfriend does not understand the reason. That is because he thinks that they just have a good time on their first Valentine's Day. But when the girlfriend explains what exactly she feels unhappy about, the boyfriend concludes the same way, and also refuses the "one more chance" offer given by the girlfriend.

No preparation was made by the boyfriend

The boyfriend is first puzzled. What he feels bizarre is: that his girlfriend requests to break up after the movie and the dinner at the hotel. But the girlfriend thinks that the boyfriend did not have any preparation for their Valentine's Day (not reserving movie tickets for the movie, not reserving booth at the window for dinner, and not ordering a dozen of her favorite flowers.) The boyfriend thinks that their first Valentine's Day is a day of fun and rest but the girlfriend expects him to make many preparations like working overtime.

Different perceptions of the Valentine's Day

Once the girlfriend voices out what she is unhappy about, the boyfriend realizes the different ways they perceive the Valentine's Day, so he draws the same conclusion as his girlfriend does.

Eventually, there is one thing they both agree on.

Applying to essays

You have to go deep enough to reveal the underlying reasons

If you fail to clearly state the reasons for conclusion, the grader of your essay would feel the same way as the boyfriend felt when he was first told that they needed to break up. Bear in mind that verbal expressions on the face may not be sufficient to reveal the real reasons . Please explain step by step and also go deep enough to reveal the underlying reasons of your conclusion in an essay.

Here, from the girlfriend's perspective, the underlying reason of breaking up is not about what movie to watch, what seat to take for dinner or what flowers or how many flowers to have, but the lack of preparation by the boyfriend.

All layers of reasoning and impact have to be completed

When you explain "why" in your essays, you have to realize the layers of reasoning and impact and then point that out in an organized manner to complete your explanations. All layers have to be completed before a conclusion is made.

Crazy conclusions can be devastating

Six ladies, including Alicia(A), Bianca(B), Cherry(C), Daisy(D), Elaine(E), Faye(F) are chatting in the pantry of their office.

A: "Teresa brings lunch to work everyday and never eats out with us. She is a cheapskate."

B: "Maybe she likes to cook."

C: "Maybe she does not want to walk in and out of the office when we have one hour for lunch only."

D: "Maybe she wants to be punctual to the meetings after lunch."

E: "Maybe she wants to save money to buy a house."

F: "Maybe she does not like one or all of us."

T: "No. You are all wrong."

Teresa just happens to come in for a cup of hot water.

T: "I am just allergic to MSG, so I have to cook myself to avoid sickness."

Explanations:

Alicia made a crazy conclusion:

Her rule: Employees who do not eat out during lunchtime are cheapskates.

Alicia fails to realize other possibilities. What other people point out are other possibilities, which sound more reasonable and probable, but none of them are close to what Teresa claims to be the truth.

11) Presentation

How to answer a question?

Do you know how to answer a question, regardless of the context of the question? I am not talking about the knowledge you have but the methodology of answering a question. The Chinese people from Hong Kong have the slang "nine does not match the eight," meaning what you answer is out of the scope of the question, or it is offtrack. The quality of your answer is just like somniloquy: you wake up in the middle of the night, and your spouse asks you a question next to you, then you mumble and fall asleep again.

Example: Which buses?

Q: "Which buses go to the wharf?"

A: "Number 8, 10 and 49."

Regardless of whether the bus 8, 10 and 49 actually go to the wharf, the methodology of answering the question is correct.

How about if you say, "the buses in the city are very unsafe, and robberies happen every day. Do not take buses. Please call Uber"? Regardless of your good-faith suggestion, the methodology you use is not answering the question.

Q: "How far is the wharf from here?"

A: "Three minutes if you take a taxi; ten minutes if you take the bus; and forty minutes if you walk."

When you answer one single question, you tend to be clear in your answer, but when you keep answering questions for three hours, you may start going off track, partly because you are tired. Hence, you have to practice maintaining your focus for three hours to stay on track.

Every sentence needs an added value

Writing a long essay does not mean you have to drag the paragraphs long or the sentences long. The context has to be rich, the discussion can be deep in depth, but the words should be concise. Every sentence is supposed to have an added value to the explanation or the analysis. Those words only take up space and increase word count but not elaborate the analysis are actually redundant "fats" in our essay. We have to get rid of them.

A legal writing should have thorough explanations with the arguments from both sides, plus supporting facts. It is good to have many good points, but not a few points only being explained in many words. Conciseness is stronger than redundancy. If you spend three pages talking about the same point with different vocabularies, and different examples, you must have spent a lot of time and effort, but I would be sorry to tell you that you have one point only. I would also feel sorry that you waste your own time and also my time reading those words.

When you become an attorney, the Judge would not like to waste time reading a few pages of words which, in fact, can be stated in a few sentences only.

When you practice writing, please proofread your own essay to find out which sentence is redundant, useless or pointless. Some extra sentences are able to make one single point clearer or more in-depth in the meaning, but not all of them. We have so many IRACs in one essay, so please do not waste time typing useless words.

Is it a complete and thorough explanation?

When you explain why, your words may not completely and thoroughly explain why while you think they did.

Example: Julie is going to have a breakfast meeting tomorrow

Julie just finished the dinner with Olivia at 8 pm.

Julie: "I have to leave."

Olivia: "Why do you leave so early tonight? I expect we are going to chat after dinner."

Julie: "Because I have a breakfast meeting tomorrow at 8 am."

Incomplete explanation:

Julie fails to explain why she has to leave now because the breakfast meeting will not take place until 12 hours later. She fails to directly address the question of why she has to leave immediately.

Can you help her complete the explanation?

Julie: I need to drive home, and then take a shower and also finish some trivial works before I go to bed at 11 pm. I would have to wake up at 6 am in order to show up at the breakfast meeting on time. If I do not go to bed before 11 pm, I would not have enough energy to concentrate on the breakfast meeting tomorrow.

One point at a time

When you write a contract essay, the same contract may have a few issues: Statute of fraud; Parol evidence rule, etc.

But when you talk about Statute of fraud, just focus on "MY LEGS" and whether the situation given needs a writing to be effective; and when you discuss parol evidence rule, you can focus on the evidence of prior or contemporaneous negotiations and agreements that contradict, modify, or vary the contractual terms of a written contract.

When you explain about MY LEGS, do not also mention the prior or contemporaneous negotiations in the same IRAC. Talking more rules in one IRAC is not going to show that you are more knowledgeable.

Subjective feeling vs. objective description

Subjective

Tenant: "The noise is loud. It is just like killing someone."

Tenant: "The landlord just wants us to move and tries to find something to justify his act."

Objective

Tenant: "He plays music at midnight almost every day."

Tenant: "One year before the landlord handed us an eviction notice, she made many excuses to try to get us to move out of the unit, such as remodeling. But when we asked when we could come back after remodeling, she said she does not want us to come back."

12) Words and Phrasing

*Semantic change in words

As time goes by, the meaning of the same word to the general public would indicate different things.

The evolvement of words

In the past, the word "Amazon" made people think of the forest, but recently, most people think of online shopping; in the past, the word "apple" was a kind of fruit, but now it means more about electronic devices; In the past, a notebook means a paper notepad or an exercise book which you can write on; but in this generation, a notebook means a laptop to most people.

Hence, when we use a particular word, we have to be clear to convey what we exactly mean.

How you phrase the sentence matters

Example: Police Station - To be accurate, neutral and honest

Here is a scenario at the police station:

The defendant, his lawyer and the police officer are all standing inside an open office.

Police: "All evidence show that your client is likely to be the person who killed the victim. There is no evidence showing that your client is innocent."

Lawyer: "To be accurate, so far, you failed to find any evidences to prove the innocence of my client while unfavorable evidences exist."

A delivery man just walks by.

Delivery: "To be neutral, so far there is no evidence, regardless of who found it, showing the innocence of the defendant; but there could be sufficient evidences showing he is guilty."

Defendant: "To be honest, I am innocent, regardless of the absence of any favorable evidences to me. Without finding favorable evidences to disprove the possibility of killing the victim by me, I could be labelled "guilty" under the current legal system. "Guilty" is just a legal conclusion based on more unfavorable facts, but I am, in fact, innocent. "

Pay attention to what the adjectives are trying to modify

When an adjective is placed at different positions of a sentence, with different connecting words, the modification can be for different acts or people.

Example: Recent

Judy watches a video about scams.

Recently, Judy watches a video about scams.

Judy watches a video about scams made recently.

Recently, Judy watches a video about scams made recently.

Recently, Judy watches a video about scams made 30 years ago.

Explanation:

Judy may watch the video about scams recently but the video was made 30 years ago. There are huge differences in meanings in the context of the video.

If the video is made recently, the scam tricks could be new and ongoing, and the general public has to be careful; but if the video was made 30 years ago, the relevancy would be relatively lower, even though the scammers can always use the old tricks to scam people.

When we read merely one sentence, we are more clear about the differences; but in the exam, when you have to deal with three essays in three hours, and every essay question has four to five paragraphs, and each paragraph has three to ten sentences, it is possible that you would not spot the differences or you would be confused. Or your brain would just remember you read the word "recent," but what is, in fact, "recent" may not be stored in your mind. This is highly likely to happen when you drop your head and keep typing under time stress. So when you actually start typing about the facts given in the question, your eyes should go back to the particular sentence to remind yourself what the adjective is trying to modify: Is the video recently made, or does Judy watch the video recently?

13) Ignorance of the law is not an excuse for unlawful behaviors

I believe most of us are aware of that: "Ignorance of the law is not an excuse for unlawful behaviors." However, in our daily lives, we somehow try to use it as a defense against different accusations.

"I don't know" would be irrelevant if the laws are violated.

"I don't know." Everyone has said that in his or her life. But if that act violates the law, who cares whether you know or not?

When "knowingly" doing an act is an element

If the elements of the rule include the word "knowingly," then whether you know would matter. If the actor did not "knowingly" take the wrong act, he would not be held liable.

Takeaway from the above discussion:

When you analyze an essay, please be aware of this concept. Without the element of "knowingly," and when the acts are completed, and the elements are fulfilled, the person would be held liable or guilty of his act, regardless of whether he knows it is illegal.

14) Discussion of short essays

Business Association Essay: The technology Company

"Kyle is one of the three partners in a technology company, Miracle Co.. Kyle aims to maximize long-term profits, so Kyle plans to build a brandnew building with AI (Artificial Intelligence) technology to replace the old one. Due to the constantly increasing price of lumber and other construction materials, Kyle hires a construction company named Wonderful to start doing the work, instead of waiting for the bi-annual meeting at Miracle for approval.

Wonderful also hires Parker, a structural engineer, to assist with the work. Kyle especially trusts Parker because they both like the same brand of vehicles, watches and shoes. Parker reviews the plans of the building with Kyle. During the construction, some heavy materials hit a pedestrian due to unusually strong wind. Some damages are also caused to the adjacent apartment buildings.

The other two partners of, Miracle are very concerned about their liabilities, and Kyle also worries whether he would be held liable personally.

Please discuss."

Here is part of a student's answer

Are partners liable for partnership debt?

Each partner is always personally liable for every partnership debt, regardless of the profit and loss sharing percentage.

Here, the facts show Kyle and his two partners are partners in general partnership defined supra, which shows that they will be liable for the partnership debt because each partner is personally liable for every partnership debt. Kyle made the decision to hire the company, so he should be personally liable, not the other three partners. But it does not matter who is making the decision in general partnership since all partners are liable for the partnership obligations.

Therefore, Kyle and his partners will be personally liable for general partnership business. <You repeated the same phrase or meaning three times, but did you actually explain why?>

Duty of loyalty

Duty of loyalty requires that partners act in good faith, treat each other fairly, and that partners avoid conflicts of interest. <This definition is not accurate. The essence of duty of loyalty is putting the partnership's interest on top of one's or other people's interest.>

Here, the facts show that Kyle recognized that <unclear>in order to maximize long-term profits. One might argue that Kyle made the decision without consulting any other partners and he acted in self-interest <This opposing argument is not supported by any facts or examples>, which is not true because facts did not show that he was trying to help himself. In fact, he was trying to improve the business. <Without the support of facts or examples>

Kyle was acting alone without consulting with other partners, which shows that his acts were not fair to other partners <without consulting with other partners does not necessarily lead to unfairness> because there is a possibility that they did not want to demolish the building since there was an increased liability of adjacent apartment buildings. <This sentence is unclear and convoluted. You have both "because" and "since" to explain the reasons. >The facts did not show that the partners were in agreement with Kyle. However, Kyle can argue he acts fairly because he was trying to increase the profits of the business which would benefit everyone. But increasing the liability of the partners without notifying them is not a fair act of Kyle and it did not avoid conflicts of interest because facts show that other partners were concerned about their liabilities.

Therefore, Kyle is liable for the duty of loyalty.

Was there a full disclosure and notification by Kyle?

The partner must always notify the partnership of all the material facts that are relevant to the subject matter of the partnership. The partner must disclose every fact <too broad: How about if a stapler is broken? It costs money to buy another one, and it would somehow reduce the profit of the partnership, but you would not need to disclose this small expense to your partner. > that he knows or should know as it will be imputed to and affect the partnership interest.

Here, the facts show that Kyle's decision is a material fact that is relevant to the subject matter of the partnership because the building is the only property of the partnership, <That explains the importance of the building to the

partnership.> and any major decision regarding the partnership property must be disclosed by notifying the partnership by the partner. <That is why Kyle should have disclosed, as opposed to when the building is merely one of the assets owned by the partnership.> Kyle was making business decisions for the business. <This sentence sounds meaningless: “making business decisions for the business.” Almost any work-related decisions are business decisions, except something very personal. Thus, you should rephrase this expression. Do you mean if the decision is wise, for the sake of the business, or intended to expand the business and increase the profit? Please specify.> and was acting in good faith <Then you bring up another opposing idea: acting in good faith may not need to disclose. Is it the argument raised by Kyle? Showing arguments on both sides is good, but the way you expressed sounds contradictory more than providing “balanced views.” > for the company therefore, he did not need to notify anyone. His decision was going to affect the partnership interest because it was going to increase the partnership liability <This is an opposing argument, so you should have the right phrase to lead in, such as “other partners may argue…”> due to the apartment buildings nearby therefore as a partner, he must notify anything <too broad: Please think about that. Does it make sense? How about a few pieces of used tissues being tossed in the hallway? That affects hygiene but it does not mean you need to disclose that to other partners. That would be too trivial.> he knows or should have known the partnership, and he failed to notify other partners. <Convoluted>

Thus, Kyle violated the duty of full disclosure and notification."

Comments:

The heading should be rights, duties and obligations, or just partners, and then talk about the three mentioned above.

When the rule has already specified that all partners are responsible for the decisions others make, there is no need to argue about the rule, but you can argue about other facts available. In fact, it is not up to you to argue about the rule.

You should not start from "debt" because the main issuc is not "debt," which is the outcome of borrowing from others. Here, the issue is the liability for damages incurred. Please use the exact term.

"The partner must always notify the partnership of all the material facts that are relevant to the subject matter of the partnership. The partner must disclose every fact : " This is over-generalized and over-broad. The partner must disclose every material fact only. That means facts that a partner knows or should know as it will be imputed to and affect the partnership interest. For example, someone offers to buy the partnership, or the cost of supply of certain products increases, or the impact of the change of the relevant government policy on the partnership.

You did not use the best words in the analysis: "The partners are supposed to have liability for decisions made by other partners. The amount of damages they could have paid would increase when the explosion is involved, up to the amount they have invested."

However, facts show that Kyle especially trusts Parker, who is a new hire by Wonderful, without objective reasons. The trust is built just because they both like the same brand of vehicles, watches and shoes. When Kyle trusts Parker based on subjective feelings or personal preferences, he has violated his duty of loyalty because he has put his own preference on top of the benefits of the partnership with Miracle Co.

The following facts should go to the duty of communication: It is reasonable for Kyle not to wait till the team meeting since the lumber price is rising, but it would be so easy and quick for Kyle to merely send the other three partners of Miracle Co. an email or make a phone call, which could take less than 30 minutes. But Kyle failed to do so. Thus, Kyle has violated his duty of communication.

<Compare: Limited partners are not expected to participate in any daily operations or business decisions, but they would also be held liable up to the amount they invested. Thus, the three other partners are also held liable to the damages incurred if the partnership is held liable instead of Wonderful.>

<You can explore more: All businesses are aimed to maximize their profits, and K's acts are for the sake of the partnership in the long run, which is important because, without long-term profits, the partnership would not sustain for long time.>

<No need to repeat the whole long sentence: which shows that as a partner, James was acting in good faith because he wanted to increase the profits of the business which will ultimately benefit the other partners and the company. >

<Even though you use the same facts, please try to adjust the way you write to fit the category: Duty of care; Duty of loyalty; Duty of communication.>

<Kyle needed to act quickly because the price of lumber was increasing. You need to argue about whether the need to act "quickly" justifies his failure to discuss with the other partners. Even though the price of lumber changes quickly, calling or emailing a partner should be quicker. Kyle should have made reasonable efforts to notify other partners, and if the partners do not respond in 24 hours or 3 days, then it would be more reasonable for Kyle to act on his own decision.>

<u>Contracts Essay: Annual pass for the baseball season</u>

Question:

"Hugo has recently bought an annual pass for the baseball season at $1200. However, he drank some alcohol inside the stadium in the second month of the baseball year, and he almost started with a fight with another man.

A male security guard tried to calm him down but he was resistant to his effort. Eventually, he was eliminated from the arena the day of the incident, and later, he received a letter notifying him that his annual pass for the rest of the baseball season would be cancelled. Also, no money would be refunded."

Please discuss.

<u>Here is part of the student's answer:</u>

"<u>Does Hugo (H) have a revocable license?</u>

A license is revocable at will.

Here, H was removed by the security personnel from the premises, and his annual pass will be no longer honored. His license was revoked when he resisted attempts by the security to calm him down. His license was for a limited purpose to watch the game and not to disturb others. If he abuses his privileges, then his license can be revoked because he is not using it appropriately.

He might argue that he has an annual pass, and it is irrevocable because neither the game nor the season is over yet. <This opposing argument is weak not supported with sufficient facts.>

Therefore, H has a revocable license. <This conclusion is not supported with sufficient arguments>

Can H transfer his license?

A license is presumed to be personal to the original licensee and nontransferable unless the licensor/licensee has the intent to make it transferable.

H's license to enter the property has been revoked. He may not transfer his license because it is personal to the licensee and nontransferable. He may want to contact the licensor to transfer the pass because it can be made transferable if either the licensee or the licensor has the intent to make it transferable.

Therefore, H might not be able to transfer his license.

H's license can be removed. He has the above rights, and he can make the above-mentioned arguments." <This conclusion is not expressed in a persuasive manner.>

Sample answer for comparison

A license is revocable if certain terms are violated.

Here, people who are admitted into the stadium are expected to act appropriately, especially when it is a public place involving public safety. In other words, one's act should not interfere with others. Hugo drank alcohol and almost started a fight, which falls on the borderline of right and wrong. It is not absolutely wrong because he "almost" started a fight, but he did not start yet. That means it could be just a fierce argument with some gestures.

When fans get emotional, excited or upset, misconduct within a range would be expected, even though those acts should not be encouraged. But, placing too many limitations may also deter people's desire to come to the stadium watching the game. In this situation, Hugo had some misconduct due to his alcohol consumption. No facts show that he had a previous record of bad conduct. This is just a one-time incident, so he deserves a chance to correct his fault. It would bc more reasonable to merely give him a written warning: "If you have the same misconduct again, your pass could be cancelled, Mr. Hugo." But it would be unreasonable for the stadium to cancel his costly annual pass just because of one single minor mistake, which is almost starting a fight.

Covenant of Good Faith and Fair Dealing

Each contract has an implied Covenant of Good Faith and Fair Dealing, meaning every party in a contract has to implement what is intended in the agreement instead of dishonestly undercutting the purpose of the transaction.

Here, the intended agreement for the stadium is to provide access for 12 months in total. If the annual pass for Hugo must be cancelled for any reason, the stadium should allow Hugo to transfer it to other people. The pass costs $1200, and it is supposed to cover the whole year. Hugo just used the pass for about two months, and the right to use it for the remaining ten months should remain valid. If his conduct is the concern of the stadium, transferring the pass to another person with no previous record of misconduct would be a desirable solution. Then, the pass can be fully utilized without the risk of having the same misconduct. If the stadium does not allow Hugo to transfer the pass to another party, it may have violated the implied covenant of good faith and fair dealing, which is to implement what is intended in the agreement. Moreover, the stadium would be unjustly enriched by charging Hugo money but not allowing him to use it.

Thus, the stadium should allow Hugo to transfer the pass to another person.

Remedies

Restitution

Here, there will be an unjust enrichment if money is not refunded to Hugo, and the pass cannot be transferred to another individual. Hugo paid $1200 for using the pass for 12 months, but only two months have passed. That means the remaining value of the pass would be approximately $1000. If the stadium has decided to cancel his pass, $1000 should be refunded to Hugo. Otherwise, the stadium would be unjustly enriched by receiving the $1000 without providing any services to Hugo.

Hence, $1000 should be refunded to Hugo.

Remedies: The famous love song singer

"Gigi is a famous love song singer in San Francisco Bay Area who enters into a valid written contract with Zion, whereby she will perform at his Valentine's Day concert at SF Auditorium for $200,000. On January 10th, Yammie, one of Zion's competitor, told Gigi that Zion is having financial difficulty paying for the necessary expenses before a concert can be held, which upsets Gigi. She worries that her concert may not be held eventually.

Yammie offers to pay Gigi $150,000 to perform for Yammie in Oakland, about 20 miles from San Francisco.

Zion told Gigi that words regarding his financial difficulty were untrue. However, Gigi still has doubts about Zion's words and tells Zion that she may accept the offer of Yammie.

Worrying that Gigi may perform for Yammie, Zion files suit seeking to require Gigi to perform for him on Valentine's Day and to prevent her from performing for Yammie or anyone else anywhere.

From the legal perspective, what issues are raised, and how should they be resolved in a reasonable manner?"

Here is part of the student's answer:

Is injunction available?

An injunction is an equitable remedy in which the court issues an order commanding an action or preventing an action.

Here, Zion wanted to prevent Gigi from performing for Yammie or anyone because she would breach her contract. Since Gigi's performance is not unique, the court might not be able to award specific performance, but it can award an equitable remedy of injunction commanding Gigi not to perform for either Yammie or anyone else. Gigi might argue that Zion could mitigate his damages by hiring another singer. Her reason for canceling the contract was Gigi believed Zion would not be able to perform financially if he did not have enough money to make the concert happen.

Therefore, the court might award an injunction.

Does the permanent injunction apply?

A permanent injunction would be granted or denied after a full hearing and the court must balance the hardship for both sides.

Here, facts show that Zion wanted to prevent Gigi from performing for anyone else on Valentine's Day. He may want to get a permanent injunction against Gigi, which the court might grant after the hearing. The contract between Zion and Gigi is about Gigi's singing performance, and she does not cancel it in bad faith. Hence, the court must balance the hardship for both parties. She signed one contract with Zion does not mean she would not be permitted to perform for other people. The court might not grant a permanent injunction to Zion against Gigi. <You failed to explain why a permanent injunction should not be granted. Gigi just promised to perform for one night for Zion, so the court may grant an injunction for performing for other people for that particular night at most. The injunction should not restrict Gigi for more than one night, and the night has to be Valentine's Day only, while Gigi's contract states that she has to perform for Zion on Valentine's Day..>

Therefore, the permanent injunction might not apply. <This conclusion is unclear. You can use stronger words: The court is very unlikely to grant the permanent injunction.>"

Comments:

The biggest problem: the analysis for both parts is contradictory to each other.

Furthermore, the court is not going to issue a "permanent" injunction for the breach of a contract that was only going to last for one night. The court may prevent Gigi from performing for Yammie, but the restriction would not be everlasting. Facts show that Gigi is a famous love song singer in the San Francisco Bay Area only, so it does not make sense for Zion to seek to prevent her from performing for anyone else and at places other than the San Francisco Bay Area. The more reasonable outcome would be: The court would grant an injunction to prohibit Gigi from performing for Yammie on Valentine's Day in Oakland, but the injunction would not go beyond the San Francisco Bay Area, and it would not be more than one day, and that day has to be Valentine's Day.

Furthermore, the court cannot issue an order to force Gigi to perform for Zion, which would amount to involuntary servitude, but Gigi may be required to pay the damages incurred by Zion.

Section 3

For CA Bar Exam takers and repeaters

Psychological aspects

Do not underestimate the psychological aspects

Psychology has an impact on almost every task we do. For example, before your public speech, if someone criticizes your work performance harshly or your boss hands you a layoff letter, there must be some impact on your mood, level of confidence, or mindset. If we have high emotional intelligence, we can try to hold the emotion inside instead of spreading that out.

Probably half of the bar exam takers took the exam three to nine times before they eventually passed. If they do not believe in their own abilities, or they are swayed by people who tell them they are not going to succeed, they could permanently stop taking the exam after two attempts. Then, there would be zero chance for them to be attorneys. When you sign up for an exam, regardless of the outcome, at least you give yourself a chance of success, and then you can work on boosting your abilities in different areas in order to increase the likelihood of passing the bar.

It does not matter if other people do not trust your capability unless you have to borrow the exam fees from them. You have to be candid with yourself about your own ability: Do you understand the meaning of the legal doctrines? Do you understand why the correct answers to the MBE questions are correct? Do you see too many unknown vocabulary in the essay questions, in the performance test or in MBEs? If yes, you may have to first improve your English competency before you sign up for the bar again.

Your life is yours: Whether you are going to be an attorney, a legal assistant, a delivery man, or a plumber, it would be your own choice, your fate and your life. It does not matter, as long as you enjoy it. You should make your own decision with your own wisdom, not to be controlled by any gossips, or swayed by others 'opinions.

English as the second language

Speaking English as a second language is not the biggest barrier to passing the bar because reading and writing skills can always be improved. Whether you will succeed just depends on how much you want to be an attorney. If that is something on your bucket list, just do it and your determination will guide you to resolve all little problems. If you have been a paralegal for a decade and think that it would be easy and convenient for you to get a license, then you may have to reconsider it when you find the exam is not easy at all. The attorney's license is not something you can just easily grab on your way without making sufficient effort and sacrifice. You have to stay determined.

Retaking the bar is not a wild goose chase

The exam is a chance for us to demonstrate how well we are able to organize reading material, understand complicated information, make judgments, present our arguments and rebut counter-arguments under time stress. It would be a big challenge to put yourself under an enormous amount of stress, but it would also be a milestone in your life if you succeed. Besides, it is also fun to see yourself growing by receiving more points in every exam. But if you never try to improve your writing skills or MBE scores, retaking the exam would be merely a wild goose chase for you.

Bad luck is not an excuse for everyone's failure

Emotional support

Emotional support is important to keep ourselves motivated and energized to fight the battle. We can share our fun, pain and frustration with other exam takers. But seeking emotional support does not mean finding excuses for yourself to escape from the responsibility.

Bad luck?

If you are less than ten points away from passing the bar, I agree that you have bad luck because a good guess to get one more correct MBE answer would immediately change your title to Esq. But if you are more than fifty points away from passing, I would say "luck" may be in play only if you fail merely in the MBE sections, while your score in essays is more than 1400. If most of your essays are below 65, your failure is not about "luck."

We all know a grader merely spends a few minutes on an essay. Then what would make them give a passing score? I do not personally know any graders. But logically, I would think the structures and the headings of the essays are controlled. If the structure looks organized, and the headings hit the main doctrines with thorough analysis, you could easily score 60 or 65. If you do not explain everything well enough or miss the analysis of some foundational concepts before you jump into the main issue, you may get a lower score in the second read of the same essay. Either good structure or good analysis is likely to bring you a good score in at least one read. If you are good in both structure and analysis, it is likely you would get high scores; If you still see your scores, meaning you failed, your weak part could be PT or MBEs.

I would not attribute success or failure to "luck" regarding study. I believe 80 percent is about your own effort, and another 20 percent would be some external forces. Unless you encounter big events such as 911 in New York in 2001, or the collapse of an Overpass near San Francisco caused by a tanker truck fire in 2007, or the Manila hostage crisis in 2010, please do not say "bad luck" again if you fail the bar. It simply saps your energy which could be reserved for studying.

Do not rush!

If you are impatient and short-tempered, please do not include this aspect of your personality into the process of writing your essay. You need to explain the doctrines with facts step by step: If there are five layers of explanations, you need to do all five to make it comprehensive. If you try to take a short cut and skip two layers in the middle, the base of the analysis would be constructed on a ground of soft and loose mud. Then the missing arguments would be similar to missing pieces of Lego building blocks: the whole thing will collapse.

Writing one essay takes one hour and this hour would be your "show time." Whoever performs a show cannot rush to finish the task. Explaining the unknowns in detail and in layers would be the context of your show. The "audience" needs to see how you showcase your knowledge and skills. If you are too eager to finish every "show 'without meeting the standard, your bar exam adventure may never end.

Enjoy the torture?

The two-day exam is torture, but before the new path to be an attorneys is available in California, the only way to end the torture would be to overcome it. Besides skills, one of the ways to achieve better performance would be enjoying the exam.

Please try to enjoy every second of your own show.

Example: Confession

A confession must be voluntarily, and knowingly made by the defendant.

Here, Deborah's confession was voluntarily and knowingly made because she said "I started thc fire."

Thus, Deborah's motion should not be suppressed.

Explanation

The analysis here starts with a conclusion, and then quote one phrase from the defendant without any explanation. Merely saying "I started the fire" does not indicate that the statement is made without coercion. There could be other circumstances leading to this statement. Someone could have taken some intimidating acts to the defendant.

Also, the conclusion is that the motion should not be suppressed. But what motion is the conclusion talking about? It is unclear, and it has to be clear.

Introspection Philosophy

Chinese people have an idiom about reviewing one's own mistakes: "Use other people as a mirror to introspect and reflect on yourself." We always see others 'mistakes, but we may fail to see our own mistakes. But that's fine because it is just human nature, and we can take advantage of the human nature to benefit ourselves: When we realize other people's mistake in logics, explanations or arguments, we can ask ourselves: Did I ever do the same thing?

You do not have to tell others your answer, but you can think about it yourself. In fact, it is not something we need to be ashamed of. No one would think that is a big problem if you tell him or her that you made a mistake and you admit the mistake.

Nobody would be perfect

If you do not believe me, we can play a game: Today, you can walk out of your house and tell everyone you come across on your way: "I am perfect. I am perfect. I am perfect." People may not argue with you. But I am sure there would be a lot of ridicule. Why? No one would believe that you are perfect. If you say so, that just means you fail to perceive your own defects. The word "perfect" simply turns up the volume of your defects.

Learning from mistakes

Passing the bar requires skills in writing essays, answering MBEs and handling performance tests while learning from mistakes is one of the strategies you need to perform well in the parts mentioned above in order to pass the bar and to succeed in your career and in your life.

Predicting what could go wrong and trying to avoid it:

Common mistakes of bar exam takers

Problem: Failing to address all elements before conclude in one single IRAC.

When exam takers are nervous, they may forget analyzing some elements before they conclude.

Solution: Making sub IRACs

Example: Veggie soup

When you prepare a veggie soup, you have to cut many ingredients: carrots, cucumber, tomatoes, etc. Some ingredients require us to spend longer time and effort to cut, and that is fine, as long as we remember cutting all of them and then pouring all of them into the cooking pot. However, while we turn around and around in the kitchen, we may forget to pour the tomatoes into the soup after we cut the carrots and cucumber. Then, the finished veggie soup would not be the complete soup of what you plan to have.

In order to avoid forgetting any ingredients for the veggie soup, please first write a list of all ingredients on a piece of paper; and also display all your veggies on the table; then cut or peel each of them and then pour each bowl of shredded ingredients into the big pot. Before you put on the lid of the pot, please check if all the veggies on the list are already poured into the pot.

Check the list of headings to avoid missing parts.

In the essay, you can first write a list of headings of elements when you have more energy at the beginning of the exam and simply write under every heading to complete the full analysis when you drop your head typing under time stress. The methodology is just like filling in the blanks when you do an application form, but what you need to fill out is not your personal information, but IRACs. If you have enough practices, you should be able to complete one sub-IRAC in less than three minutes.

Instruction: Address all elements before you conclude in one single IRAC.

One rule may have two or three elements, and one element may take more time to explain than another. The common mistake for bar exam takers is a long explanation of one particular element distracts them from the analysis of other elements.

Example: Strict scrutiny

You do not only need to explain what is a compelling government interest but also the element of "narrowly tailored" or a "tight fit." When you spend one big paragraph to explain the compelling government interest, you may forget to explain if it is a tight fit. When you first start writing the essay, you can make sub IRACs by writing a heading for each element, and discuss if each element is met before you conclude this single IRAC.

Strategies

Study should be your first priority

Everyone at grassroots level must work to support his or her basic necessities, including housing, food and health services. Otherwise, we would not have energy to pursue our dreams. You would not be able to concentrate on your study if you just lived inside a tent under the overpass. But besides your job to pay the bills, study should be your first priority. Do not create excessive entertainments which would take away your time, energy and money. Our first priority before passing the bar should be studying. If you treat your study like a hobby, such as learning dancing or learning a foreign language for travel, it would be difficult for you to score higher than the cut score in California.

Two years before I passed the bar, I did not hang out with any friends or former colleagues. Going out with friends would reduce the amount of my time, energy and money. I had to focus on my study: writing essays, doing

MBEs, and saving the money to pay the tutors. For every dollar I could spend elsewhere, I saved them for the journey of pursuing my dream.

Meeting others was not a temptation for me

For acquaintances who did not know my plan to be an attorney, I could not share my frustration with them; for acquaintances who knew my plan, I did not want to bring up my frustration in front of them. You might think others could comfort me. But what is the point for a layperson to talk to me about the exam when they have no idea of how the bar exam is? Repeating your failures to other people would not help. Hence, hanging out with others was not a temptation to me.

Do not keep postponing your bar exam

Do not always postpone your plan to take the bar exam unless you have a real family emergency, especially when you already reach middle ages. It would take much time for you to build up your reputation in the career after you pass the bar, so do not waste time. If you plan to take the exam one year later, your first priority in the coming 52 weeks must be studying. Please stay away from those unnecessary parties or gatherings. Those occasions are usually intended for people to show off. You can wait till you swear in to become an attorney to show off your talents and achievements at any party throughout the year.

How to learn from sample essays?

Do not regard sample essays as definition sheets. If you need to study definitions, you can use flashcards or outlines. Instead, please find out how others handle the massive information given in the fact patterns; see how others interpret some facts, as opposed to the ways you interpret; see what facts are totally overlooked by yourselves; check what legal doctrines are missed by you; see which analysis in the sample answers is, in fact, unnecessary; if others support the opposing sides, see if their explanations and analysis are in fact sufficient to support their standpoints.

Practice writing a few IRACs when you do not have one full hour for a complete essay

If you have a full-time job and kids, you may not be able to write one full essay every day. Then you can try to write the outline and all headings first and complete two or three IRACs every night before you go to bed.

Writing one full IRAC takes about five to ten minutes

One complete IRAC with a few sub-IRACs should take no more than ten minutes; if one single IRAC takes more than ten minutes, it is highly likely that you wrote unnecessary stuff. When one single essay has probably more than ten IRACs, writing one full IRAC should not exceed five minutes.

Practicing IRACS is testing your own knowledge of legal doctrines

Do you understand the doctrine well?

When you practice one single IRAC, it is the opportunity to test your own knowledge of that particular doctrine. Many exam takers are able to recite the headings of the outline but do not thoroughly understand the doctrine. If you have difficulty explaining and analyzing, you may have to go back to the books to polish your own understanding. How you write your analysis demonstrates how much you understand the rule.

If you understand the doctrine, do you explain it well?

The way you explain must hit the key elements, and show exactly how the situation would be when the rule applies to the facts given.

<u>Example: Content based vs Content neutral</u>

Unclear explanations:

The public school principal does not allow the drawing of the dove on the school wall. The dove is the symbol of a local gang.

Clearer explanations:

The public school principal does not allow the drawing of dove on the school wall nor on students' own hands solely because the dove is the symbol of a local gang, while the drawing of other birds and animals on the wall are allowed.

The first explanation failed to explain the main reason of the prohibition. The principal may prohibit any drawings on the school wall and regard all of them as graffiti. Then, the rule would not be deemed content-based. It could be deemed a restriction of time, place and manner: you are allowed to draw the dove on a piece of paper.

The second explanation clearly tells you that drawing other birds or animals is allowed on the wall, so it is not a restriction of time, place, and manner. The prohibition takes place because of what is drawn, so it is deemed content-based.

<u>Do not start typing in the first 15 minutes of the essay portions</u>

If you start typing right after the exam starts, you are harming your score more than helping. That is because starting too early without fully digesting all the facts of the whole situation would only make you overlook details, which could affect the position you would like to take.

Example: Witness in the evidence essay

In an evidence essay, Walter is invited to be a witness in a litigation about construction. Facts tell you that Walter has been working in the construction industry for ten years. Then, you would have to talk about "Expert vs. Layperson witness." Without reading further facts, you might quickly jump to the conclusion that Walter is deemed the expert witness because of his rich experiences in the construction profession.

By reading more closely, you are going to reveal more facts in the scenario. The litigation is about the plumbing problem in the restrooms of the house but Walter was responsible for the kitchen area only for the past decade. Then how can Walter be regarded as an expert witness?

If you discover more facts halfway through writing the essay, you may have already wasted too much time writing unnecessary stuff, and fixing it would also take time.

Thus, my advice is to read entire facts and determine which way to go before you start writing or typing. Spending at least five minutes on each essay question before you write, which means waiting for at least 15 minutes before actually starting typing for the essay exam session.

Do not let tunnel vision block your sight

In terms of thinking for an essay in the bar exam, "tunnel vision" could be a barrier for you to think comprehensively.

You might be able to see the situation from merely one angle in the exam. If you have already failed multiple times, can you please fix your tunnel vision before you sign up for another exam?

If you can afford it, hire a good tutor to help you; if you cannot afford it, maybe you can post an essay question or a paragraph from the fact patterns into a chat group and invite participation of the discussion. Other people's thoughts may stimulate your ways of thinking, even if some people could be very impolite when they express their thoughts. It does not matter. You can just focus on their ideas and ignore their attitudes.

"Tunnel vision" could be the consequence if your focus of studying is to recite all the rules, and then, you merely "vomit" all of them on the papers or the screen in the exam. Your efforts would be spent on retrieving all doctrines from your head, and applying the rules to some facts which are able to attract your attention instead of analyzing the given situation from different perspectives. I believe we all have the ability to see a situation from different angles, but our abilities could be suppressed by our overloaded and bulging memory systems, which are holding thousands of doctrines for us during the bar exam.

Do you have a garrulous person or conversational narcissists around you?

In your daily lives, do you have a garrulous person or conversational narcissists around you? These people just like to talk endlessly without attentively listening. I believe you would not like such a person. If you keep typing what is inside your head in the bar exam without reading the question in detail and thinking thoroughly, you would be similar to the garrulous person or conversational narcissists.

Restroom break is a refreshment during exam sessions

The morning session of Day 1 takes three hours, and the afternoon session takes three and a half hours. Time is tight, but do not misbelieve that sitting on the chair for three consecutive hours without walking away would be the best use of the time.

Do you have experiences where when something big, shocking or disastrous happens, you would not be able to come up with the best solution immediately or the best way to handle it until you have left the scene or the whole incident is over? That is because when you are still on the scene, your mind is being trembled by the unexpected nature of the incident, or even when the incident is ordinary in nature, you did not expect it would really happen to you. For example, you get robbed, or your car window is broken by someone, or when you take a job interview in front of a panel of five people, the five pairs of eyeballs make you unable to respond to the questions in the best way with the best expressions, even when you have the capability. But once you have walked out of the hiring company, more desirable answers would come up.

When too much information comes into your mind at the same time, you would not be able to process all of them at that particular moment; but when you have calmed down, you might start realizing that another approach would be more helpful.

In each exam session of the bar exam, I suggest you go to the restroom at least once. If time permits, twice is even better. I used to go once after every essay. Besides my physical needs, going to the restroom is always a kind of refreshment for me. I could wash my face, refresh my mind and also walk away from the essay questions for a few minutes. But certainly, do not spend more than ten minutes in total in the restroom, and hopefully, you do not need that long. The short break could be beneficial to you if the break allows you to think of something you might have ignored due to over-concentration on the essay questions. Most importantly, we are just human beings. Our bodies need at least one restroom break in a three-hour session.

Rules

Do not bring up a rule if you do not plan to or need to explain it

Do not bring up a rule which is not going to help explain or analyse the facts at controversy, or you do not plan to or need to explain it. Why?

Example: The rules for a buffet

Henry is a 35-year-old man working full-time. He just got divorced, and he does not have any children or a new girlfriend. He does not want to be overwhelmed by the sadness caused by his divorce. He tries to make himself happy by eating his favorite food to release all his frustration and unhappiness.

When he walks into a buffet restaurant, the receptionist asks him how many are in his party, he answers, "one, only one. I am by myself." Then the receptionist told him the buffet is $50 per adult. He said, "OK, I can afford it." He also feels hungry after walking for an hour, and he is eager to get the lobster, crab, and clam chowder.

However, the receptionist keeps talking instead of bringing him to a table. She wants to tell Henry more about different charges for different people: "For a couple, the restaurant would offer a discount. The restaurant charges $80 only for a couple instead of $100; for seniors over 65, the charge is $20 per person; for a party of six or more, regardless of the ages, there would be a 10 percent discount for the whole table; For teenagers ranging from 12 to

17.5 years old who are also full-time students, the charge would be $35 per person."

Can you imagine what Henry would feel? He might feel grumpy and annoyed. He is so hungry, but the receptionist keeps telling him information about different charges, which do not apply to him today. He is still starving because of the useless rules. Moreover, he is still recovering from his divorce, so he would not want to know the buffet discount for couples.

Wrong rules are given out at wrong timing in a wrong situation

The receptionist should not give out a laundry list of charges when the customer is just by himself. If she wants to contribute more information for his next visit, just save it until the customer has finished his buffet today, and then tell him on his way out. That would be a better timing and the customers would be more patient to hear about that.

Applying to essays: Please do not bring up an irrelevant rule and make a silly argument to show that you are unworthy of obtaining the attorney's license!

If you bring up a rule in an essay just because you remember that rule, but the rule is not triggered by the facts given, you are doing exactly what the receptionist did. If the rules are irrelevant, what valuable arguments can you make in the analysis? Please do not bring up an irrelevant rule and make a silly argument to show that you are unworthy of obtaining an attorney's license.

If the rule is somehow related to the facts, but it does not apply because of a piece of unique fact, please point that out in the essay because that is important for the grader to know that you are aware of the differentiation.

For exam purposes, your goal is to attain high enough scores to go beyond the cut score. Do you expect the grading rubric would include those rules not triggered by the facts? When the rules are not included in the rubric, how can you score points? It is going to harm your essay more than help it.

The sequence of stating the details of rules:

State the main rules before exceptions or limitations

Please state the main rules first, and then the exceptions, its limitations, and lastly, other possibilities.

Example: Shopping discount rules

The Miracle Company has a big sales coming up next week:

"All regular-priced products are sold at 30 percent off. For on-sale products which are not watches and jewels, there is an extra 15 percent off. Members would have an extra 20 percent off on dresses and pants, and 2 percent off on watches. New members who just sign up today would have valid membership immediately after they have passed the credit score check.

All cash coupons or other discount coupons issued by the Miracle company apply to regular-priced products only.

Gift cards are treated the same as cash or credit cards. No checks are allowed. Returns are not allowed, but exchanges. All exchanges have to take place by the end of this month, and receipts are required for exchanges."

Logical sequence

The above sequence is logical because you talk about the purchase first, and then the mode of payment, and what options are available if customers change their mind.

Explaining the rules about discount

Firstly, you have to state the main discount. Then you can point out the extra discount for on-sale products, but subject to limitations. And then, there is a difference between members and non-members, but no difference between new members and old members. However, membership applicants must have passed the credit score check in order to have their membership approved.

Secondly, you can point out the limitations of the coupons, including cash coupons and discount coupons issued by the Miracle.

Thirdly, you can explain what form of payment is prohibited; also, there are no special preferences for any forms of payment, and all forms would be treated the same.

Thirdly, you would talk about the options if the customers do not like the products after the purchases.

The bad layout of rules

A bad layout of rules would be a failure to establish the foundation before you further explain.

Example: Hotel breakfast

Please read the following conversation between Jasmine and Kara, two classmates of a law school, at the cafeteria of the campus.

Jasmine: “Hi, Kara, do you have time tomorrow morning? Between 7am to 10am.”

Kara: “Yes, I will be available. Our second year of law school is just over, and I would have one week of free time before the first assignment of the third year becomes due.”

Jasmine: "Flora has just finished her fourth year of law school. We would have a celebration for her law school graduation.”

Kara: “Great. How are we going to celebrate for Flora? I would see if I am interested in your arrangements, and if there are food I like.”

Jasmine: “We have many activities. One of them would be the buffet breakfast tomorrow. The food are delicious, including pancakes, sausage and omelettes.”

Kara: “Wow. All are my favorite food. But I have only five dollars left for this month.”

Jasmine: "The buffet is going to be free."

Kara: “Oh, really? It sounds too good to be true. Where is it going to be? I do not have a car.”

Jasmine: “Just two blocks away from here.”

Kara: “That sounds good. Are we going to meet at the restaurant or somewhere else tomorrow?”

Jasmine: “Everyone will go down from their rooms at about 7am.”

Kara: "Going down from their rooms? Do you mean they all live upstairs from the restaurant?"

Jasmine: "Yes. Ten of us are going to stay at that hotel tonight and we would eat at the restaurant together tomorrow morning. But I believe some of us would rather stay late in bed and they would miss the breakfast. That would not be a big deal. There is no extra charge for the breakfast."

Kara: "Do you mean the breakfast is complimentary for hotel guests only?"

Jasmine: "Yes, of course. It would not be free for other people or homeless people hanging around there. I do not think they serve people who are not the hotel guests, not even if you offer to pay because there are no cashiers."

Kara: "But I am not staying in the hotel tonight."

Jasmine: "Oh, I have assumed everyone knowing Flora would stay in the hotel tonight."

Kara: "No. I told you that I have only $5 left. How can I join you? How can I celebrate for Flora with all of you?"

Jasmine: "You can contribute $5 to sign your name on the' Congratulations' card we have bought."

Kara: "No, thanks. I would just give Flora a call to say 'Congratulations." '

Takeaway from the above dialogue

What do you learn from this dialogue? What could be the problem if the rules are laid out in the incorrect sequence?

What are the rules for joining the free breakfast buffet tomorrow?

From the hotel's perspective:

Have to be the hotel guest

Have to be available tomorrow between 7am to 10am

From the perspective of Kara:

Have to be something she is interested

Have to include food she likes

Have to cost $5 or less

Have to be within walking distance

What did Jasmine do wrong in laying out the rules for Kara?

Jasmine fails to state the biggest rule: Have to be a hotel guest to join the breakfast buffet

Jasmine should first say or ask Kara:

Are you staying in the hotel tonight with us?

Can you wake up early tomorrow to attend the breakfast buffet between 7 am to 10am?

Jasmine never told Kara that being the hotel guest is the prerequisite to attending the breakfast buffet, so it caused a misunderstanding between Jasmine and Kara.

Applying to the essays: Build up the foundation first before explaining limitations or exceptions

Please state the main rule first and then talk about other requirements, limitations or exceptions. Build up the foundation before you further explain. Some students are too eager to go into the exceptions or minor details before they explain clearly what the doctrines are actually about. It just confuses the graders.

The nature of the gathering: For hotel guests only

In the above example, if Kara first knew that the breakfast gathering was actually for those who stayed at the hotel, then she would not ask about the time or location or the cost of the buffet because they would not apply to her situation anyway. But Jasmine has wrongly categorized it as a free breakfast when the food is, in fact included in the hotel room charge.

On the other hand, Jasmine should first find out if Kara is staying at the hotel with them. Then, she can further explain to Kara that she has to be able to wake up by 10 am in order to have breakfast. If Kara likes to stay late in bed till noon, then Jasmine does not have to tell her what kind of food would be provided in the breakfast.

If the breakfast buffet is also available for non-hotel guests

If whoever pays $35 can have the breakfast, then the rule would be making the payment of $35: If Kara can afford $35, then she would need to know the time because she may have to do homework or study. If she is available, she then has to know the location because she does not have a car. If she is able to get there and she has time, she would need to know the type of food provided in the buffet because she may think the buffet does not deserve $35 if only donuts and coffee are provided.

Imagine if you are the person writing the exam questions

Imagine if you are the person writing the exam questions: That would be the wishes of many exam takers. Merely imagining would make you happy. It is always good to create some excitement when we study in distress. This would be a helpful imagination.

Example: Miranda warnings

"Miranda warnings apply to custodial interrogations and a suspect is in custody when a reasonable person would believe that they are not free to leave."

How would you design the fact pattern if you are given the authority?

I would say:

"The police officer allows Damon to leave but Damon wants to finish the game he is playing online. Then Damon says something related to the crime at issue. "

Show the unique/controversial aspect:

Damon is free to leave the police station, but he chooses to stay to finish the game. When he is free to go but he chooses not to, then Miranda's warnings may not apply, even though you still have to talk about it in the analysis.

Example: Common law burglary

"It is the breaking and entering of someone else's dwelling at night with the intent to commit a felony therein. "

How would you design the fact pattern if you are given the authority?

I would say:

"Someone climbed into a commercial building at 7pm in the summer time to try to steal the cash from their accounting department, and also use the restroom when the door is unlocked."

Show the unique/controversial aspect:

The structure is not for residential but commercial, then the exam taker would have to talk about this point. Does "burglary" still apply here?; The incident happens at 7 pm in summer, when it is not dark yet, so is it deemed "night time"? The exam taker also needs to talk about it; the door is unlocked, so does it constitute "breaking"? (Breaking does not mean something has to be broken or damaged. You have to explain that.) Is trying to steal cash a felony or misdemeanor? However using a restroom without permission would not be deemed a felony. The exam taker also needs to talk about it.

If you put yourself into the shoes of an exam writer, you would know what facts you would need to discuss for full credit. Then you might not miss similar points in the exam.

Reinforce your memories when you study the elements

When you study the elements for the rules, please also imagine that you are given the authority to write exam questions: What tricks are you going to create for the exam takers? I guarantee that the imagination would help you to remember the numerous elements of the rules well.

Using the opposite words to emphasize the main characteristics of the rule

You have to explain the main characteristics of the elements of the rule, and one of the ways is to use the opposite words.

Using the opposite words to emphasize the main characteristics of the elements

Example: Vagueness

If you want to explain whether a rule is vague, you can use the opposite word: Is the rule clear in several aspects: do you know what exactly is banned under this rule; do you know what is allowed and what is prohibited; is the dividing line clear?

If you are unable to find the answers to the above question, it is likely to be vague.

Rules which are always useful

Example: Contracts - Good faith and fair dealing

All contracts have an implied duty of good faith and fair dealing, so parties must make good faith efforts to comply with all conditions.

When you write a contract essay and have time left, you can always talk about whether the parties have fulfilled such an obligation.

Example: Professional Responsibility - Duty of loyalty

For PR essays, you can always talk about the duty of loyalty, duty of communications, and duty of diligence because such obligations are required in dealing with all clients, regardless of what facts are included in the question.

If you have time left, please check if you include the discussion of the above duties.

Facts handling

Facts sorting is like playing shape-sorting cube

Example: Shape sorting cube - Selecting the right pieces

Do you or your kids ever play shape sorting cubes? Do you remember how to do it?

You have to pick the correct shapes to put into the corresponding holes, including the square, star and triangle. Otherwise, the shape plastic would not fit.

Applying to the essays: Extracting the right piece

When you use your facts in the essay, you need to do what you did in playing the shape sorting cube: Select the right pieces.

If the big chunk of facts contains the "triangle" you need, just extract the "triangle" from all the shapes on the table. You cannot put the triangle plus the square plus the star into the hole of the triangle. They do not fit.

When the paragraph includes seven or eight pieces of facts, they can be used in different spots for different purposes. Be sure to extract the useful part from the big paragraph. You do not need to repeat every part in every IRAC.

Making use of the facts is not penmanship

The professors or tutors always remind us to make use of the facts. But making use of the facts does not mean repeating the whole paragraph of key facts without making a point or adding value to address the call of the question. It just means applying the rules to the facts given.

Please do not repeat the whole paragraph given in the fact patterns in any of your IRACs. You can quote some words or use the whole statement made by someone if that is important. But repeating the whole paragraph is meaningless. This is not a typing contest or a penmanship assignment. The bar exam is aimed to test your ability to be a competent attorney, and an attorney would not just do typing.

Extraction

Instead, please extract the helpful and relevant facts to support your arguments, which is very similar to a "matching" game: matching the facts with the rules; and the particular facts you would choose would be similar to the shape sorting cube mentioned above.

After you have finished the "matching," you are not done yet. You still have to explain the connection between the rule and the facts and also analyze for the purpose of addressing the call of the question.

Please read the following example and extract the relevant facts.

Example: Parking fees

Rules:

The parking fees would be $4 per hour. Once the cars enter the parking lot, the clock starts ticking even though the car owners are still looking for a parking space. The lot has installed a system to count how many cars are outgoing and how many spaces are left. If there is no more vacancy, the gate of the entrance will be closed automatically. In other words, if your cars are able to enter, there must be a vacant spot.

Three minutes after the first hour would be deemed the beginning of the second hour. The time spent on waiting in line for the availability for the paying machines would also be charged.

After customers have paid for their parking tickets, their cars must leave within 15 minutes.

If the customers 'cars stay beyond 15 minutes after payment, they have to pay for one more hour. But if they cannot leave for reasons beyond their control, and they are able to prove it or the manager determines that it is believable, the charge for that extra time would be waived.

Ten minutes after the exact time the extra charge is waived would be considered the starting time of a new parking ticket, and every new parking ticket would be charged for at least one hour, regardless of the actual time parking or merely staying inside the lot.

Facts:

"Yolanda entered the parking lot at 3:03pm, and parked at 3:08p.m. She planned to leave at 5:05pm.

However, there was a long line waiting to pay at the machine. She made the payment at 5:09 p.m.

Then she ran to her car but her car was blocked by two cars which just collided. The owners of the two cars in the accident talked for 20 minutes and also had to take pictures. They tried to call the police, but the phones had no reception.

A friend of one car owner tried to look for the security guard or the manager of the parking lot, but nobody came. Eventually, they decided not to wait and moved the cars away from the accident spot at 5:34 p.m. There were a few surveillance cameras around the accident scene, but there were also blind spots. It was unclear whether the videos have actually captured the two cars involved.

Yolanda got into her car and organized something for five minutes. She also felt thirsty and went out of the parking lot at 5:40 p.m. to walk across the street to the grocery store to buy a can of soda. Then she drank the soda and rested a little bit.

Finally, Yolanda's car left the parking lot at 6:12 p.m."

How much does Yolanda need to pay for the parking fees? Please discuss all possibilities.

<u>IRAC 1-6</u>

Six IRACs would be used to discuss this question here. Facts would be repeated but there would be a purpose when the facts are mentioned.

IRAC 1

The time of entering the parking lot is deemed the starting time instead of the actual time car owners are able to get a spot.

Here, Yolanda parked at 3:08 pm but the starting time would count from 3:03 pm because the time of entering the lot counts instead of the time she was able to park her car. So the term parking fees could be a misnomer and should be changed to the fee of staying inside the parking lot since car owners, in fact, pay for the time their cars stay inside the area of the lot. The lot owner does not care when you are able to get a spot to park as long as they know that there are vacancies. Even if the vacant space is situated between two giant cars, and you can just park without the possibility of opening the door, the lot would not care. If the situation comes up, that would also be irrelevant in the calculation of the total fees.

Thus, 3:03 would be deemed the starting time.

IRAC 2

Leaving within three minutes after the preceding hour would not be charged another hour.

She planned to leave two hours and two minutes after she entered the parking lot. The lot would waive the extra time charge if the car owner simply stayed less than three minutes after the preceding hour. But Yolanda is not going to benefit from this buffer term because she simply planned to leave but did not actually leave the lot. Her desire to leave does not count.

Thus, would not be deemed the leaving time.

IRAC 3

Moreover, the time spent for waiting in line for a machine would still be charged.

Here, Yolanda spent minutes in waiting, but the charging time would not stop until payment is made, even though she did not choose to wait in line and she would rather pay earlier. When she successfully made the payment, the third hour started, so she has to pay for at least three hours.

Thus, would be regarded as the leaving time. As such, she would have to pay for three hours up to this point.

IRAC 4

Staying for more than 15 minutes after payment is made would incur a charge of another hour unless the reasons are beyond the control of the car owners and have to be proved or the manager determines that is believable.

Here, Yolanda was unable to leave immediately because of a car accident unrelated to her. The two cars blocked her car. This is something out of her control but no managers were available to verify that. However, Yolanda May have taken some pictures as proof, or the managers can watch the surveillance videos to verify that Yolanda's car stayed inside the lot for reasons beyond her control, meaning she could not control where the cars crashed, and she cannot control when the two car owners drove their cars away.

However, it was unclear whether the videos have actually captured the accident or the cars staying there after the accident because blind spots existed inside the lot. It is possible that Yolanda herself or other people are able to verify the truthfulness of the car accident.

Or if the manager determines that Yolanda's story is believable, the extra charge for the fourth hour can be waived.

IRAC 5

After customers have paid for their parking tickets, their cars must leave within 15 minutes to avoid extra charges unless something out of their control stops their car from leaving.

Assuming the manager agrees to waive the extra hour charge due to the car accident or adjusts the payment time to 5:34 pm instead of 5:09 pm, then she would not be held responsible for the extra time after payment is made.

However, her car did not leave right after the accident was cleared Her mere physical body has walked out of the lot six minutes after the accident scene was cleared but the time 5:40pm does not count because the rule clearly states that the car has to move out within 15 minutes of payment, not the car owner.

Thus, she may still be held liable for the extra time staying within the lot after the payment is made.

IRAC 6

Ten minutes after the exact time the extra charge is waived would be considered the starting time of a new parking ticket, and every new parking ticket would be charged for at least one hour, regardless of the actual time parking or merely staying inside the lot.

Here, facts do not show the exact time the extra charge was waived, assuming it was waived. If the manager waived it six minutes after the cars were driven away, which was 5:40 pm, then she would have to leave by 5:50 pm to avoid being regarded as starting the second parking ticket.

However, she left at 6:12 pm, 32 minutes after the presumed waive time, and then she would be charged one more hour on top of the previous hours in the first ticket.

Even if the manager agrees to waive the extra charge of the fourth hour because of the accident, it does not mean the waiver would still be effective when Yolanda chooses to buy soda herself and retain the car inside the lot. Yolanda may argue that she felt thirsty just because of the long wait, which was beyond her control, so the extra charge should be waived. But this argument is unlikely to succeed. She can simply leave the lot before she buys a soda. Walking out of the lot to buy a soda is entirely within her control, so the extra charge should not be waived.

However, even if the manager refuses to waive the extra charge due to the car accident, Yolanda may also need to pay four hours in total because from 3:03 pm to 6:12 pm, there were only three hours and nine minutes. Any extra time of more than three minutes would be deemed one hour. Hence, three hours and nine minutes would be charged the same as four hours. Without waiving the extra time staying, there would not be a second ticket.

Thus, regardless of whether the extra time of staying is waived, Yolanda would have to pay for four hours of parking only. While $4 is the hourly rate, she would have to pay $16.

Applying to the essays: Step by step; layer by layer

Example: Contract essay

Expectation Damages

If the singer Aria performs for Connie instead of Paul, she would earn $10,000 less, which would be her expectation damages. But such a loss is unlikely to be covered by Connie because Aria and Connie have agreed with this price, and Aria chose to perform for Connie because she does not like the possible arena chosen by Paul. The $10,000 loss would not be covered by Paul either because Aria failed to fulfill her promise to perform for Paul, and Aris chose to do so. Paul suffers loss due to her breach, so it makes sense for Paul to pursue damages from Aria. However, if Paul eventually had no arena for Aria to perform, and Aria was forced to perform for Connie on the same day to minimize her loss, then Paul would have to pay Aria $10,000 to compensate for the reduction of income.

Be skeptical of the statements in the fact patterns

All objective facts given in the essay questions are true

When the facts tell you Pedro is a man, then Pedro would not be a woman; when the facts say Mary is telling the truth, then Mary would not be lying. when the facts point out that the vase is worth $1 million, then it would not worth less than that.

Instruction: Be skeptical of the subjective thought

However, it does not mean you cannot be skeptical of some statements in the fact patterns. A verbal statement or an expression of emotions made by a certain party is not equivalent to a conclusive fact.

Example: Feb 2022 Torts essay

Subjective thought

"Diana explained that the facility could not survive economically without rock concerts and that rock concerts were, by their nature, loud."

Diana said so but that seems to be her subjective perception only. She thinks that rock concerts must be held for the facility to survive financially, but it does not mean there are no other alternatives. It just means that she does not consider or try other alternatives. Or she is too narrow-minded to explore other means of financial survival.

Thus, do not allow these subjective thoughts to limit your own analysis. It does not mean you cannot give other suggestions in order for the facility to survive.

Objective data

How about objective data, then? Does it mean the results are conclusive?

Example: Ten restaurants closed in four years

Facts show that only Italian restaurants are able to survive in this area. Ten restaurants serving Chinese, Korean and Japanese food have all closed in these four years.

The closure of the ten restaurants are objective facts, which would not allow you to dispute the existence of the facts. However, what are the causes of the closures? The causes are not confirmed yet.

Question:

Does it mean all residents here like only Italian food?

Answer:

Probably.

But many reasons would be possible to lead to closure of a business. The type of cuisine is one factor, and the quality of services can be another; Or the language abilities of the servers also matter; and the location with safety concerns, the availability of free parking spaces, the demographics of the population in this area all count.

Please write down all other possibilities you can think of merely to stimulate or activate your ability to explore other possibilities:

Suggestions:

The ten restaurants are in fact owned by the same person, and he gets arrested by the police, and nobody helps him to manage the restaurants.

Certain food, including rice and noodles, served by the ten restaurants are provided by the same supplier, and those food has caused a big incident of food poisoning four years ago and people nearby cannot forget.

Manipulating the facts is like shaping the mud rubber

In the essays or in reality, facts remain unchanged, but what you can change is the interpretation of facts. The facts given in the question would not change, just like what already happened to your future client would not change, and also the acts he already did. But what you are able to change or control is how you interpret or use these facts. When you shape the mud rubber, the same material can be made into different figures.

Example: The sale of a Rolex watch

You are a new sales associate in a store selling jewels and watches. Today is your first day of work. You sell nothing but one Rolex watch.

If your supervisor would like to encourage you, she would say: Good job. You sell one Rolex watch on your first day. But colleagues who do not like you may say: Do you know how much rent our store costs every month? You sell only one watch today!

The fact you sell one Rolex watch would not change. But you can manipulate it by emphasizing that you are selling one expensive watch today or downplaying your contribution by emphasizing you just sold one watch, and the profit is not going to cover the store rent.

Thus, manipulating facts is just like shaping the mud rubber: You can shape it like a ball or pressure it to be flat. The weight of the mud rubber mass would not change, but the outlook can be modified to fulfill your purpose.

One fact can be used for more than one purpose

Example: Argument between a married couple

When one fact can be used for more than one point……

Scenario:

The husband has been unemployed for a year.

The wife (W) has an argument with her husband (H). The whole dialogue is about one fact: The husband has been unemployed for one year. But there are many reasons for the wife's anger:

W: "You did not work for one year."

H: "Many companies have layoffs now. Too many people fight for limited jobs."

W: “I have been working hard to pay the bills. I also have to tap our savings to make the payments.”

H: "There is no job. I have no income.”

W: “You just repeated the problem. Did you try to share the burden with me? Did you try to find at least a part-time job? Did you try to do some housework while I was working?

You are also part of our family.”

H: “I do not feel motivated.”

W: “But you have the motivation to hang out with your bad friends all day long.”

H: “They are also unemployed. We are in the same situation.”

W: “What is the purpose of hanging out with unemployed friends? To show that no job is not your own fault?”

H: “Just to kill time.”

W: "You killed a lot of time by drinking and smoking. You have some friends who own restaurants. Why don’t you approach them for a possible job position?”

H: “I do not want to be a waiter. I was a manager before I lost my job.”

W: “So you would not work unless you find another manager position? You cannot adjust yourself to adapt to the changes of the economy?”

H: “A restaurant is so different from an office.”

W: "Did you ever try to learn new skills? You have been sitting at home for a year but did not spend any time learning anything?"

H: "I miss the day I was a manager."

W: "I understand that. But that is part of your memory in your head. Your boss is not going to hire you again as a manager. You have to move on with your new life."

The points of the wife:

When the husband remains unemployed, there is no money to pay the bills; the wife is unhappy that the husband just repeated the problem without trying to solve it; he has no sense of responsibility; he always hangs out with unemployed friends; he did not try to accommodate to the change; he just wastes time drinking and smoking; he did not take advantage of the time to learn another skill for survival; he just remembers the days of being a manager; he refuses to face the reality.

Applying to the essays: When the same fact can be repeatedly use

When the same fact can be repeatedly used in different IRACs, you have to explain the same fact with different descriptions and explanations from different perspectives in different IRACs. The words have to be adjusted to fulfil that particular purpose.

Please do not just repeat the descriptions without adding value

Add a value and make a point

When someone told you a fact, you would not just repeat like a GPS device: "You have arrived. You have arrived."

Instead, you would think about it, make an inference or judgment.

The logic on suggestions

Problem A:

Imagine if your friend Stephanie tells you the following facts when you have a coffee with her. How would you respond or conclude? Or what questions you may ask to clarify?

-John wants his teenage son to be a medical doctor, but his son is not interested in studying. He liked to play online games and go out with girls.

Solution A:

Your response: He is a typical teenager focusing on playing games and dating. If John wants his son to put more effort into preparing for medical school, maybe he needs to help him get a medical school student as his girlfriend. Then he may spend less time on online games and more time on studying. A male needs a clear goal to be motivated.

Regardless of whether your suggestion is actually working, your idea is to find a logical way to fulfill John's purpose. His son could be influenced by his girlfriend, so this suggestion could be a realistic way to make his son work hard to be admitted to medical school and graduate. What his son likes could remain unchanged for a few years and that would be difficult for his father to change. If he likes dating with girls, perhaps he would adjust himself to match the girl he likes.

Problem B:

-Daniel worked for three jobs in the past three years. He is unemployed now. He worked for a restaurant, a coffee shop and a gym.

Suggestion B:

Your inference could be:

-"Daniel must be a lazy worker or a server with bad attitude."

More information:

The three businesses the same Daniel worked for are all located in the downtown of San Francisco. Since many companies closed after the pandemic, and many employees work from home, the amount of foot traffic has greatly reduced.

Then your inference has to change to:

"Daniel should try to find some jobs which have more businesses after the pandemic, such as food delivery or grocery delivery. "

Paying attention to trivial facts

Every paragraph should be read at least twice before typing.

In a fact pattern, almost every word has a purpose to the discussion of the main issues, except the verb to be “is” or “are,” or the article “the” or the preposition “to.” Hence, every paragraph should be read at least twice before you start typing in order not to miss the key facts, which are the backbones of your analysis, and trivial facts, which are the ingredients for you to increase your score from 65 to 70, or 75.

Example: Cy-Pres

It means as near as possible to the settlor's intentions when these cannot be precisely followed.

Then you have to find out the intention of the settlor when the trust is made.

For example, the settlor wants to donate $100,000 to an organization helping dogs, but that organization no longer exists. Then, would an organization helping cats close enough to the settlor's intention? Maybe or maybe not.

Then we can try to find if there are facts in the scenario explaining why the settlor chose the organization helping dogs. If he wants to help the organization just because his former girlfriend, who died of cancer, like dogs, then your second choice could be different. If the late girlfriend also liked birds, then probably an organization supporting birds would be closer.

Beating around the bush

When your client tells you something about his case, he may be beating around the bush, either because he is afraid, or he does not know what is relevant, and what is irrelevant. As his attorney, for relevant facts, you have to ask more; for irrelevant facts, you can sort them out and ask them to stop there unless something favorable or unfavorable to his chance of prevailing comes up.

When the facts are described by related parties, those facts could be incomplete or biased when the related parties try to shift the blame to others.

Example: Three brothers and the vase

Three brothers play, fight and also dance in a closed room. The oldest brother is Tam; The middle brother is Sam; and the youngest brother is Ram. Suddenly, the mother heard the sound of something breaking.

The mother went in and saw the pieces of a broken vase. She asked what happened.

Tam: Sam got my crackers.

Sam: Ram got my chocolate.

Ram: Tam got my ice cream. I chased after Tam.

Tam: I chased after Sam.

Tam: Sam hit the table.

Ram: I tried to save the vase from falling.

Sam: I tried to help holding the table too.

Tam: But the vase still fell.

Ram: Yes, the vase fell too fast.

Tam: If the vase has a pair of hands to hold the table, it would not fall.

Sam: Yes, I think so.

Ram: Yes, we all stretch our hands to save the vase but the vase fails to do anything.

Sam: Yes, the vase just sits there.

Explanation:

Tam, Sam and Ram are chasing after each other, and hit the table with a vase on, so the vase breaks. But the way they explain to their mother is: that someone tries to grab his food and he has to chase after the person. They try to make the chasing sound more reasonable than it is, and everyone contributes effort to save the vase but the vase does not do anything to save itself. We know that the three brothers try to shift the blame to the vase, which has no life. The vase would not be able to defend itself so the three brothers try to phrase the words to protect themselves.

As future attorneys, we have to be able to detect the bad side of human nature to extract the objective facts from the descriptions.

Do not allow others to mislead you.

Facts given are like lines drawn on the floor around your body

The facts given in the fact pattern are like lines drawn on the floor around your body: you cannot go beyond the lines, but you are free to move within the lines.

Example: A tattoo of dove

John has a tattoo of a dove, and a dove means peace to most people, and the police say it is a symbol for a particular local gang members.

When you analyze, you have to stick to what tattoo John has, what dove means to most people, and it symbolizes gang members from the perspective of the police.

But why John has a dove tattoo or what a dove means to John is unknown. There are many possibilities. You can infer from other facts or you can state a few possibilities and then pick one most fitting the situation.

What do the facts mean?

Digestion test

The output is the outcome after digestion.

When we have nausea due to stomach upset, the vomitus may look almost the same as how it was before we swallowed the food because our stomachs do not function properly. If we are able to digest, the output is definitely different from the form of input. Your "output" in the restroom must look different from the form when you took "input." If they look the same as each other, you should go to see the doctor.

Applying to the essays: Explaining "why" in three to five sentences

Do not just say the attorney's act is a violation of a duty of diligence or communication because of this fact or this act. You have to explain that. Before you have fully grasped the skill, try to write three to five sentences to explain "why" in the analysis section instead of merely repeating the words given in the scenario or paraphrasing the words given.

Facts are "starting points" only

The facts given are only "starting points" for you to think. You must contemplate the "impact" of those facts instead of repeating the words or paraphrasing the descriptions.

Workplace gasconade

Workplace gasconade also teaches us something about facts implication.

Example: Lunch meeting with the CEO

Connie and you are working for the same company but for different departments.

Connie: I had lunch with the CEO yesterday. You were not there.

Explanations: Showing that Connie is more important than you are

Regardless of whether the lunch with the CEO actually happened, the motivation of the colleague Connie telling you this is to show that she is more important than you are in the hierarchy of the company. The CEO had lunch with her, but not you.

Question:

Do you have to record this in your work notes?

Answer:

Probably not.

She might have to record that lunch meeting in her own notes or calendar because that was important to her or at least meant something to her.

But her lunch with the CEO means nothing to you as an employee in another department. It might mean something to your own feeling that you were not invited. But in terms of work issues, there is no importance to recording other staff‘s lunch meetings with the CEO.

Or the CEO met Connie‘s team because of an ongoing project and you would have a similar lunch meeting with the CEO two months later when the big project in your department starts. So you are not unimportant. Your turn has not come yet.

But if the CEO just visits the city for two days and he would have a lunch meeting with one department only and he chose Connie‘s department, that may indicate that Connie's team is the most important or profitable to the whole company.

When we handle the facts, we have to deal with the facts with the same methodology.

The implication of the facts:What the facts given actually mean is important in analysis

Example: Murder Essay - The death of Victor

When the essay is about murder, what do these facts mean?

Fact 1: The defendant Danny hangs out at the bar for two hours before the death happens

Fact 2: The bar is two blocks away from the residence of Eric, which is named Rabbit Manor.

Fact 3: The security guard saw Danny sitting outside the manor 30 minutes before the death of Victor.

Fact 4: Victor and Eric went home at almost the same time.

Fact 5: From the kiosk for the security guard Sam, Sam witnesses someone with the gold hat and the gold T-shirt pointing his finger at D outside the gate.

Fact 6: V was killed at the garden of Rabbit Manor.

Fact 7: V was stabbed twice.

Fact 8: The weapon was a broken glass bottle.

Fact 9: D did not carry anything with him, according to Sam.

Fact 10: Eric was picking up his mail from the mailbox when the death happened.

Fact 11: The victim Victor who gets killed is wearing identical gold T shirts, and wearing identical gold hats as the enemy of the defendant. The T-shirt and hat is worn by the main character of a recent popular movie, so many people buy and wear recently.

Fact 12: The defendant had mental problem three years ago

Fact 13: The enemy Eric argued with the D two days ago.

Fact 14: Eric is good at Taekwondo.

Fact 15: When the police officers watched the surveillance videos, they believed E was the one having a quarrel with D, but not absolutely sure because the two people have the same clothing.

Fact 16: The surveillance camera system does not monitor everywhere. About sixty percent of the area is covered.

Fact 17: Eric has his tattoo on his arm while Victor does not have.

Fact 18: D's fingerprints are found on the weapon.

Fact 19: D said he understand that killing people is wrong.

Fact 20: D did not admit or deny killing V.

Fact 21: There is no surveillance video showing how V gets killed.

Fact 22: E said E talked to D for two minutes but does not recall any gestures he made.

Answers to the implications of the facts

Fact 1:

The defendant Danny hangs out at the bar for two hours before the death happens

That means:

-He could get drunk

-voluntary intoxication

-specific and general intent crime

Fact 2:

The bar is two blocks away from the residence of Eric, which is named Rabbit Manor.

That means:

D could be waiting for E (lying in wait)

D could walk there without plan because two locations are close to each other

Fact 3:

The security guard saw Danny sitting outside the manor 30 minutes before the death of Victor.

That means:

-D could be waiting for E (lying in wait)

Fact 4:

Victor and Eric went home at almost the same time.

That means:

-There could be mistake of identity

Fact 5:

From the kiosk for the security guard Sam, Sam witnesses someone with the gold hat and the gold T-shirt pointing his finger at D outside the gate.

That means:

-V or E May argue with D. There might be a quarrel

Fact 6:

V was killed at the garden of Rabbit Manor.

That means:

-Here is the crime scene.

Fact 7:

V was stabbed twice.

That means:

-The killing is not a mistake.

Fact 8:

The weapon was a broken glass bottle.

That means:

-The weapon could be brought by D or Grabbed by D on the ground

Fact 9:

D did not carry anything with him, according to Sam.

That means:

-It is more likely that D did not bring the bottle with him, but it is also possible that the bottle is hidden so Sam cannot see

Fact 10:

Eric was picking up his mail from the mailbox when the death happened.

That means:

Eric may not see what happened

Eric could be the target but he walked away

The victim, Victor who gets killed is wearing identical gold T shirts, and wearing identical gold hats as the enemy of the defendant. The T-shirt and hat is worn by the main character of a recent popular movie, so many people buy and wear recently.

*There could be mistake of identity

Fact 11:

The defendant had mental problem three years ago

That means:

Insanity defense may apply

Fact 12:

The enemy Eric argued with the D two days ago.

That means:

-D may have motivation to kill E

Fact 13:

Eric is good at Taekwondo.

That means:

-E may also use force

When the police officers watched the surveillance videos, they believed E was the one having a quarrel with D, but they were not absolutely sure because the two people have the same clothing.

-The identity cannot be confirmed by authorities.

Fact 14:

The surveillance camera system does not monitor everywhere. About sixty percent of the area is covered.

That means:

-The murdering is not recorded

Fact 15:

Eric has his tattoo on his arm, while Victor does not.

That means:

-The tattoo could be the main characteristic differentiating E and V‘s physical appearance on the day the murder happened

Fact 16:

D’s fingerprints are found on the weapon.

That means:

-D touched the weapon, but it does not mean he was the killer.

Fact 17:

D said he understand that killing people is wrong.

That means:

-Some insanity defenses may not apply to him

Fact 18:

D did not admit or deny killing V.

That means:

-D may not remember exactly what happened.

Fact 19:

There is no surveillance video showing how V gets killed.

That means:

-There is no concrete evidence of the killing

Fact 20:

E said E talked to D for two minutes but does not recall any gestures he made.

That means:

E may or may not be the one in quarrel with D before the murder happened.

Arguments Formation

You are not working for the legislative branch

You are a future lawyer. Assuming you have already passed the bar, you are just a lawyer. You are not working for the legislative branch! It is also possible but if you have to practice bar essays, that means you have not reached the legislative level yet. Please do not try to create a rule which you think we should have.

You have no authority to abolish or revise the rules

Also, please do not try to defeat or abolish the rules when you write the essays because you are not the one setting up or revising the rules.

What would help you to increase your chance of prevailing the argument?

Example: Submitting the enrollment form to the 6th floor

Scenario 1.1

"You walk a little slower than usual because your legs got injured in a football game one month ago. The DMV also issued you a temporary disabled parking placard. Today, you do not drive.

You walk to the blue building to submit an enrollment form for a singing contest to a certain organization on the 6th floor.

The deadline is 5pm today, according to the form. The blue building does not allow visitors to use the elevator after 4:58pm.

You get to the elevator at 4:54p.m. but the security guard at the lobby stops you from using the elevator and says "you are not allowed to use the elevator." The time of the clock at the lobby is 4:59 p.m. which is five minutes faster than the time shown in the cell phones, including the guard's and yours."

Question A:

What would be your strongest argument to the security guard?

Argument:

"It is not 4:58pm yet."

Supporting facts:

-The clock at the lobby is five minutes faster than the smart phone of the security guard and your own cell phone.

Scenario 1.2

Same story in the same building:

You are allowed to use the elevator eventually, and when you get to the organization on the 6th floor, the receptionist says you are one minute late, so you are not allowed to submit the enrollment form. The clock's time is 5:01 p.m., which is the same as her smartphone and your cell phone.

Question B:

What would be your strongest argument to the receptionist?

Argument:

"The security guard at the lobby stopped me for five minutes to figure out if it was before 4:58pm and if I could use the elevator.

Hence, this was not my fault to come one minute late"

Is the argument going to work?

However, this argument may not work because the enrollment form states that the deadline is 5 pm today, and the form does not say whoever comes late, not because of his own fault, would be granted an exception.

Thus, you can argue, but it may not succeed.

Scenario 1.3

Same story:

While the receptionist stops you from turning in the form, you see a person in a wheelchair is allowed to go into the office to submit his form. Then the receptionist tells you people with mobility issues would have an extra 15 minutes as a buffer.

Question C:

When people with mobility issues have extra 15 minutes as buffer, what would be your strongest argument to the receptionist?

Argument:

"My legs also got injured one month ago. I do not walk with a cane but I am unable to walk at my usual speed. The DMV also issued me a temporary disabled parking placard."

Is the argument going to work?

It is very likely that the argument would work because "people with mobility issues would have 15 minutes as a buffer" and you were just one minute late to submit the enrollment form. You have your temporary disabled parking placard as supporting document.

What arguments would be invalid?

You cannot argue with the security guard that the elevator should not be locked at 4:58 pm. (Because the rule is set by the blue building); or the deadline for submitting the form should not be 5 p.m. (Because the deadline is set by the organization organizing the singing contest.); or the singing contest should not be held after you get injured. (This is totally off track because you have no control of the contest. You have the right to participate or not participate, but you do not have the right to change the plan of the organization.)

Arguing within the range

All arguments in an essay have to be sensible and within a reasonable range.

Example: A traffic rule of 55 MPH for vehicles

"The freeway has a sign of 55 MPH."

If you receive a driving ticket, you cannot argue that the maximum of 55 MPH is too slow for the traffic on freeways. You do not have the authority to change the laws.

However, if there were three seconds only you reached 56 MPH, you may argue that your average speed was only 53 MPH and only the average speed should be taken into account when a citation is issued.

Example: John's reimbursement forms

Here is a rule for the organization:

"All reimbursement forms have to be submitted to one's immediate supervisor within 15 work days of incurring the expenses unless your immediate supervisor is on vacation or not working due to personal reasons. Then the same forms should be submitted to the accounting department within 30 work days of incurring the expenses."

Scenario:

"John paid $300 for a dinner with one client. The dinner took place at 7pm on September 1st."

Let's think:

What you can argue and what you cannot argue

You cannot argue whether the rule is good or bad; sensible or ridiculous, whether 15 days or 30 days are sufficient for employees to organize and complete calculations of the total expenses in a particular time period. If you want to rescind the rule, you have to talk to the upper management for revision.

You are not working for the branch of legislative body

When you are an attorney at law, what you can argue is whether the acts of defendants met the elements of the rule., not whether the rules are good because you are not working for the branch of the legislative body. You are not invited to make a new law or amend the existing law. If you want to do so, do it on another occasion, not in the court trial for your client.

Let's think:

What is relevant and what is irrelevant

The total dollar amount spent on the dinner would be irrelevant because the rules do not mention any restrictions on the maximum dollar amount, or the expenses above or below a certain dollar amount would be an exception to the rule.

What would be relevant includes the date of incurring the expense.

Let's think:

According to this rule, which elements or terms are the most arguable to make a difference on the validity of John's reimbursement form?

What are arguable?

Terms with many different definitions or variations

Please read the rule again:

"All reimbursement forms have to be submitted to one's immediate supervisor within 15 work days of incurring the expenses unless your immediate supervisor is on vacation or not working due to personal reasons. Then the same forms should be submitted to the accounting department within 30 work days of incurring the expenses."

"Work day"

In my opinion, that would be the term "work day." For people who work from 9 am to 5 pm, submitting the form at 5:30 pm of the 15th work day would make the form invalid because the deadline would be 5 pm. But for a person who must finish all scheduled appointments on any day of work, the time of completion of the last appointment would mark the end of her work day. For example, if an employee met a client at 7 pm and finished at 9 pm, her work day would end at 9 pm, indicating that she would still be allowed to submit the form from 5 pm to 9pm, as opposed to other 9-5 workers.

"Submit"

The second most arguable word is the definition of "submission." The rule does not specify how the staff should submit the forms. When we argue, we can talk about reasonable means of submission: It can be done electronically, in person, or by mail if either side works from home. For electronic submission, the exact time of submission would be accurately recorded; for regular mail, there would be a date stamp on the envelope. But for in-person submission, there may not be any receipts, so that would be the most arguable point among the three manners of submission.

Submitting the form in person to Samantha

If John submits the form in person to his supervisor Samantha, and. Samantha receives it in person, the moment of Samantha's receipt could be deemed the time of receipt.

Question:

How about if John places the reimbursement form on the desk of Samantha but she will be out of the office for three days? When she eventually received the form, it was the 17th work day. Does it matter?

The rule simply says the form has to be submitted within 15 work days and did not mention the time of receipt, while the time of receipt or acknowledgement by the supervisor is out of the control of the employees. In other words, the form should not be deemed invalid when the employee does not do anything wrong. As such, the form should be deemed valid.

What to do when Samantha is not in office

However, the direction of the argument would change if Samantha already gave John instructions about what to do when she is not in the office: All forms have to be scanned to Samantha's work email address on the same day if she is not in the office. If Samantha has made this instruction, failing to scan the form to Samantha on the same day would be deemed unsubmitted.

Scanning the form to Samantha's personal email address

How about if John scanned the form to Samantha's personal email instead of work email? Regardless of whether Samantha checked her personal email while she was out of the office, she could regard John's form as unsubmitted because she had already clearly specified that the form had to be submitted to her work email.

As such, John's reimbursement form would be deemed invalid, meaning he would be unable to get reimbursed.

What is a legal argument?

Not a quarrel on the street

A legal argument is not a quarrel on the street. It has to be based on the elements of the rules. It is not anything opposite to the standpoint of the opposing side or something you wish could happen.

Example: Opal borrows money from Alem

"Opal owes Alem $500, and Opal is supposed to return the money to Alem on the coming Friday, according to the written agreement between them."

Not a wish

If Opal says, "I would rather return the money to Alem in two years," the statement would be her wish only, instead of an argument, as there is nothing of value supporting this two-year postponement. In other words, Alem would have no incentive to accept the postponement.

A promise inconsistent with the written agreement

If Opal says when she borrowed the money from Alem, Alem said she could take her time to repay him, and "no rush," then that could be an argument for Opal, even though it is inconsistent with the written agreement. Eventually, Opal may not prevail since the written agreement is more likely to control, but that is an argument she can bring up.

Reasonable expectation to be treated the same way

Or if last time Alem borrowed Opal's money, Alem also returned it to Opal in two years, then this time length could be a sound argument for Opal because it would be reasonable for Opal to expect Alem to be equally flexible to her regarding to the deadline of returning the money to him. She did him such a big favor, so it would be reasonable for Opal to expect Alem to return favor to her. Certainly, Opal's argument may not work for the current loan since what is stated on the written agreement is more likely to control, but at least, this would be an argument based on reasonable and logical reasons.

Use the strongest argument first

Please always use the strongest argument on the top of the analysis: (1) To be exam-oriented, you would not want the grader to miss your strongest point. (2) Moreover, you would not want the grader to have a bad impression on you at the upfront because of the starting weak points. (3) In addition, it also flows logically to have the strongest point on the top.

Example: The top salesperson gets fired

Scenario:

Your occupation is a salesperson for brandnew vehicles at a dealership. The manager has the idea of firing you but he has not made up his mind yet.

Question: What would you say to try to save your job?

The following is the dialogue between you (the salesperson) and the manager:

Salesperson: "I have been the top salesperson for the past decade. Last month, I sold twenty-five cars, while three of them are luxury cars."

Manager: "But you lost the biggest client last month. The company lost about half a million dollars in net profits."

Salesperson: "I have been working here for twenty years, and I am also the mentor for the new hires. I contribute my experiences to the training sessions."

Manager: "But the new hires know more than you do in terms of new technologies."

Salesperson: "I always come to work on time, and I even cancelled my trip to Europe last year just because the store had something urgent to deal with."

Manager: "Thank you for your help. But the company has already paid for your loss of money, including the air tickets and hotel room charges. That urgent situation is unlikely to happen again; even it happens, the new hires would be trained to handle it."

Salesperson: "Manager, my daughter is just admitted to a famous university and the tuition costs a lot."

Manager: "Congratulations to your daughter. She will have a bright future. You can rely on her for your living when you no longer work for us."

Analysis of your arguments:

The strongest argument: You made a lot of sales so the company received high revenues and net profits.

The second strongest argument: You also helped training the new hires, meaning you also contributed in building more assets for the company. In future, the junior employees would have great potential to create revenues for the company. In other words, you also contributed to the future earning capacity of the company.

The third strongest argument: You are a disciplined employee as you always come to work on time. In the urgent work situation last year, you even sacrificed your personal trip for the sake of the company.

(This argument is not strong because coming to work on time was part of the employer's ordinary expectations when you got hired. This point would not strengthen your bargaining power. Besides, the sacrifice you made was already compensated by the employer, including hotel rooms and air tickets.)

The fourth "argument," which is the weakest:

Your daughter's tuition is expensive, indicating that you need money but it has nothing to do with the well-being of the company.

In fact, the fourth "argument" is not deemed a valid argument. That is just a point merely to trigger the sympathy of the manager. Bear in mind that paying the expensive tuition for your daughter is not going to benefit the business of the company at all. (You might argue that would benefit the company because you would have stronger sense of belonging to the company if you are able to pay for your daughter's tuition with the income earned at the dealership. But come on, the manager wants to fire you. Who cares about your sense of belonging?)

Reminder: Your argument has to be something benefiting the employer

In conclusion, when the company is contemplating firing you, your argument has to be something benefiting the employer and making sense for them to save your job from the business perspective, not how devastating your life would be if you have no income. No one would care about you when money is concerned!

Avoid making a strawman argument

A strawman argument is a fabrication of someone's real argument, which then becomes a distorted and weaker version that can be easily refuted. That is the informal fallacy of refuting an argument different from the one which is actually under discussion.

*Example: Brenda refuses to contribute her money to buy gifts for colleagues

Anna, Brenda, Charlotte, Daisy, and Elizabeth are colleagues at the OOO Company.

Anna: "Charlotte said everyone has to contribute $10 to buy a gift for Daisy, who is going to marry next month."

Brenda: "Is it mandatory? I do not want to make this contribution because I am not close to her. She is just like a stranger to me."

Anna: "No one has any objection so far. Also, Elizabeth is going to have a baby shower next week. Please also contribute another $10 to buy a gift for Elizabeth."

Brenda: "I do not want to pay for it either. I have too many expenses."

Anna: "But you seem to be very close to Elizabeth."

Brenda: "I have my own plans. I do not want to spend money on any gifts to anyone."

Anna: "In future, when you marry or have babies, other colleagues will also buy you gifts. Why don't you marry? Then you can have babies, too."

Brenda: "I do not have to explain to others about whether I am going to marry or have babies. I just do not like the idea of buying gifts as many gifts are useless and just waste money. Furthermore, I feel so uncomfortable that others try to control the way I spend my own money. This is the suggestion of Charlotte, so she should pay for it."

Anna: "Charlotte said buying gifts to the brides-to-be or mothers-to-be has been the tradition of the OOO company."

Brenda: "Then the owner of OOO should pay for the gifts, not us."

Anna: "The owner of OOO never paid for any gifts in the past two decades. The employees are expected to fulfill this tradition."

Brenda: "What a ridiculous tradition and expectation! The OOO company makes itself look generous by creating a tradition of buying gifts but never funding them."

Question: What are the strawman arguments here?

Answer:

Why Brenda does not marry or have babies?

Anna tries to distort the argument and make it a problem of Brenda when she does not marry or have babies, so she cannot benefit from the tradition of the OOO Company.

The real arguments:

The real arguments would be: Whoever suggests the gifts should pay for them. Some of the employees may feel uncomfortable having their own money tapped by others or when they are told that they have to follow the company tradition to spend money on colleagues whom they are not close to.

Applying to the essays: You need to have the wisdom to distinguish the real standpoints of the opposing party when you formulate your arguments

You need to have the wisdom to distinguish the real standpoints of the opposing party from the strawman arguments, and also the points of view for yourself when you are being attacked, or your arguments are being distorted purposefully when you formulate your arguments.

Be clear about everyone's standpoint

Both Anna and Brenda have stated reasons to support their arguments about contributing money to buy gifts.

Brenda's concerns:

1. Is the contribution mandatory?
2. Is she close to the colleague?
3. She has her own plans, which cost money.
4. Whoever made the suggestion should pay for the gifts.

For Brenda, the main reason she does not want to pay is:

She wants to save her money for her own plans, which are more important to her.

Applying to the essays: Formulating the corresponding counter-arguments

When we prepare our arguments, we need to figure out our real arguments or the genuine standpoints of the opposing party. Otherwise, your effort would be wasted on formulating the wrong counter-arguments.

Here, Anna tried to formulate her argument based on the responses of Brenda:

Anna first thinks that "not close enough" to Daisy is the real reason for Brenda to refuse to pay for the gifts, then Anna argues that Elizabeth is, in fact, close to Brenda. (In fact, regardless of whether the person is close to Brenda, Brenda still wants to reserve money for herself.)

Afterwards, Anna thinks that Brenda does not want to pay because she is stingy, then her argument turns out to be the possible rewards in future: What Brenda is going to pay now would be offset later when Brenda marries or has babies in future. That is because other colleagues would also buy Brenda gifts. (But Brenda thinks that gifts are in fact useless and merely wasting money.)

When Brenda's argument turns to "whoever suggested should pay," Anna's argument then changes to: Charlotte is not the real decision-maker, but the OOO Company. However, no facts show that the owner plans to pay for this so-called company tradition, so Anna believes that its employees have to share the expenses.

When you are too conclusive, all you get would be distorted or over-generalized truth.

Example: Lisa lost a $100 dollar bill

Scenario: In the drinking bar

"Lisa, a young and beautiful lady, claims that her $100 dollar bill inside her wallet is missing. According to the bartender, you are the only one who has approached her purse. Hence, Lisa accuses you of stealing her money."

Lisa said, "You stole my $100 dollar bill because you were the only one approaching her purse. You are the thief!"

Question A: How would you respond to Lisa's accusation?

You can simply call the police, and the police is very unlikely to press charges on you.

Question B: Why?

There could be no relationship between the two acts - "Lisa lost her bill" and "you walked close to her purse."

Reasons:

You could have walked close to her purse because of many reasons, for example, there was a box of napkins close to her purse and you merely wanted to grab a piece of napkin for your running nose.

What are the other possibilities which Lisa has failed to realize?

She already spent the dollar bill but she forgot about it.

Someone else approached her purse, but the bartender did not see it when his eyeballs focused on the cocktails rather than her purse. The bartender just subjectively believed that he saw everything, and in his memory, you were "the only one" approaching the purse. But in fact, you were one of a few dozens of customers who have approached the purse. What the bartender means by "you were the only one" is you were the only one he saw, assuming he is not lying.

Please also write down other possibilities:

Reminder: Do not make an accusation without sufficient support

If you are too conclusive in your analysis, you would become "Lisa," who made an accusation against you without sufficient support.

A two-way argument acts more than a pendulum

We can go two different ways in the arguments of one single fact, but merely realizing the need of two-way argument is still insufficient for you to make a thorough discussion. You would not just sway left and right like a pendulum. Instead, you have to go far and deep enough to bring a value-added point before you sway another way. In short, your task is not only to demonstrate that you know this argument can go both ways but also to think deeply enough to explain the two opposite and also rational possibilities. Most of the time, the arguments on two sides also make sense, but one is more likely to prevail because of certain reasons. Imagine two counsels arguing in the court trial: Even if one side has a stronger case, it does not mean another side has nothing sensible to say.

Do not "groan when you are not sick"

The common mistake of many exam takers is: they have presented a paragraph looking like a two-way argument just because they know they have to do so, but one of the arguments does not make sense at all. In Chinese, we call it "groan when you are not sick." That means you create some arguments merely to fulfill the requirement of a "two-way argument," but the points in the context do not hit the issues at all, or the points simply make you look dumb rather than supporting your argument.

As a future attorney, you have to demonstrate arguments which are rational, reasonable and supported by rules. As such, both analyses in a two-way argument must be strong and solid with sufficient explanations.

Let's try to convert our thoughts into body acts for a second

Imagine our bodies are our brains, and we would regard the lateral exercises as the process of analyzing: When we move our bodies, we would not just swing from one side to another side; when we move our bodies to the left, and before we move our bodies to the right, we would raise our arms to the side, or bend our bodies to hit our toes. We would fully stretch our muscles on one side before we move our bodies to another side.

When we analyze both sides 'points of view, we have to go deeper and make a sensible point on one side before we talk about another side. Then, we would pick our side based on a certain reason.

Example: Manslaughter

Manslaughter is the killing under provocation, and the defendant is still under the "heat of passion," while a reasonable person would not have enough time to cool down, and the defendant is, in fact, not yet cooled down.

Scenario: A insults B

If A insults B, and B walks away from A for two hours; and then they meet each other at the bus stop. B kills A with a knife he grabs from the nearby store selling fruits.

Is the period of “two hours” long enough for a reasonable person to cool down?

For the nature of the “two-hour period”, you can, and you have to go two ways. Whether a period of two hours is a long enough time period for a reasonable person to cool down is very subjective, and for whatever side you pick, you have to think from the perspective of the opposing counsel, too. Hence, you have to include both sides' arguments.

Do not just say:

“Some say ‘two hours ’is a long period, but some say ‘two hours ’is too short.” (This is not a meaningful argument because this is not backed up with any or sufficient explanations)

Compare:

“Two hours consist of 120 minutes, which are equivalent to 7200 seconds. Many things could happen in 120 minutes or when we count from 1 to 7200. When B walks away, he should have seen many different people, items and facilities on the road, which would be able to distract him from the insult made by A. Those distractions would help to calm him down from the anger created by A.

Thus, a period of “two hours” could be deemed long enough for B to calm down.

However, it may also be true that when someone gets insulted and feels upset, whatever appears on his way would be completely ignored by him. That means even though many acts and incidents could happen in those two hours, B could still be overwhelmed by A's insulting words or gestures. B could keep thinking about those bad words, and those words would keep replaying in his mind. As such, the two hours may not be sufficient to calm him down. On the contrary, B could get more upset two hours later because those words are being replayed in his mind over and over again in 120 minutes. In other words, the impact of those bad words on B could have magnified after two hours.

As such, the two hours may not calm him down at all or could even make him more emotional.

<u>Find a reason for you to pick a side</u>

Then you have to find a reason to pick your side since both ways are possible. For the above argument, you ended with a point that B could be more angry, but there should be some facts in the question to help you pick a side.

For example:

“Since B seems to be distracted for at least 10 minutes by a cute baby on his way to the bus stop, B should be deemed calmed down already before B meets A again.”

Conclusion:

You have to show how both ways go and then pick a side based on the facts given. Which side to pick depends on which argument sounds stronger to you.

When two subjective thoughts clash

Litigation always comes up when two parties believe and insist that their acts are correct.

When we explain their points of view, we need to fully state the standpoints of both sides. You cannot shorten or simplify the arguments just because you plan to take the side of the opposing party. You have to show the main points of both sides' arguments or what makes them insist on their own standpoints, and then point out why one side is more likely to prevail unless the argument of one side is completely ridiculous and ungrounded.

Example: A contract of "Apple"

Bobby and Cindy entered into a verbal contract. B agreed to sell C the Apple(s) to B has at $50 only. Later, C did not receive what she wants. When C contacted B, C found that there are inconsistencies in their thoughts. What C means is the Apple brand laptop B has, but B means the apples he grows himself in his own garden.

There is not "a meeting of minds."

Thus, the contract may be invalid. If the contract is valid, reformation may be needed.

Instruction for students: Explain the misunderstanding

Walk into the shoes of both parties

When you argue, you have to explain the misunderstanding clearly, instead of merely repeat the wording in the fact pattern given. B and C have to state why they think their interpretations of the word "Apple" make sense. You have to walk into the shoes of both parties to feel the subjective "reasonableness" of their thoughts:

<u>Why B thinks "apples" refers to the fruits grown by himself?</u>

B would argue "apples" mean the fruits in his garden because he is well known for the wonderful apples he grows, and $50 would be too low for an electronic device of Apple brand that C would think the word "Apple" refers to. Moreover, B and C discussed the contract in B's garden, so it makes sense for B to indicate "apples" in his garden. Besides, B is certain that he used the plural noun "apples" instead of "apple," so it was "apparent" that the word "apple" would not mean a single laptop made by Apple company.

<u>Why C thinks an "apple" refers to an electronic device?</u>

However, C would argue an Apple laptop which is three versions behind the current version is just about this price, and it would not worth more than $100. Moreover, C may have never heard that B grows apples in his own garden. It is merely a subjective thought for B to believe that he is well known in the community for growing apples in his garden, but in fact, many individuals are not aware of that. Furthermore, the location of discussion does not matter to the context or the terms of the contract, and has no relevance to the validity or the context of the contract between B and C. It is merely B's subjective thought to infer that a conversation taken place inside his garden would be equivalent to selling something grown inside his garden. Most importantly, C always thinks that B is a person speaking without grammar, so C never pays attention to the plural form of "apples" B claims to have used in their conversations.

No "meeting of minds"

Since B and C have never shown any samples of "Apple" or "apples" in their negotiation, both parties have no reason to detect the differences. Neither B or C seem to be more wrong than another one. Most importantly, it is apparent that there is no "meeting of minds." As such, a valid contract is never made.

Reminder: Try to be fair to both parties

Please do not subjectively conclude that $50 must be for fruits instead of an electronic device before going through the analysis. Try to be fair to both parties to feel each side's subjective reasonableness.

Analysis

-Either soliloquy or "product description" is not an analysis

An analysis is not a showcase of products

Some exam takers have a wrong idea of analysis. An analysis is not like a showcase of products: opening the package, talking about its features and closing the box. This kind of "product description" is not analysis.

Example: General Partnership

"A General Partnership is formed by two or more individuals who associate for profit.

Here, the facts state that Danny, Brenda and Grace operate under a general partnership agreement.

Thus, this is a General Partnership."

The above example shows that the analysis and conclusion is almost saying the same thing.

The facts say that they operate under a general partnership agreement, so this is a general partnership. This is also like soliloquy.

This is similar to:

"A mother-daughter relationship exists between a mother and daughter.

Here, you are my mother and I am your daughter.

Thus, there is a mother-daughter relationship between you and me."

Explanation: Lacking a real explanation and analysis

The above section lacks a real explanation and analysis. The whole section keeps repeating the same words, and nothing has been explained. Who is a mother? Who is a daughter? What are the definitions? How do you know you are the daughter of your mother? Just because when you are born and you start having the ability to recognize people, someone told you a particular woman is your mother? Or just because you look like the woman and she told you she is your mother? Did you ever verify that biologically?

I use the "mother-and-daughter" relationship as an example just because that is something many people would assume to be true without thinking. I do not mean to offend anyone. I am merely talking about this from the perspective of logic and inference. If you never think about it, please start thinking now. What makes you draw this conclusion?

<u>The misconception about issue spotting: You have to go through a full analysis afterwards</u>

We are always told that "issue spotting" is important. Yes, it is. But this is the first step only. Once you have spotted the issue, you have to go through a full analysis before you conclude.

For many essays scoring 55 I have read so far, they have one common mistake: they define all terms or doctrines they find in the question, or repeat the facts given like a parrot, and then conclude that the legal concepts apply to the situation given. Do you think merely repeating the facts like a parrot would be the complete job description for an attorney?

A parrot does not do analysis. If you just repeat what the question tells you, this is absolutely not an analysis. If this is, a parrot can also be an attorney.

<u>Example: Is this a homicide?</u>

<u>Homicide</u>

Homicide is the intentional killing of one human being by another human being.

Bad example:

"Here, both Warren, the suspect, and Vivian, the victim, are human beings but Viola is not.

Anyway, there is a homicide."

Explanation: Reaching the conclusion without analysis

The "analysis" just says the suspect and the victim are human beings and then conclude without talking about anything else.

Compare:

Here, Warren is suspected of killing Vivian and her puppy Viola. Warren is a human being and Vivian is also a human being, while Viola is a dog. The death of Viola would not be deemed a case of homicide, regardless of whether Warren has actually ended the life of Viola. That is because it is not a human being, despite Vivian always tells her friends that Viola is her lovely daughter.

For the death of Vivian, she was stabbed five times and the weapon is believed to be a bone cutting knife. The knife with Vivian's blood and Warren's fingerprint was found at the house of Warren. However, there are no witnesses so far, and Warren never says a word after he was arrested, so the whole story was still unclear. There are still many possibilities: For example, Warren knew who was the murderer but tried to conceal the identity of the real suspect, so he took the knife and hid it.

It is clear that being stabbed five times would not be an accident or caused by the worsening of one's health condition. Although the identity of the killer is still unconfirmed, the occurrence of a homicide is apparent.

Thus, homicide occurs, while Warren is the suspect, or he would be the defendant if the police charges him of murder or involuntary manslaughter, and Vivian is the victim.

Explanation: Someone tries to end her life on purpose

The gist herc is whether there is homicide, not murder or involuntary manslaughter. (You can talk about murder or involuntary manslaughter below homicide if it is a full essay.) The main point of homicide is the intentional killing of someone by another person. If someone passes out and then passes away, the death could be caused by his or her own health condition, assuming no other wounds are found. Furthermore, it is also possible that someone attacked him one day ago and caused internal injury, and the injury takes time to produce an impact on his body.

Here, the victim was stabbed five times, so her death would not be a natural cause, or an accident (one-time cut could be an accident, or something heavy and sharp falls on her). The main point is: Someone tries to end her life on purpose, and stabbing is a means to fulfill this goal.

Do not make the analysis a conclusion

When something is very obvious to us, or is so easy to understand in our daily lives, we always tend to skip the explanations in our conversations.

Example: Bringing an umbrella

It is 8 am now. The weather forecast says it will rain after 6p.m.

"I bring an umbrella with me because it may rain this evening." That is enough for our daily conversations. The reason is clear. If you further explain, people would think you are stupid or you are insulting them because you think they are stupid.

But in the bar exam, the above explanation is not clear enough. That is because it is supposed to rain ten hours later. Why would you carry something with you only when it would be useful ten hours later?

In the bar exam, you have to explain like this:

"It is not raining now. But I still need to bring my umbrella with me now because the weather forecast predicts that it is going to rain this evening, which will be ten hours from now. Since I always work for more than eight hours a day, it is very likely that when I finish my work and start going home tonight, it will be raining on my way. As such, I may get wet if I do not carry an umbrella. Moreover, there are no conveniences stores selling umbrellas close to my office. In other words, if I need an umbrella ten hours later, I would have to bring it with me now.

Thus, I am bringing an umbrella with me now even when it is not raining."

Or you can also say: "Sometimes the weather forecast may not be accurate. I could buy an umbrella on my way home if it really rains, but I already have over a dozen of umbrellas at home which were purchased when the rain suddenly came. I do not want to have any more umbrellas, so I would rather bring an umbrella to prepare for possible later use, rather than buy another umbrella if it suddenly rains."

Explanation: Why I am carrying an umbrella when it may rain ten hours later

The second explanation is much clearer to explain why I am carrying an umbrella when it is not raining, and it may rain almost ten hours later.

Bringing an umbrella with me is basically intended for use tonight. For people who prepare to buy an umbrella when it rains would not need to bring an umbrella now.

Example: Studying and HOA

"I did not study for the bar exam this morning because the HOA had to do inspection in my unit."

But you are the one to study, which has nothing to do with the HOA. Hence, the above explanation did not hit the main point.

Please provide a complete explanation:

____

____

____

Suggested explanation:

"When the HOA came to the apartment complex, they did not come first to my unit. They went to my neighbor first. Nevertheless, I did not want to start doing anything else when they could come into my unit anytime. Also, I observed how the people from HOA inspected other units then I would know how to prepare for their inspection inside my unit, for example, what furniture or electrical appliances to remove, or what keys I may need to ensure access for the HOA people. I heard they also asked questions of history of some facilities, equipment or residence so I also needed to look up for some previous records, invoices, documents, letters and notices, in order to be able to answer their questions.

Thus, I spent my morning accommodating to the inspection of HOA. As such, I did not study for the bar exam this morning."

Get a panoramic view of the situation

Do you ever take wedding pictures or portraits in the traditional studios?

That would be the common memories of the older generation, who are at least middle-aged people now.

When the bride-to-be take wedding pictures at the studio, the backdrop can be Royal gardens or a palace, or Athenian constructions. The backdrop would make the lady look so elegant, just a like a princess waiting for the prince to pick her up with a "Disneyland-style" vehicle.

But if you look towards another side, you might see a lot of boxes, camera equipment, or the cameraman is eating a hamburger, an employee is cleaning the floor with a broom and a dust pan. What you see in another side would not match the princess in the Palace, so the bride-to-be would not want you to include the above people and stuffs in her wedding picture.

However, in the bar exam, you have to show the "dust pan" and the "princess" in order to have a full picture and a comprehensive analysis of the situation. What I mean is: Some facts are inherently more eye-catching and distracting than others. Just like everyone would be attracted by the face, the hair, and the tiara of the "beautiful princess in the palace." Who cares about the hand gloves or the uniform worn by the janitor sweeping the floor? But as a director, the person in charge of the photo studio, he or she has to see the panoramic view, and manage the whole situation. If the backdrop has the risk of collapsing, he or she has to clear the scene by asking the princess, the janitor and other staff to walk out. If fake snow or soap bubbles are needed to make the backdrop look more romantic, then other staff may have to help producing these effects, and the director in charge of the production has to coordinate.

Do not just get fascinated by the beautiful princess! You will miss a lot of the reality!

Elaborating the vague words or descriptions and exploring the unknowns

We always see many unclear terms, verbs, adjectives in the essays which could mean many things, or lead to different possibilities, and we have to spot these vague terms, which are intended to give us room to develop our analysis.

Please pull out one essay from the past exams and circle all the vague terms. That vagueness allows you to argue both ways with different defenses. Then you can pick one side which you think would be stronger, meaning they are supported by more concrete facts and compelling arguments.

Elaboration is not equivalent to making up facts. If the essay never mentions a certain situation, do not drag too far by saying if this happens, then……if you go offtrack, it would just waste your time as it is very unlikely to hit the issues offering you points in the grading rubrics.

Example: Suing the ex-girlfriend on behalf of the client

"Attorney Alex is hired to represent Pamela to sue Doris in the defamation lawsuit, when Doris was the girlfriend of Alex when they both went to high school. Convinced that he is able to handle the conflict well, Alex did not tell Pamela."

What is the vague word worth paying attention?

"Convinced"

That would be "convinced."

I would ask "convinced" by whom, and based on what foundation?

Three possibilities:

He can be convinced by some previous real experiences: He handled a few cases involving his former girlfriends and his clients were all happy about his performances.

When he dated Doris in the past, she was pretty cute and skinny but she has become old, ugly and fat now, so Alex does not believe his mind would be swayed by an ugly woman who is not attractive.

Alex knows Pamela very well, and he believes Pamela would not hire another attorney even if he tells her that Doris was the girlfriend of Alex .

You would be able to think of many possibilities for sure. Whatever the reason is, the main point is: Pamela is never given a chance to make the decision of continuing to hire Alex or hiring another one.

If you say "Alex is convinced that he would be able to handle the situation well, so he has not violated the duty," that would be a problem because the perspective of the client is completely ignored.

<u>How the acts are phrased in the fact patterns matters in understanding what exactly happened</u>

Please read carefully about how the acts are phrased in the following descriptions:

Example: Kelly started running when the police officer spots her big bag

"Around the bus terminal and the train station, Kelly is walking and carrying a big bag. But she starts running when the male police officer spots her big bag. The male police officer stops Kelly because she looks so suspicious to him."

Do not be misled by misleading statements

The misleading statement here is: "she starts running when the male police officer spots her big bag." Pay attention to how the sentence is phrased. Kelly did not start running when she spot the police officer; Instead, when the police officer paid attention to her big bag, she started running.

What is the difference between the suspect spotting the police officer and the officer spotting the suspect?

The difference is: Kelly could not control when the police officer spot her. In other words, Kelly did not run because of the police officer.

The main point is: Kelly could start running just because she thinks of something important that she needs to rush.

Geographical location

Furthermore, please pay attention to the geographical location: There is a bus terminal and a train station nearby.

What does that mean? Kelly could simply see a bus coming, or the phone app indicates that a train will arrive in three minutes, so she has to run.

Do not assume an inter-relationship between two acts

Two acts could happen at the same time coincidentally without any relationship.

Here, Kelly's act of running could have no relationship with the police officer's discovery.

"Suspicious to the officer"

As such, the phrase "suspicious to the officer" would be reasonable only from the perspective of the police officer, but not from the perspective of a regular person, or people always have to run to catch a train.

Kelly could have never discovered the presence of the officer. She just focused on her own route to her destination. Just because the officer saw her running, he thought that her act was suspicious. Subjectively, it was suspicious from the perspective of the officer; but objectively, it was unreasonable.

Takeaway from the above discussion: How the acts are phrased matters

How the acts are phrased would affect the ways we should and we can argue.

Helpless repetition :Do not keep repeating the same condition just because it is a foundation

Foundation is needed for some doctrines or rules.

Example: Late Fee as penalty

When we have to pay a fee, we would receive a bill or invoice or notice from the merchants or the organizations, with a due date. If we fail to pay by the due date, there would be late fee plus interest.

However, if no bill or invoice is ever issued, should the merchant or the organization charge you a late fee or interest?

They should not have charged you.

If they do, you might call to tell them you never receive an invoice to pay, then they may credit you back the late fee and interest.

Hence, the original bill with the due date provided is deemed the "foundation" of charging the late fee.

That would be the same as the discussion of many legal procedures in the bar exam.

Example: Motion to compel

If no discovery request to a certain document is ever made, the motion to compel would be too early and inappropriate.

"P did not provide a certain document to D."

But did D ever request?

Motion to compel is used when the opposing side refuses to produce the document. However, if you never request it, that would be your own problem.

It is just like your boss forgets to ask you to do something but then he accuses you of not doing that particular task. In order to save your job, you might not directly tell him "you never asked me to do that" or "you forget to tell me that, stupid!" But you know that there should be a foundation of asking you to do the job before he can blame you for failure to do so.

Takeaway from the above discussion: Build up the foundation first

We have to build up the foundation before further analysis in an essay, and then do not go back and forth without a strong reason.

For contract essay, if you already discuss whether a contract is valid, do not repeat the discussion for the remaining parts of essay. If there are two different conclusions due to the validity of the contracts, just say: ....if the contract is deemed valid; but as mentioned above, the contract may be deemed invalid because of… then…

Should we discuss the elements of a contract when the contract is valid......

We are told that only issues need to be discussed and we have to answer to address the call of the question.

But some sample essays also talk about non-issues.

How should we deal with that?

This is your own decision.

If you think those rules are too important, and you do not want to miss them, then just do a small IRAC, and make an analysis including not more than five sentences. But please also provide some added values to make the section more valuable, instead of repeating the exact words given in the fact pattern.

For example, when the essay question points out that the contract is valid, some students still discuss the elements of the contract. Is it redundant? How can we handle it wisely without taking the risk of missing big points?

Offer, consideration, and acceptance

In my opinion, it could be helpful to state what is the offer, consideration and acceptance in the scenario given because you may have to later talk about other issues, such as mutual mistakes, rescission, sham consideration in the essay. Hence, the previous mentioning of the elements of the contract would be a foundation for you to further discuss other developments of the story.

You may write like this: "As mentioned above, the consideration is only $1 paid by A, which is used in exchange for the diamond ring contributed by B. There is a huge difference in the values of two sides 'consideration. It is more likely that B just wants to give A the diamond ring as a gift, regardless of the price. As such, it is very likely that the court would say what A paid is only a sham consideration."

In order not to give the grader an impression that you simply repeat the words without thinking, you can identify what is the offer, consideration and acceptance in a more analytical way, which can show your understanding and insights after contemplation.

Do not make a silly conclusion when the fact pattern already told you that

It would be a silly conclusion if you write "the contract is valid" because the fact pattern told you "the contract is valid" at the beginning. Do not make such a conclusion after analyzing for the whole paragraph. It would make you look so dumb. If you want to build a foundation as mentioned above, please try to make the wording of the conclusion more sensible:

"Thus, the contract is valid from the moment she signs, or from the moment he starts doing the work for the house owner." Even though the fact pattern says the contract is valid, it does not specify from what point the contract has become a valid and legally binding agreement. Then such a conclusion would add a value to your essay.

Later in the essay, if you need to talk about reformation as a remedy, you can refer to how the contract was first made: Which part appeared to not truly reflecting what A wants or what B expects.

There is no standard to analyze if the elements are never used

What would you analyze when you are not using the elements of the rules? There is not even a standard for you to analyze if elements are never used.

Please bear in mind that what is an analysis: It is a systematic way to determine whether some acts are right or wrong, or if certain acts have met a certain standard.

Therefore, you have to know and point out the standard, which is expressed in the elements of the rules.

Example: Black Jack with Snoopy

In the casinos, whoever has a total value closer to 21 than the dealer would win in the game of Black Jack. It would be a tie if player's hand and dealer's hand have an equal value. All winning bets are paid 1/1, but when you get Blackjack, you would get 2.5 times the amount you bet.

But how about if you see the cartoon characters Snoopy, Hello Kitty or Mickey Mouse when you open your card? The deck of 52 cards are all Cartoon characters, and there are no Ace, King, Queen or any Spades, Diamonds or hearts, or any numbers in the card.

Then how to determine who is winning and who is losing?

There is no way to make a determination without the type of cards worth a value mentioned above to count the total value.

But if there is a chart showing the value of cartoon characters, you may continue the game: For example, "Snoopy is equivalent to Ace;" or "Hello Kitty is equivalent to Queen."

Applying to essays: Discuss how one's act has fulfilled the elements of the rule

When you write an essay of criminal law, you may say the defendant is guilty of robbery.

But why he is guilty?

That is because his act has fulfilled all the elements of robbery.

Thus, you must point out the elements of the rule and discuss how his act has fulfilled the elements.

Financial conditions as defenses?

You may be able to bring up the financial conditions of the defendant of a robbery, and then say they are not valid defenses.

Why they are invalid defenses?

That is because being poor or an urgent need for money is never a defense for robbery. The law would not justify a crime just because the defendant needed money.

In order to explain why the defenses are invalid, you may have to say what would be the valid defenses first, and that would be the standard for you to make a determination.

Applying to the essays- Example: ABC Company

"A General Partnership is formed by two or more individuals who associate for profit.

Here, the facts state that Amy, Bob and Carl operate the ABC Company under a general partnership agreement.

Thus, it is a General Partnership."

Explanations:

The segment above does not use the elements at all. Although three names are mentioned implying that there are three people, we still have to use the same elements mentioned in the rule to show if it is a GP: The elements used in the rule are "two or more individuals." Then we have to say "there are three individuals in total, which is more than two."

"Who associate for profit"

Furthermore, the segment above did not analyze the part about profits.

"Here, Amy, Bob and Carl operate the ABC Company for the business of ......for the purpose of earning money to make a living, which is making profit, as opposed to running a charity.

Thus, the element of associating for profit is met."

Applying to the essays:

Example: The qualifications for the special subsidy

Rule: Seniors who have monthly income $1000 or less are eligible for applying for the special subsidy from the government.

Notes: "Seniors" indicates people who are 60 years old and above; Food stamp would also be deemed income: $2 food stamp is equivalent to $1 monetary income.

Information about Yolanda

Yolanda has $950 monthly income and a food stamp worths $180. She will have her 60-year-old birthday on the 1st of next month.

Question A: Is Yolanda eligible for the special subsidy?

Age

Seniors means 60 years old and above

Food stamp would also be deemed income.

Facts show that Yolanda will be 60 years old on the 1st day of next month, which will be within 30 days. Although she will be 60 years old soon, she is still not yet eligible.

Thus, she will be eligible next month, in terms of age, but not now

Income

Seniors who have monthly income less $1000 or less are eligible for applying for this special subsidy. For seniors receiving food stamp, $2 is equal to $1 monetary income.

Here, Yolanda has $950 monetary income, which is below the threshold of $1000 income; but she has $180 food stamp, which would be deemed $90 income. As such, she would have $1040 income, which is higher than $1000.

Thus, Yolanda is not eligible for the special subsidy, in terms of income.

Elements must be fully discussed and get it done in the same IRAC

Without full discussion of all elements, the outcome of the scenario cannot be determined.

Example: Vaccination before boarding the plane

Rule: "People are not allowed to get on the plane if they do not get vaccinated."

The first step: finding out if the person is vaccinated

You need to first find out if the person is vaccinated.

The analysis would be for the purpose of finding out if a person gets vaccinated.

How would you define "vaccination'?

The definition of getting vaccination matters. It could mean getting vaccination from authorized agencies, and with the proof of vaccination card. That means if someone gets vaccinated from unauthorized agencies, or agencies with uncertain background, it would be arguable that if the person is deemed vaccinated. Or if someone gets vaccinated but lost the card, then he may be deemed unvaccinated from the perspective of the government.

Without knowing the definition of vaccination, you cannot determine whether a person is deemed vaccinated.

Getting on the plane vs. Going to the airport

Definition: Vaccination may not be required if a person merely appears inside the airport

Does it matter if the person boards the flight to work or to travel? Or if the person just goes to the airport but not boarding the flight, then the requirement could be different. That means vaccination may not be required and you have to point that out. You may say D only goes to the airport to see his friends off. He does not plan to fly abroad. In other words, he merely appears inside the airport without boarding the flight. Thus, he should be allowed to walk into the airport without vaccination, but not allowed to walk beyond a certain point.

Thoroughness of explanations are important

One of the important skills of analysis is being able to explain thoroughly.

Are you able to explain thoroughly?

Example: Stephanie's expenses last month

Stephanie has $3000 monthly income, and the following list shows how she spent her money last month.

$1000 rent

$800 food

$300 gas and parking

$200 utilities bill

$200 car insurance and life insurance

$300 clothing

$200 entertainment

Borrowing money from Tiffany

Stephanie runs out of money this month, and she wants to borrow $500 from her older sister Tiffany.

T: Why do you need to borrow money from me?

S: Because my house rent has increased.

Can you find out why Stephanie needs to borrow $500 from Tiffany?

The following list shows how Stephanie spends her money this month:

$1200 rent

$800 food

$300 gas and parking

$200 utilities bill

$200 car insurance and life insurance

$300 clothing

$500 entertainment

Total expenses: $3500

Analysis: The increase of her entertainment expenses is the gist

By taking a closer look, we find that her house rent has increased by $200 only, while she wants to borrow $500 from her older sister. The main reason she lacks money is the increase of her entertainment expenses, which could be very flexible. She has increased her entertainment expenses from $200 to $500 this month. Entertainment itself is not a necessity, and when her rent has already increased by $200, she should have saved the $200 entertainment fees in her budget, or adjust her expenses on food or clothing, while other expenses cannot be eliminated due to its essentiality, including gas and parking.

Full explanation: An increase of entertainment expenses must be mentioned

If Tiffany wants a full explanation, Stephanie should tell her that is because her entertainment expenses have increased by $300, and the rent has increased by $200, so she needs $500 more this month.

Merely blaming on the increased rent is not a full explanation. It is also possible that Stephanie does not want to be blamed by Tiffany so she tries to hide that she spent more on the entertainment this month, and also failed to reduce other expenses such as clothing in order to retain the money for the increased rent.

In other words, the main reason of Stephanie's need to borrow money from Tiffany is: Stephanie failed to reduce unnecessary expenses.

Applying to the essays: (1) Evaluate the reasons leading to the outcome

When we try to explain something in an essay, please read the facts carefully. When someone claims that this is the reason, you need to insert your own thoughts and evaluate if this is the real reason leading to the outcome.

Applying to the essays: (2) Explain the impact on the facts given

An analysis is a description of how the rules apply to the facts. When you analyze, you have to explain about how the rule applies and the impact on the facts given.

Explanation is not yet complete if the unique aspect is missed

When you explain, you have to explain the key feature or the most unique aspect of the doctrine or the situation. If you fail to do so, you do not explain at all or your words would not count as a full explanation. In other words, an explanation is not yet complete if the unique aspect is missed.

Example: A layperson witness

You have to explain why the witness may be deemed a layperson because he does not have the specific education.

On the other hand, he could be deemed an expert when he has multiple years of work experiences with a certain skill.

Example: An attorney for work compensation

Shirley has been an attorney for work compensation for ten years. She could be deemed an expert in those laws about injury as an employee.

But regarding to general labor laws about minimum wage, sick hours, discrimination, she could be deemed a layperson.

Explanations: Do not promptly conclude from the face of the words

When you see the words an "attorney," or a "doctor," or a "professor," do not promptly conclude that she is an expert. Find out what exactly she does. The argument could go both ways. Then you can choose a way to go based on sensible reasons.

Example: Rita's certificate in immigration laws

Rita just received a certificate in immigration laws, so in terms of education, she could be deemed an expert; but she never completes one immigration case on her own, then in terms of actual experience, she could be deemed a layperson.

Since actual experiences are important for attorneys to know how to deal with the immigration department, Rita may not be deemed an expert in this area because she would be able to talk about what she learns from the course but not actual examples of how Immigration department would react to certain applications.

Exaggeration in choosing adjectives or description is not going to make your analysis more persuasive

You have to support your standpoints with the facts given.

Each fact pattern has some unknowns or missing facts. But you can still infer from the facts given or point out a few reasonable possibilities developing out of the facts given.

If the person just did something wrong, make sure you use the correct words to describe that: some acts are careless, unreasonable, but may not be bad-faith. Do not use the description which would make the problem more serious than it is, just because you think he is playing the role of villain in the essay.

A regular rule may not perfectly fit into the particular situation given

You have to seriously think about how a rule applies to the particular situation. Do not just randomly connect a fact with a certain rule by merely writing a few sentences. You have to think whether the rule works in the given situation or if it makes sense in the real world.

Example: What "status quo" you would like to protect with a TRO?

When a person tries to stop another party from doing something, students would think about TRO. However, TRO is aimed to mainly protect the status quo, then you need to think about what exactly you want to maintain.

An old tree vs A singer

If someone wants to cut an old tree, you might want to have a TRO to protect the status quo; but if someone wants to stop a singer from performing for a certain boss or a particular venue, what kind of status quo you would like to protect? If you have a contract with this singer, she may not be deemed violating the contract until she actually violates the contract. Then what status quo do you need to preserve? You cannot request the singer to stay home everyday to maintain a "status quo" of not performing for other people.

Stopping an actress from having a tattoo

You have a movie contract with an actress, and she would be required to show her full body naked, and demonstrate her perfect and smooth skin to the audience. However, another contract requires her to do tattoo on her body. If she has tattoo, the tattoo would jeopardize her role in the movie requesting her to show her full naked body. Then you might want to get a TRO to stop her from having a real tattoo because once she has the tattoo done, there would be a mark on her skin forever. Thus, you would need to maintain the status quo of not having any tattoo. Then another boss could consider making a fake tattoo like painting on her body in order for the actress to fulfill both contracts.

Defenses

Valid defenses are not equivalent to the reasons for pleading in sentencing

If you rob a person for money, and all elements are fulfilled, then you would be guilty of robbery. Even if you have your mother staying at the hospital, your father having a big gambling debt, your younger brother being unemployed for three years, the above points would not be valid defenses for robbery. Your attorney may be able to mention your devastating situation in the sentencing stage at the court to minimize your penalty or jail time.

When you write an essay, you may be able to bring up the financial conditions of the defendant, and then say they are not valid defenses. When those facts are given, the grader expects you to discuss them.

Defenses are not counter-accusations

If someone accuses you of breaking a cup, you cannot defend yourself by pointing out that he also breaks a plate. This is not a defense for what you have done. Your defense should be something out of your control made you break the cup, so that is not your fault. For example, a cat suddenly jumped on me.

Applying to criminal law essays: You killed two but I killed one only?

If you are charged of killing one person, or your neighbor Albert claims that he witnessed that you killed one person, your defense would not be the fact that Albert has killed two people. The killing act of Albert would not negate your own killing act, or make your wrongdoing or offense looks less severe.

When you think about this, you may understand it; but when people are crazily typing different IRACs, their so-called defenses could be anything they can think of under stress. Please be aware of that.

Defenses are based on the rules established by the government, not your own moral judgments

Defenses are based on the rules, not from your own preferences.

For example, in criminal law essays, you can use defenses such as defense of oneself, defensc of others or insanity. These defenses are valid because the rules allow this.

The defenses are not rules of your own moral judgment. For example, "he did this and that, so he deserves to be killed, and the defendant only beats him up, so he suffers less than he deserves." This defense is not going to work.

For example, goods transaction of $500 or above need to be in writing in order to hold both parties liable. If your goods worth only $499, then you do not need writing to hold another party liable. But if your goods worth $501, you cannot defend yourself by saying something like "inflation has been high in the past years, and $500 is nothing so it does not even deserve a piece of paper to make writing." This is not going to work.

Although what you say is sensible, you can write to the government to change the rules, but you cannot adjust the rules with your own value judgments.

Be the "God of details"

"The devil is in the details" is an idiom indicating that the details are complicated and likely to cause problems. So please make yourself to be the "God of details" and make use of the trivial words or elements of the rules properly.

Please take advantage of what the rules failing to specify

Example: Mary has to wear a sexy dress

"Mary has signed a contract with the Fashion Company to be a model for three months. Her job is "to wear all the clothes provided by the company and walk around the store every work day to show them to the customers. "

Today, Mary is given a dress which she thinks is too sexy to wear on. But if she does not follow the instructions, she could be held liable for breaching the contract.

<u>What must Mary do to fulfill the contract?</u>

The rule of the contract specifies that she must wear clothes provided by the company, which means she has no choice of what to wear and what not to wear.

<u>What is not included in Mary's contract?</u>

The contract does not specify how Mary has to wear the clothes.

<u>What would be Mary's options?</u>

Mary can consider wearing the T-shirt provided by the same company and then wearing a dress on it. Then it would not be too sexy to her.

Certainly, the company does not like that.

But at least Mary has not violated the contract by doing so.

<u>Applying to defenses: Please try to come up with defenses from the lack of specifications</u>

When a rule just tells you what you need to do, please find out if they say how, where, by what time, and in what way? These are important because they leave room to argue, even though the original purpose is to maintain flexibility for both parties.

Here, the rule says that Mary has to wear all clothes provided by the company and walk around the store on work days to show them to the customers. The act required is walking with the clothes worn, on work days, and the purpose is to show the customers the fashion. But how to walk, what facial expressions and gestures are required are not specified. That means if Mary walks too slow, or does not smile, her act would not constitute the breach of contract.

When you try to come up with a valid defense for a party, please pay attention to what she literally has agreed to and what she has not specifically agreed to.

In the above example, if the boss wants to sue her because she does not smile when she walks in the clothes, he may not succeed because the contract does not specify she has to smile, and she never agrees to.

Be aware of the correlation between the rules and the defenses

Do not merely recite the templates without understanding the correlation. In the baby bar, students always recite the templates for torts, criminal law and contract, and recite all of them. Many exam takers even write out the whole template with all headings, regardless of the facts, and define all of them and then write they "do not apply."

In the General Bar, there are so many variations and possibilities, and you cannot survive with the same trick. Moreover, more subjects, rules, and defenses are involved. You need to understand the correlation between them in order to have a good presentation.

For example, "unclean hands" are the defenses to equitable remedy such as specific performance. If you want to or need to talk about unclean hands, please place the analysis of unclean hands right after the equitable remedies.

Moreover, you may remember a lot of defenses, but they are defenses to what? Are you clear about that? You cannot say the defense is for the whole situation, and we are going to prevail because of that. The defenses we have are not catchall defenses. They would not be valid regardless of the facts. The defense usually works because of a particular element and no longer effective when it is out of the scope. For example, defense of oneself is the defense to battery, but only to the scope that you are no longer in danger. If you use excessive force, the defense would not work anymore, and you need to specify that in your analysis. Do not throw things at the wall and see what sticks.

Conclusion

Showing instead of telling

Do not "tell" the graders about your conclusion but "show" them all the steps with supporting facts, and sufficient explanations. Then the conclusion would naturally and smoothly come. Certainly, you have to type it to make the conclusion visible. But before your grader reads your conclusion, they should be able to predict it. If you would like to make a surprising conclusion, that is fine if sufficient reasonings are provided. For example, an exception comes out because of……

However, without sufficient explanations and supporting facts, the "surprising" conclusion would be just "shocking" to the grader.

Example: Miscalculation of your refrigerator payments

Scenario:

You have to pay a refrigerator by installments for 24 months, without interest. There is a regular payment of $100 every month. Your job brings you unsteady income. Sometimes you pay $150 when you earn more, and sometimes you pay $60 when you earn less.

This month, you find that there could be mistakes in calculation but you are not sure. Hence, you go to talk to the manager of the billing department.

After 15 minutes of readings and calculations, the manager said "there is no miscalculation for your refrigerator installments. Next customer, please."

What would you feel? You might feel angry, confused and unsatisfied. You come because you believe there could be a miscalculation, even though you are not 100 percent sure, and you might get some refund, but the manager just said "no miscalculation" and asked you to leave.

You are not begging for money, and you are not saying the billing department must be wrong, but you just want to clarify the possible mistake or what led to the misunderstanding.

Then what would you need? You would need the manager to show you how they do the Mathematics. You want him to show you after making a few payments of different amounts, why the balance would be this dollar amount.

You would not want to walk out of the billing department just because someone merely gives you a conclusion. You need a person to show you the steps of calculations, in order to confirm that the dollar amount in the balance section on the monthly statement is correct. Then you would leave the billing department happily and with satisfaction.

Applying to the essays: Are you able to persuade the graders?

That would be the same rationale when we conclude our bar exam essays. You need to be able to persuade the graders that this is the correct conclusion based on the above explanations.

What are senseless or groundless conclusions?

A senseless or groundless conclusion would be one generalizing statement based on ridiculous reasons or biased thoughts of a narrow-minded person.

Does your conclusion make sense?

Example: Who pays for the smog check?

Amy plans to sell her car and she would like to know which party is supposed to pay for the smog check of the preowned car before the sale takes place.

A dialogue between Amy and Billy

The following is a dialogue between Amy and Billy:

Amy: "I would like to sell my old car, and the prospective buyer wants me to complete the smog check first. Does the law require the seller or the buyer to pay for the smog check?"

Billy: "I never paid for it when I sold my old car."

Amy: "Then I should ask the buyer to pay himself."

Explanation: Amy's conclusion does not make sense at all

Why?

Amy would like to know if the law requires the seller to pay for the smog check. Billy does not provide Amy with the answer about the particular rule. Instead, he describes his own experiences: he never pays for that. Amy simply makes a conclusion based on Billy's personal experiences. How can Billy's own experience speak for the laws?

In fact, Amy's senseless conclusion was brought by the wrong rule and the lack of analysis. The standard she used was, in fact, the personal experience of Billy and it has nothing to do with the existing laws. The choice and act of Billy could be wrong.

It is possible that the laws do not have any requirements: As long as either side agrees to pay and they agree with the price of the car, the government may not care. The buyer or the seller can even split the expense. (I do not know whether there are any laws governing that.) Assuming there are no such laws, it makes more sense to request the seller to pay for it because once the seller has completed the smog check, the seller can sell the car to whatever buyer; but if the buyer pays for it and the car does not pass the smog check, then the buyer may not even want to buy it. Then the buyer would have spent money on a smog check of a car not belonging to her and gain nothing eventually.

However, the seller may also claim that she would sell her car "as is," and if the buyer does not want to buy the car due to the result of the smog check, that would mean the buyer has paid to get rid of the potential trouble, which also has a value.

Whatever the rule is, Amy cannot conclude just because Billy did not pay for the smog check in the past: (1) Billy's history has nothing to do with Amy's car; (2) Billy's situation does not apply to Amy's at all.

Billy's history has nothing to do with Amy's car

If the law in fact requires the seller to pay for the smog check, who cares whether Billy paid when he sold his car?

Billy's situation does not apply to Amy's at all

The only thing common for Billy and Amy would be the sale of old cars. Other than that, nothing from Billy can apply to Amy.

Perhaps Billy's car was popular in the market, looking fantastic, and in good condition, so the buyer was willing to pay for the smog check, regardless of what the law requires. Billy may have bargaining power to request the buyer to pay for it.

Even if both Amy and Billy have the same model of car, the years can be different, or the conditions can be different, Or one has crash history, and another one does not have; or when Billy sold the car, the supply of cars are limited but when Amy sold her car, the market has too many cars of identical models.

But Amy's car may not look as good as the car of Billy. Amy should have her own analysis based on the laws; if no law governs that, she should make her analysis based on the totality of the circumstances, including the attractiveness of her car, the price she requests for the car, the number of prospective buyers. If more buyers want her car because her car looks great, the buyer may offer to pay for the smog check in order to defeat other competitors, or if the car costs a five-digit dollar amount, the seller may not even care about the expense of a two-digit dollar amount for smog check.

Regardless of whether the buyer or the seller pays eventually, the factors considered should logically lead to a sensible conclusion.

Conclude after all the unknowns for all layers are found

The conclusion is not ready if there are unknowns yet to be explored. Please solve problems in every layer before your conclusion because a conclusion is a summary of your findings or your legal advice. If there are important unknowns, you would not be able to draw a sensible conclusion; if there are some kinds of uncertainty, you can conclude like this: "This argument is likely to prevail if……Otherwise……"

Each layer is determined by certain factors

Each IRAC addresses a layer of issues, and after all layers are addressed, you would be ready to conclude. To make it simple, a layer could be a factor leading to a final decision, and each factor also depends on other variations.

Example: Is Eva going to travel out of the country in the coming Christmas?

It is July now.

Eva (E) lives at San Francisco, CA. She is an interior designer. Dylan(D) is talking to her about her possible vacation plan.

D: Are you going to travel out of country in the coming Christmas?

E: I have to see if the current project can be completed by the end of October.

D: Florence is a difficult client. Hope she is happy with your work.

E: We are waiting for a kind of marble tiles from Italy. If everything is smooth, completing the project by the end of October should not be a problem.

D: But you told me you lost your passport.

E: Yes. Without an old passport, it would take longer time to get another passport.

D: I heard that the majority of the staff in the passport office are sick due to food poisoning. The office may not do the normal work for the coming two weeks.

E: Yes. That could cause a long delay. But everything should be clear in November, then I would order air tickets to probably Vienna or Paris, if it would not be too late.

D: I think it would be late. It would be almost impossible to get a direct flight.

E: For indirect flights, there would be a big risk of flight cancellations due to the weather. If one flight is delayed or canceled, I would probably miss the second flight and also other reservations, such as hotel rooms and rental cars.

D: If you would decide that late, a road trip may be better for you because that would be more flexible.

E: Yes. Then I can make my final decisions just a few days in advance. If have more time, I can drive to Los Angeles; If I have less time, I can at least drive to Sacramento. I will see if we are going to have the annual bonus by then.

D: This year has been financially difficult for our boss. We may not even have the annual bonus.

E: Even if we do, I think the amount could be less than a few hundred dollars.

D: Probably. But at least it would be enough for you to drive to Oakland for a meal and come back to San Francisco on the same day.

E: Yes. At least a meal in Oakland. Not too bad.

D: A vacation is just a mental break from the work. How far and how long are not the most important.

Explanations:

Please pay attention to the structure here:

From the above dialogue, we learn that Eva would like to travel out of the country, probably to Vienna or Paris. But it depends on at least a few factors: (1) the time she will complete the current project for Florence; (2) the time she will receive her new passport.

However, by the time she can confirm she can travel, it could be too late to order air tickets, and she does not like indirect flights because delay or cancellation of one flight could have an impact on the second flight and other hotel reservations.

Hence, she may change to road trip instead because of flexibility. Then she can make her final decision at the last minute. If she has more time, she prefers going to Los Angeles; if she has less time, she might go to Sacramento.

Moreover, money is also a key factor in determining the destinations. She is not sure whether she will have the annual bonus from her employer and it sounds like the expenses of her trip all rely on the bonus. A trip, including gas, hotel rooms and meals, may cost over $1000, but they expect the bonus could be just a few hundred dollars for each employee. Thus, she may simply drive to Oakland for a day trip, and she expects she can afford at least one meal.

Conclusion

The conclusion here would be:

"Eva may take a road trip within California instead of traveling out of the country due to her need for flexibility because of the unpredictable nature of her work and the possible delay of receipt of her new passport. Which cities to go to would depend on the amount of time and bonus Eva is going to have. "

The final sentence would be:

"Eva is not traveling out of country in the coming Christmas due to her expected inability to get direct flights to fly to Vienna or Paris."

"In conclusion" does not necessarily mean a real conclusion is coming

Writing the preceding conjunction "in conclusion" at the beginning of a paragraph does not mean that the following words really constitute a conclusion.

Conclusion does not just mean the last sentence or the last paragraph of the essay. It has to be a logical judgment or decision reached by reasoning. In order to reach a logical ultimate conclusion, you have to resolve all unknowns in all layers.

A conclusion is supported by the backbones, not the embellishments

A conclusion states the outcome of the analysis, without leaving room to be challenged. Whether you conclusion works, it depends on the preceding paragraphs.

Example: Holding an admission ticket to a concert

Everyone has to pay to attend a concert. But the staff would only check if you have an admission ticket, without asking whether you paid or how you paid.

That is because holding an admission ticket is the "conclusion" of making payments unless other inconsistent proof is found.

Other inconsistent proof - the bleeding man's accusation

For example, someone with his head bleeding points his finger at you and accuses you of hitting his head and grabbing his wallet with the admission ticket. Moreover, he is able to tell the serial number of the ticket. The staff has confirmed that the number he says is exactly the number shown on your admission ticket. Then, the staff may ask you more questions, including your proof of payment, to verify who actually owns the ticket.

Without this bleeding man, a valid admission ticket would be a "conclusion" of owning the ticket, without doubt, or challenges by the staff.

Applying to the essays - Did you successfully rebut the bleeding man's accusations?

You have to find out if all unknowns or conflicting arguments are completely rebutted by you before you conclude.

When you make a conclusion, you have to be aware of whether there is a "bleeding man" pointing his finger at you. If such a "bleeding man" is present, you are not ready to conclude yet. You have to show more concrete proof, such as your credit card receipt, in order to prove that you, in fact bought the ticket when the admission ticket alone is no longer equivalent to the conclusion that you paid for the ticket.

Example: Partnership essay

In a partnership essay, facts show that Sam is not a partner in the partnership agreement of the law firm. Can you conclude Sam is not a partner? Please read the facts carefully. You might find some conflicting facts: Sam shares 30 percent of the profit of the law firm even when he is just a tenant attorney because his presence in the building helps attract more clients to the law firm. Then, you have to deal with the conflicting facts before you conclude.

Example: Wendy's car crash

Wendy works from 9am to 5pm, Monday thru Friday. She crashed her car and injured someone at 1p.m. on Saturday. Can we conclude that Wendy's crash was out of the scope of her work? Not yet. More factors need to be considered, and more conflicting facts need to be found out before a conclusion is made: Was she driving a car provided by her employer? Was she driving to meet a client? Did she crash the car because of any work-related phone calls or text messages?

Phrase the conclusion in the way the questions are asked

A conclusion is unlike a signature at the end of a letter. It is not just a symbol but a real answer.

A conclusion is the answer to the essay question

When you draw a conclusion, you are also answering a question. Be sure to phrase the answer in the same way the question is asked. Otherwise, you are not directly answering the question.

Example: Pets 1

This is a dialogue between you and a friend.

Q: Do you have any pets?

A: I am afraid of all pets.

Explanation: You did not answer the question

Even though we can infer that you have no pets (Because you are afraid of all pets), you did not answer the question. The correct answer should be: "I do not have pets."

Example: Pets 2

Q: Are there any pets in your house?

A: I am afraid of all pets.

Explanation: The rest of the house is not within your control

This answer is not address the question, and we do not know the answer, even though we are aware of the fact that you are afraid of all pets. That is because you may live with a roommate, or you just rent a bed space on a bunk bed while the rest of the house is not within your control. If that is the case, there could be pets owned by someone else in your house, even though you are afraid of all pets. Other people would not give up their pets just because you are afraid of them.

Applying to the essays: Read every word of the call of an essay question when you conclude

When you are ready to conclude an exam, the last time you read the question could be almost an hour ago. For safety, you would better read the wording of the question one more time to make sure you are actually answering the question and you are writing in the correct direction.

Example: Did the court err in ruling that?

First, you have to find out what the decision should be under the existing law; Second, you would see how the court ruled in the fact pattern; thirdly, Lastly, you can figure out if the decision was correct or incorrect.

If you have a gut feeling that party A would prevail, but your analysis does not show it, then your so-called "conclusion" is not actually a conclusion but a groundless prediction.

Example: You are the attorney for party B

If the question said "You are the attorney for party B. What would be your advice? " how should you answer?

Then you have to point out the legal doctrines, analyze the situation, figure out the chance of prevailing and how to put your client into the most favorable position: What cause of action can he take? What valid defenses the opposing side would have? After analyzing the chance of prevailing for your client, you can decide whether he should proceed with the litigation, take the settlement offer, or make a settlement offer. The conclusion could be stated in one short paragraph, but the backbone are the preceding analysis and explanations.

A short and brief conclusion is acceptable

When we spend much time writing rules and analysis, it is very likely that we will have less than five minutes left for the conclusion. Hence, the conclusions are always short in the exam; But being short and brief itself is not a mistake, as long as they make sense.

If you do enough practice, and your analysis is thorough and in-depth, you can simply write, "based on the foregoing discussion, she would be held liable for…..but not liable for…"

Wording

Writing like a lawyer: Wording should be appropriate

Graders would like to see lawyer-like writings. Hence, it would be helpful for us to use appropriate words in all sentences.

If you use "therefore" or "hence" already in the same paragraph, try to use "as such" for the last sentence. For the final conclusion, please use "based on the foregoing reasons."

If you need to refer to something you already discussed, please use "as mentioned above."

Some students like to use "facts show that, "…But that preceding phrase is only used to emphasize something in the fact patterns, and those words, perceptions or act descriptions are from the plaintiff, the defendant, or the exam question writer, not from you. That is to show the grader that you quote something from the facts given: "That is exactly what happened."

If you just talk about something ordinary or not controversial, and it does not need emphasis, you do not need the phrase "facts show that." If I say, "the surveillance video shows that" you had lunch, but you never denied you had lunch, then what is the point of adding "... show that?"

One might say…another might say…

When you discuss a controversial public issue, you can use the preceding phrase mentioned above.

For example, when the government plans to implement a new policy; or when the management team of the huge parking lot has decided to increase the fee by 80 percent

But when you have two identified parties in a certain litigation, please use the name or alphabet symbolizing the plaintiff or the defendant.

Example: Quincey occupies the land of Rafael

Rafael claims that the use of the piece of land by Quincey does not constitute adverse possession because the use is not open and notorious, and Rafael never knows her use;

But Quincey would argue that Rafael could be the only one who does not know the use by Quincey, while other residents have already regarded Quincey as their neighbor. For whatever issues related to that piece of land, most residents would talk to Quincey.

Whether adverse possession takes place is an issue between two identified parties R and Q. They would have opposing arguments to each other. Neighbors could be laypeople witnesses, and attorneys could be expert witnesses. You would not quote people who talk about the land occupation as gossip. Those words are not useful in a legal dispute.

Imagine if you argue with your spouse……

Moreover, imagine when you argue with your spouse and your spouse says, "one say that...and another say that…" it does not make sense at all. That is because the issue is between you and your spouse. Why would I care about what other people say about a matter between me and my spouse?

Adjust the wording for your particular purpose

Words are used to convey our meanings, and in order to be more persuasive, we have to manipulate the use of words. The wording has to be adjusted for your purposes.

The same meanings could be expressed with different ways of phrasing.

Example: Peter returned money

"Peter returned the money to me three years after he borrowed it from me. Before I received the money back, I called him seven times and even waited outside his workplace in rush hours."

Rephrased version:

"After Peter borrowed my money for three years, and after I called him seven times, he still refused to return my money. I was unable to get it back until I waited outside his workplace in rush hours."

The rephrased sentence emphasized the reluctancy of Peter to return money to me and how much effort I spent on urging him to do so. He did not return money to me until I did something which he might feel embarrassing. In other words, he returned money to me not because he think he should do so but he just wants to avoid the embarrassment he might have outside his workplace. He is a jerk.

How to present different opposing arguments?

The wording is important, especially when the grader simply spends a few minutes only on your essay. The wording you choose is a kind of roadmap for the graders to predict what is coming up in the next sentence or paragraph.

When D says something to state his point of view, and E says something opposite, then D wants to argue again about what E just said.

Use "rebut" instead of "argue" for the second time one expresses his standpoint opposing another one's

When D expresses his views the second time, please do not use the word "argue" again to avoid confusion. I would use "rebut." Do not let the grader think that you are turning around and around.

The structure would be like this: Clearly indicating the opposing views of the opposing sides with different verbs and conjunctions

Diana went to Pedro's house without the consent of Pedro, which constitutes trespass to land (You can also talk about intent, act, causation.). The fact that nothing is damaged or disturbed is irrelevant as long as Diana entered it without permission from Pedro. (The above sentence is about definition.) Diana may argue that she simply went into Pedro's backyard to take some measurements solely for the purpose of installing sound-deadening materials, which is for the health and well-being of Pedro. (The above sentence is about defense.) However, Pedro may also rebut that measurement is not something urgent to justify her act of trespass to land. (The above is stating the defense fails, and the elements of trespass to land do not include bad faith.) In other words, entering the land without Pedro's permission would be sufficient to establish trespass to the land, even though it is motivated to protect Pedro's health. (Still "trespass to land" even though there is good faith.)

Also, avoid the structure "but...but...but..."

Also, avoid the structure "but...but...but..." to express the opposing views of two parties. It may be acceptable in daily conversations, but not legal writing. Legal documents are supposed to be prepared by professionals or attorneys, so the wording should be formal.

How to handle the difficult subjects

Make the abstract rules more tangible - Civil Procedures.

There are many rules in Civil procedures. If you never work for a law firm, and never get involved in real litigation, it would be hard to remember all of them.

Walking into the shoes of the defendants

Try to imagine if one of your neighbors sues you for making loud noises: Then you might argue that you never play loud music at night. You merely have conversations at reasonable sound level with family members after dinner, but you always stop talking loudly by 11pm.

Rule 12b(6)

Rule 12(b)(6) permits a motion to dismiss for failure of the complaint to state a claim on which relief can be granted.

Imagine that you have to prepare a motion to dismiss for failure to state a claim and try to think of what facts are favorable to you and what facts are not.

Use your imagination and formulate your arguments

Your neighbor Nancy thinks that she is disturbed by noises coming from your unit, so she is unable to sleep. But you think it is ridiculous because you live with your parents, who usually go to bed at about 10 pm, and you might talk to your friends on the phone, but you would stop any phone conversations by 11 pm.

What the plaintiff needs to prove

In order to sue you, Nancy has to at least point out (1) what kind of noises she hears every night and (2) she has to show that the noises actually come from your unit.

Check if she is able to show the above two points.

If the noises come from the vehicles on the street or cats or dogs owned by other people, then that would not be your obligation. If Nancy claims that she hears noises of pigs but you do not have any pigs at your home, then she would be unable to establish her accusation. If Nancy accuses you of the noises just because your unit is closest to hers, that would not be sufficient to support the above claim.

Summary Judgment

Assuming 12b6 does not work for you and the case proceeds to the court trial, maybe you can try requesting a summary judgment. Please recall what a summary judgment means: A summary judgment is a judgment entered by a court for one party and against another party without a full trial when there is no genuine dispute.

If you think there is no genuine issue of dispute, then you can request summary judgment.

Nancy says she heard people talking loudly at midnight, and she believes that the noises come from your unit, but you always go to bed and fall asleep before midnight. Some other witnesses say two people living at Apt Y like to stand outside your apartment smoking and talking at the same time. If these conversations are the exact noises mentioned by Nancy, that would not be your fault. Apparently, this would be something out of your control. Perhaps Nancy can talk to the security guard of the apartment complex and try to stop the two people living at Unit Y from talking outside your unit. The property management may suggest they talking elsewhere, which can be the garden or the fountain, far away from the residential units.

When the noise is proved to be caused by the two people living at Unit Y, the trial against you would not need to continue, so a summary judgment may be granted.

You can also create your own example in order to remember the function of every pre-trial and trial procedure. Think of something you care about the most. Then, that mental picture would be more impressive to you.

There are a lot of rules in CP. If this is your weakest subject, try to think of a scenario every day with different rules, and if you keep doing it for three months, your understanding in this subject will greatly improve.

<u>Interpret the essay questions into a way less abstract for you</u>

<u>Constitutional law</u>

Imagine if you are the plaintiff who is adversely affected

Talk about the three levels of scrutiny somewhere

Have a checklist of headings in your head and check which one applies

<u>Essay Example: July 2022 Constitutional Law</u>

In the Con law essay, imagine you are the person having a dove tattoo on your wrist, and the authorities ask you to have it removed or cover it, or you will be suspended. That is because one of the gangs 'symbols has birds.

If you are a person with tattoos, you tend to think that the instruction is ridiculous, or you might even have a lot of bad words in your head. Try to get rid of those bad words and extract the gist from it:

<u>Different meanings to you and to the school</u>

The "dove" means peace to you but the school interprets it as the cause of violence between gangs.

<u>Support your standpoints with different doctrines</u>

Then you have to use different doctrines to explain your standpoints.

When I first studied Con laws, I thought the rules were abstract. But when you are targeted by the authorities and suffer, you would feel its actual existence. It would be something solid, concrete and tangible.

<u>Visualize the scenario</u>

In order to make the images more visible to you, try to remember some good MBE questions to strengthen your understanding and memory about the three levels of scrutiny or the concepts of ripeness and mootness.

<u>Example: The concept of mootness</u>

If the student is no longer pregnant, is the issue moot? No.

Why? Because the issue is capable of repetition. Try to pick those MBE questions and answers that you believe you would still remember ten years after you pass the bar. Those would be good MBEs, in my opinion.

Example: Three levels of scrutiny test

There are three levels of scrutiny test. Do you understand what they are and what their purposes are?

They are used to evaluate the constitutionality of statutes or the reasonableness of a government act. But it is still abstract to many people.

Easier to understand the scrutiny test if the test is dragged into the private sector

The Constitutional Laws apply to the government only, but we can borrow the rules into the private sector for a minute.

Let me talk about some examples in private sectors, and apply the test to them, then you could feel more substances.

***Tight fit= narrowly tailored**

"Tight fight" means the acts taken are necessary and do not create more burdens than necessary to achieve a goal.

Some acts in our daily lives may intrude into our privacy but they are necessary when certain works need to be done, including works in the private sectors.

Example: Providing SSNs to prospective employers?

Our Social Security Numbers (SSN) are deemed confidential, and we cannot disclose it to others, including friends and colleagues. But when we work for an employer, we need to provide that in order to get paid and verify our legal status to show that we are allowed to work in this country.

Thus, asking for your SSN can be deemed a "tight fit" when your employer needs to pay you for the work you do.

However, if thousands of people are applying for five vacant job positions, asking for SSN in the first round of job interviews may not be deemed a "tight fit" because most of the candidates would not be selected eventually. Writing down the SSN would create the risk of loss and risk of identity theft, which could be avoided.

How about people who check in to stay at a hotel? Is asking for SSN a "tight fit?" No. It is not necessary at all, as long as the identity card of the guest is provided and payment is made.

Reminder: The "tight fit" concept applies to government acts only,

Certainly, the "tight fit" concept applies to government acts only in the bar exam and in real life. The above example is aimed solely to help you understand more about the concept of "tight fit."

Whether your own act is necessary to achieve a certain purpose

Example: Rummaging through drawers

You rummage through your drawers, boxes, containers in your house, turning many items upside down to look for the following items:

You lost your passport, and you have to board the flight tomorrow morning.

You lost a picture you took when you were a teenager, and you are 50 years old now.

You lost a $5 supermarket coupon, which is going to expire in three weeks. When you use the $5 coupon, you must spend another $5 out of your pocket to make the coupon valid.

You lost the winning lotto ticket which would give you $10 million.

<u>Question:</u>

Is the act necessary? Is it a “tight fit”? Do you create more burdens than necessary?

Number 1 is a "tight fit." You have to board the flight tomorrow morning and you would not have enough time to apply for an express passport. So you must be able to find it, or you will miss the flight and waste your money on air tickets, hotel and other reservations. In other words, rummaging through your house and turning everything upside down would be more reasonable, as opposed to the risk of missing the flight and losing money in all other reservations.

Number 2 would be necessary to find the lost picture because of its precious value: You are 50 years old now, and your appearance must have changed a lot when compared to how you looked when you were a teenager. You would not be able to take the picture again with the same setting or the same people. Everything happened more than 30 years ago.

However, there is no urgency. You can take your time to find your old picture. In other words, your goal of locating the old picture does not justify your act of turning almost everything upside down. It is not a "tight fit." It burdens more than it is necessary.

Number 3 is unreasonable, in my opinion. You still have three weeks before the expiration date of the coupon, and even if you are unable to find it, you will lose only $5. Most importantly, you have to spend another $5 out of your own pocket in order to use the $5 coupon. So, the $5 dollars coupon is not actually worth $5. If you do not spend $5 more, the coupon is a piece of trash only.

What are you going to gain if you can locate the coupon? A chance to spend $5 more out of your pocket. As such, losing the coupon is not necessarily a loss because you would save the $5 you are required to spend. In other words, turning everything upside down to locate something pushing you to spend more money would be equivalent to “give a lark to catch a kite.”

Number 4 would be a "tight fit" for most people because with $10 million prize, your whole living standard would change. You would be able to afford a luxurious house and car; you can quit your current job and start your own business; or you can travel around the world or give a big sum of cash to each of your family members. The goal of fulfilling all your dreams mentioned above would justify the acts of rummaging through your house and overturning your storage boxes.

In a nutshell, the three levels of scrutiny are a system to evaluate if your goals are able to justify the craziness and intrusiveness of your acts. Certainly, in the bar exam, you would not use the word "craziness."

Student Essays

Feb 2023 Professional Responsibility

Overall comments:

Your biggest problem is: Your approach to write an essay is merely copying elements from the rules from the books of outlines, without paying attention to the facts given. There are many sub-rules under a big umbrella of rules or doctrines. You have to pull rules directly responsive to the facts given.

For example, there are no deaths in the fact pattern, so there is no need to mention a rule about the attorney's disclosure of information regarding to death.

You fail to understand the nuances between different duties. Duty of competence is the ability to handle a case, or whether you are capable of taking the job, but not the fulfillment of all other duties. You also need to spend more time studying definitions.

Also, please be sensitive to the facts given. You cannot write independently of the fact patterns. You cannot just recite all the rules about PR without reading the facts in detail. There are reasons for exam writers to include certain facts. The essay portion is to test exam takers' abilities to apply rules to the facts given, instead of reciting a whole bunch of rules and typing on the screen, regardless of what the questions ask.

The way you go shows that you are not familiar with the facts: You have to clarify who is a client and who is not a client.

I rewrote a lot of analysis for you. Please read them carefully, and also the sample answers released by the State Bar.

Furthermore, please focus more on the issues rather than non-issues. You might not even have enough time for real issues, so do not waste time on non-issues.

Take it as a real case, and think about the details more seriously.

<u>What ethical violations, if any has Andy committed? Discuss.</u>

Representing LawnCare ("LC") to defend a personal injury suit from Paula ("P")

<This heading is unnecessary, unless there are more than one lawsuit in the essay, then you would like to make it clear.>

<The question is asking about the ethical violations by Andy, so focus on that: The heading should be the duty, and the conclusion should be whether Andy has violated such a duty. Do not put the conclusion in the heading. It is not entirely wrong but IRAC is the standard format. You do not know the style of the graders, so you should be more conservative.>

An attorney-client relationship with LC <This paragraph is useful to make a foundation. Without such a relationship, the ethical rules may not apply. But please explain more if you have decided to include this paragraph. Each paragraph is expected to have value in contributing useful information or valid arguments.>

An attorney-client relationship begins when the client retains the attorney to represent her. <Please check the rule: The relationship starts when the client talks to the attorney for the purpose of obtaining legal advice, regardless of whether the attorney gets hired eventually.>

Here, there is an attorney relationship (You made the conclusion in the very first sentence in the analysis, which makes the following analysis meaningless. Save this for the conclusion part. That would be more logical. Besides, the relationship is known as an attorney-client relationship.) between Andy ("A") and LC because P is suing LC for personal injury when her children developed LA's weed killer. A is defending LC from the lawsuit. <Please read the above paragraph again. Your reason is not a reason. The relationship exists not because P is suing LC, but A represents LC in LC's case, which is the main point. You have to pay attention on how to present your arguments, and how to write sentences to quickly hit the point. >

<Compare to how I would explain:

Here, LawnCare is being sued by Paula and LawnCare would need a lawyer to defend the Company. Facts show that a valid retainer agreement is already made between LC and Andy, meaning that the existence of the attorney-client relationship between LC and Andy is already reduced into writing, which is formal and confirmed by both sides. Thus, there is an attorney-client relationship between LC and Andy.

Non-issue – valid retainer agreement <This part is not necessary, but you can do that if you have time. It is not needed because the focus is Andy's ethical violation, and he already has a valid agreement with LC. In order to save time, you do not have to do that in an exam.>

Under ABA, there is no writing requirement for regular fee agreements, but preferred to be in writing.

Under CA, it requires a fee agreement over $1,000 to be in writing unless the client is a corporation, the agreement was made during an emergency, the client waives the writing requirement in writing, or the service is for a previous client with similar services in which the fee can be implied, or it can not be illegal or unconscionable. <This part shows your problems: you state the rules without any analysis. Moreover, the rules, the explanation, and the conclusion are not connected. >

<Your conclusion is: There is a valid retainer agreement, but you failed to explain why it is valid. Your conclusion also failed to address the ABA part.>

Here, since the retainer fee agreement is valid,<the facts already say the agreement is valid, so what you should do is either not talk about it, or talk about it but also provide an added value.> it meets both the ABA and CA requirements.

<Compare:

Here, no facts indicate whether the litigation takes place in CA. If it does, the rules mentioned above apply. For a personal injury case involving breathing problems and chemicals, many reports from the experts would be needed. It may also take a few months to complete the legal proceedings, plus all the paperwork. It is very likely that the attorney fees charged by Andy would exceed $1000, so an agreement would be necessary. >

(Please also write an analysis of other elements you brought up, but it would waste much time in the exam. I say "waste" because the conclusion would be there is no violation.)

Thus, there is a valid retainer agreement.

<Even though there is a valid agreement, it is stupid to say so because that is exactly what the fact pattern says. Then, what is the added value of your analysis? >

<Compare: Thus, the retainer agreement already fulfilled the requirement of CA, and also, it has also done more than what ABA requires. >

A is a member and financial supporter of C2AC.

<Please check the rules: in my memory, when an attorney works pro-bono, it is less strict. No formal attorney-client relationship is developed. But free service would not affect the establishment of such a relationship.>

An attorney-client relationship with C2AC

Supra

<Contradictory to the facts given: The facts clearly state that there is no formal attorney-client relationship with C2AC. >

<Please pay attention to the fact patterns.>There is an attorney-client relationship here because A provided pro-bono-free legal advice to C2AC in an unrelated corporate matter. Providing pro bono-free legal advice is the same as representing C2AC in legal matters.

Thus, there is an attorney-client relationship. <unnecessary discussion>

<The point about the pro bono to the whole essay is Andy never tells LC, so the main concern is the duty of loyalty.>

Breach of Duty of Loyalty <Just say "duty of loyalty" in the heading>

<it is good that you talk about potential conflict of interest, but please read the definition of the following rule:>

A lawyer has a duty of loyalty to his client that requires the lawyer to put the interest of his client above all other interests and to avoid any conflict of interest ("COI").

<Duty of loyalty

-put the interest of his client above all other interests

-to avoid any conflict of interest

You stated the elements of duty of loyalty, but you concluded before your analysis of conflict of interest. That is the problem.>

Here, there is a breach of duty of loyalty because LC is A's client. <The above sentence does not carry a complete message. You can say something like A represents both LC and C2AC, while LC and C2AC have opposite standpoints on weed killer.> LC is making weed killers and selling them in the market. C2AC is also represented by A, and it is lobbying for environmental regulations to remove LA's weed killer due to unsafe products. A is a member of C2AC and believes in and is concerned about chemicals made by LC. A's interest is in conflict with LC's interest. <This paragraph has fulfilled no purpose, and there is no explanation. You merely repeated the facts given. Please use the facts to fulfill your purpose instead of merely repeating the words.>

<Compare:

Here, Andy should place the interest of LC on top of his own interest. LC may feel uncomfortable having an attorney associated with a group lobbying for environmental regulations that would remove chemicals to represent LC in litigation with the subject matter of breathing problems, which could be caused by chemicals. Facts show that "Andy is convinced" that his representation would not be affected, but it is unclear based on what reasons he would make this conclusion. Moreover, Andy can convince himself does not mean LC would have the same thought. LC is never given a chance to make the decision of whether the representation should continue. Regardless of what supports Andy's thought, Andy has been deprived of the chance for

LC to determine whether LC wants to continue to hire Andy. Andy might not want to disclose the fact to LC to avoid trouble.

"Andy did not want to jeopardize losing LawnCare as a client by discussing his private concerns about their clients." That means he does not want to lose his income or sense of achievement. As such, he puts his own interest on top of the interest of LC. ><The last sentence has to fit the wording used in the rule.>

Thus, the duty of loyalty is violated.

Thus, there is a breach of duty of loyalty.

<You had two consecutive "Thus," and two sentences saying the same thing.>

Conflict of Interest

A concurrent conflict of interest XXX

<A concurrent conflict of interest exists if:

the representation of one client will be directly adverse to another client; or

there is a significant risk that the representation of one or more clients will be materially limited by the lawyer's responsibilities to another client, a former client or a third person or by a personal interest of the lawyer.>

It does not apply here. Andy does not represent both C2AC and LC at the same time. His association with C2AC is merely a personal aspect.

A lawyer may not represent a client where there is a conflict of interest with a current client with the attorney and among the clients.

Here, there is a concurrent conflict of interest among the clients and the attorney with his client because C2AC is A's client. C2AC is currently lobbying for environmental regulation against LC's weed product. LC is also A's client, so they are in conflict with each other. A joins C2AC and provides financial support to the organization for its causes. Thus, A's interest is in direct conflict with LC. WRONG

I would call this a personal conflict of interest:

Andy is a member and financial supporter of C2AC, so his personal preference is obvious. He personally would not like chemicals. However, Andy would argue that he is not going to exert his own personal standpoint into the litigation against Paula. It may or may not be real. But his personal affilation with C2AC should be disclosed to LC and let LC decide whether it wants to trust Andy.

Thus, there is a personal conflict of interest.

Potential conflict of interest

Andy has given legal advice to C2AC, but no formal relationship is ever established; moreover, the matter is unrelated to the current litigation.

Hence, the conflict of interest only stays at the potential level but would make LC feel more insecure.

Thus, there is a potential conflict of interest. As such, Andy should have disclosed that to LC.

A's counter(I would say defense; I would insert the defense into the above argument.)

However, A would counter that he has provided pro-bono-free legal advice to C2AC regarding an unrelated corporate matter, which is not in direct conflict with LC's weed-killer product. A's argument would fail, and the court (no court is involved; the litigation is about personal injury, and ethical violations do not rise to the court level) will likely rule against him because A is not only a member but also provides financial support to lobby for environmental regulation – so A's interest is in direct conflict with LC's interest.

Thus, there is a concurrent conflict of interest.XXXX

Potential conflict of interest

Potential conflict is when there is no conflict, but a possible future conflict.

An actual conflict of interest is missing here.

(That is when Andy responded to the questionnaire. Although the information used is public, there is actual conflict because Andy is, in fact, playing two roles.) <Please try to rewrite this part>

<please take a close look at the IRAC below>

ABA, potential conflicts do not require informed written consent.

CA Need informed written consent of each client, a lawyer may not represent more than one client in a matter in which the clients 'interests potentially conflict.

<Your rule is about whether there is written consent, but your analysis is saying they are in direct conflict. In fact, no analysis at all. The analysis is also a conclusion.>

Here, there is no potential conflict of interest because A and C2AC's interests are directly in conflict with LC.

<Compare: Facts do not show there is any written consent from LC. That is because LC is not informed by Andy about the conflict. If LC is told and it decides to continue to hire Andy, written consent is needed from LC, but that is missing here.

Thus, Andy has at least violated the rules for CA regarding informed written consent.>

Thus, there is no potential conflict of interest.

Breach of Duty of Communication

Under ABA

<duty of communication is about updating the client about new developments not about disclosure of conflicts.>

Here, no facts indicate that there are any new developments about the litigation brought by Paula. But Andy may need to contact the opposing counsel for updates, and then inform LC. No facts reveal any recent communications with LC regarding to the litigation. Andy did not talk to LC until LC initiated the contact regarding to the questionnaire.

Thus, Andy may have violated his duty of communication.

Duty of diligence

rule here

Here, Andy may need to contact the opposing counsel for updates of the medical report for the children of Paula and then inform LC. The medical condition of Paula's children could have affected the strategies used by Andy or the chance of prevailing for LC. But Andy did not do that.

Thus, Andy may have violated his duty of diligence.

An attorney has a duty to 1) Keep the Client informed, 2) respond promptly to reasonable requests, and 3) explain all matters promptly.

Here, there is a breach of duty of communication because A fails to keep LC informed that he is a member of C2AC and provides financial support to lobby for environmental regulation, which is to remove LC's weed killer product. Furthermore, A fails to explain that he previously represented pro-bono-free legal advice to C2AC about an unrelated corporate matter. WRONG

Thus, there is a breach of duty of communication under ABA.

Under CA

An attorney has a duty to allow a lawyer to delay the transmission of information to a client if the lawyer reasonably believes that the client would be likely to react in a way that may cause imminent harm to the client or others. <offtrack>

Here, there is no fact in the question stating that the LC is likely to react in a way that may cause harm to himself or others.

Thus, the CA rule does not apply.

Breach Duty of Confidentiality

A lawyer generally must not reveal information relating to the representation of a client.

Under ABA

L cannot reveal unless there are exceptions: 1) informed Consent; 2) Implied Authorized to represent the client; 3) Reasonably believes the disclosure is necessary to prevent Death or substantially bodily harm; 4) to prevent a crime or fraud; 5) to comply with a court order; 6) to secure legal Advice; 7) to establish a claim or Defense in a controversy between the L and client. <Too far><The point here is public information is used, but Andy may not pay attention to such information without litigation. Hence, somehow confidential. You can argue both ways.>

Here, there is likely a breach of duty of confidentiality because A is representing LC in a product liability sue about weed killer. The information that A obtains is likely to be revealed to C2AC, which is lobbying for environmental regulation.

The exceptions to ABA confidentiality do not apply because no fact indicates the LC gives informed consent. There is no implied authorization to represent the client, no reasonably believes the disclosure is necessary to prevent death or body harm from LA, no prevention about crime or fraud, no copying with a court order, no secure legal advice, or any defense case between A and LC.

Thus, there is a breach of duty for confidentiality, and exceptions do not apply.

Under CA

A lawyer cannot reveal unless: 1) necessary to prevent death or others, 2) compelled by court order, 3) To establish a claim or defense <Go too far><Rules are triggered by facts given. No such facts here>

Here, there is no fact in the question showing the LC is likely to cause death to others, nor any court order, no defense in a court proceeding.

Thus, there is no exception to CA's breach of confidentiality.

Duty to Withdrawal (duty to withdraw would be discussed when the client is not honest; here, the attorney is dishonest in some ways. I would change the perspective to discuss the duty of candor, and then the biggest impact would be being terminated by the client or disbarred by the State Bar. The wording has to fit the situation.)

A lawyer must reject a case if there is a violation of law or ethical rule to take the case.

Here, A has a duty to withdraw because he has breached the ethical rules like duty of confidentiality, duty of communication, duty of loyalty, having a conflict of interest, and duty of competence, etc.

Thus, there is a breach of duty of withdrawal.

Permissive withdrawal

Under ABA

A permissive withdrawal can take place when 1) the financial burdens the attorney, 2) the attorney and client have a fundamental disagreement, 3) the client is unreasonably difficult, 4) the client refuses to fulfill obligation after L has warned him you would withdraw or other good cause.

Here, the permissive withdrawal under ABA does not apply because there are no financial burdens on the attorney, there is no fundamental disagreement between the attorney and client, LC is not unreasonably difficult, and LC does not refuse to fulfill obligation nor has A warn LC with anything.

Thus, there is no permissive withdrawal under ABA.

Under CA

A permissive to withdrawal takes place when 1) the client has no good cause to bring the case; 2) the lawyer's mental and physical condition makes it difficult to continue; 3) L cannot work with a co-counsel; 4) A continuation is likely to violate CA professional responsibility (PR) rules

Here, there is no permissive withdrawal under the CA rule because there is no fact in the question indicating LC has good cause to bring the case, A is mentally and physically conditioned to make it difficult to continue, A can not work with a co-counsel, or continue the representation is likely to violate CA PR rules.

Thus, there is no permissive under CA rule.

Mandatory withdrawal

Under ABA

A mandatory withdrawal under ABA takes place 1) if continuing would violate an ethical rule; 2) if the client wants to pursue legal action solely for the purpose of harassing/maliciously injuring another person; 3) if physical or mental shape renders atty incompetent; 4) client discharges atty; or 5) If Atty discloses confidential client info to prevent death or substantial bodily harm.

Here, there is a mandatory withdrawal under ABA because if A continues to represent LA, he could continue to violate the duty of communication, the duty of loyalty, the duty of competency, etc.

Thus, there is a duty of mandatory withdrawal under ABA.

Under CA

Mandatory withdrawal is required when 1) representation is unreasonably difficult to carry out effectively; 2) L is discharged by C, or 3) frivolous litigation or to harass (known there is no probable cause); 4) using L service for criminal or fraudulent activities.

Here, there is no mandatory withdrawal under the CA rule because there is no representation from A to LC, which is unreasonable and difficult to carry out effectively. In addition, there is no discharge of representation on A; there is no frivolous litigation or harass. Finally, LC has not used A's service for criminal or fraudulent activities.

Duty of Competent <Should be the duty of competency>

Under ABA

Using the legal knowledge, skill, thoroughness, and preparation reasonably necessary for the representation.

Here, there is a breach of the duty of competent <it is the duty of competency> because A violated the duty of confidentiality, the duty of withdrawal, the duty of communication, etc. <Wrong rule><Your analysis has to use the word of elements, meaning whether Andy has used the legal knowledge, skill, thoroughness, and preparation reasonably necessary for the representation.>

These violations show he lacks the legal knowledge, skill, thoroughness, and preparation to represent his client, LC, and C2AC. <this is conclusive without explanations. Unethical does not mean lacking the legal knowledge.>

<Compare: this is a case about injury possibly caused by chemicals. It is unclear whether Andy has such expertise, or handled such cases before, and also, the bar exam never tests chemistry knowledge. It is acceptable for an attorney without the expertise to take such cases as long as he is able to find ways to bc familiar with the subject matter before the court trial. However, no facts show that Andy has hired any experts, associated with any experienced lawyers, or done any research. Without the above work, Andy may not know enough to defend LC.

Thus, Andy may have violated his duty of competence. >

Thus, there is a breach of competence under the ABA rule.

Under CA

The competency includes diligence and mental, physical, and emotional ability, duty to supervise the work of subordinate lawyers and non-lawyer employees.

Here, there is no breach of duty of competence under the CA rule because the facts in the questions do not apply to the duty of supervising the work of employees or subordinate lawyers.

<Starting from here, it is repetitive.>

A representing both LC and C2AC

Conflict of Interest

Actual Conflict of Interest

A lawyer may not represent a client where there is a conflict of interest with current client: 1) Between current clients; 2) Between current client and another client, a former client, or by a personal interest of the lawyer; or 3) materially limited by responsibilities to another client, a former client, a third party, or the lawyer's own interests.

Here, there is an actual conflict of interest because both LC and C2AC are represented by A in legal matters - LC is for personal injury in selling weed killers, and C2AC is for unrelated corporate matters, but its goal is to lobby for environmental regulation. This shows both LC and C2AC are A's current clients.

Thus, there is an actual conflict of interest.

Potential conflict of interest

Potential conflict is when there is no conflict but a possible future conflict.

Under ABA

Potential conflicts do not require informed written consent.

Here, the ABA rule does not apply because there is are conflict between LC and C2AC (see above).

Thus, the ABA potential conflict of interest does not apply.

Under CA

The CA potential conflict of interest needs informed written consent of each client, a lawyer may not represent more than one client in a matter in which the client's interests potentially conflict.

Here, there is a violation of CA's potential conflict of interest because A has not gotten any informed written consent from LC and C2AC.

A’s Counter

A could argue that his association with LC will not affect his representation of LC. Furthermore, LC is impressed with A’s reputation as a litigator. A’s argument will fail in court because he has knowledge about LC’s case. Because he is a member of C2AC and supports its mission of environmental regulation, this is definitely going to affect LC’s legal case. A’s argument that LC is impressed with his litigation performance is irrelevant when it comes to conflict of interest.

Thus, there is a violation of CA's potential conflict of interest.

Breach of duty of communication

Under ABA

A breach of duty of communication is when 1) Keeping the Client informed, 2) responding promptly to reasonable requests, and 3) explaining all matters promptly.

Here, there is a breach of communication because A did not keep LC informed about his relationship with C2AC. In addition, A did not want to jeopardize losing LC as a client by discussing the private concerns about their weed killer chemical, so he failed to respond promptly to the conflict between LC and C2AC’s lobbying to remove chemicals, including LC’s weed killer. Finally, A’s kept secret and not discussing his private concerns about LC’s chemical shows he fails to explain all chemical matters promptly.

Thus, there is a violation of ABA's duty of communication.

Under CA

A breach of communication exception allows a lawyer to delay the transmission of information to a client if the lawyer reasonably believes that the client would be likely to react in a way that may cause imminent harm to the client or others.

Here, there is no breach of communication under the CA rule because there is no fact in the question showing that LC is likely to react in a way to cause imminent harm to others.

Thus, there is no breach of CA duty of communication.

Responding to an anonymous questionnaire sent to all C2AC members

Breach of duty of communication<why you repeated duty of communication><In the exam, just say what duty he violated and then IRAC each one. Andy does not have a formal relationship with C2AC. You ignored this, and that would cause you to waste much time discussing unnecessary stuff.>

Under ABA duty of communication

A breach of duty of communication is when 1) Keeping the Client informed, 2) responding promptly to reasonable requests, and 3) explaining all matters promptly.

Here, there is the ABA violation because A response to an anonymous questionnaire sent to all C2AC members, he did not inform both LC and C2AC about what he did and his relationship with each entity, so he did not keep the clients informed. In addition, when LC CEO called A about his received call from C2AC representative regarding LC's lawsuit from P, A said he did not know where C2AC got that information. This shows A did not respond promptly to LC's reasonable request. Finally, not tell the CEO about A's response to the anonymous questionnaire sent to C2AC members and telling the CEO that he has no idea where C2AC got the lawsuit information, showing A fails to explain all matters promptly.

Under CA duty of communication

Supra

Here, there is no breach of communication under the CA rule because there is no fact in the question showing that LC is likely to react in a way to cause imminent harm to others.

<You mixed up the duty of candor and the duty of loyalty. >

Breach of loyalty – lying and disclosing LC's confidential information to C2AC.

A lawyer has a duty of loyalty to his client that requires the lawyer to put the interest of his client above all other interests and to avoid any COI.

Here, there is a breach of loyalty by lying and disclosing LC's confidential information to C2AC because when A responded to an anonymous C2AC questionnaire about LC's pending lawsuit from P, he did not place LC's interest above everything else. He fails to avoid the conflict of interest by disclosing confidential information. In addition, he lied to the CEO that he had no idea where the C2AC representative got the personal injury lawsuit from P. The representative would not know about P's lawsuit if A did not disclose the information in the questionnaire.

Counter from A

A would likely counter that the lawsuit from P is public information. He did not provide any more detail in the anonymous questionnaire. He is just fulfilling his member duty with C2AC by replying to the questionnaire.

A's argument would fail in court because there is a conflict of interest between LC and C2AC (as discussed in supra), so he should not represent both parties in the first place. Although he did not disclose more detailed information in the questionnaire, the representative knows the lawsuit and gives C2AC leverage in lobbying the regulation against LC's chemical.

Thus, A has breached loyalty to LC by lying to the CEO and disclosing LC's confidential information.

In conclusion, A has breached the duty of communication, the duty of confidentiality, the duty of competence, the duty of loyalty, the duty to withdrawal, conflict of interest, etc.

Feb 2023 Civil Procedures

Overall comment:

You did not read the facts carefully; Please pay attention to the question and answer with the keywords given in the question, meaning directly responding to the question.

The way we talk in our daily conversations may not work in essay writing:

If the waiter asks you "what would you like to eat?", then you answer the lobster looks good, in fact, you are not answering directly to the question. The way you answer in an essay should be "I would like to eat the lobster."

When the essay includes big subjects such as discovery, there should be a separate heading "Discovery", then define the rule; Here...; Thus...

A big heading "Motion to Compel" is needed, and then you have to explain what should be done before the "motion to compel" is made. Facts given are unclear, so you have to point out the uncertainties. If an initial request is already made and the party refuses to provide, then a "motion to compel" can be filed with supporting arguments.

Here, P did not produce W's statement but no facts indicate whether D has ever requested. If D never requested, a "motion to compel" may not be appropriate.

Before you start typing, please think from different perspectives and in different layers. Treat P, D, M, W as real people. Then you would be able to handle the essay more comprehensively.

Dura Tires' motion to dismiss Compulsory Joinder - Rule 19

THE FIRST QUESTION:

DID THE COURT PROPERLY DENY DURATIRES 'MOTION TO DISMISS?

<Firstly, you need to find out if DuraTires should file motion to dismiss.

The alleged reason is "for failure to join Maurice" as a defendant. But Maurice is just a mechanic who installed the four new tires but this litigation appears to be a product liability case between the manufacturer and the buyer, and the user. M, a mechanic, is an intermediary who can be held liable too. But M is not necessary to the litigation between P and D. M can be sued later, and does not have to be in this claim.

However, P filed the claim for "breach of warranty and negligent installation and manufacture of the tires." If M is the mechanic hired by D, then M could be an important witness to testify in court, but still not a necessary party.

Assuming the installation is negligent, P would be suing D on the theory of respondent superior. M's testimony would be helpful in explaining how the tires are installed. But even if M does not testify, the negligence can be shown by examining the tires.

Thus, Maurice is not a necessary party. Either M is hired by D, or not hired by D. Without her, the claim can still go on. As such, DuraTires should not file a motion to dismiss. So the court properly denied DuraTores 'motion to dismiss. >

At trial, a party may joint <wrong word; should be "may join">

a mandatory joinder. If such mandatory joinder fails to join at the trial, the other party is allowed to file a motion to dismiss for failure to join the mandatory joinder, or it can also attach such motion in its answer.

Here, Maurice is an employee of Duratires <Facts never say M is an employee. M is just a mechanic of any company>, and he is responsible for the installation of the tire which caused the accident. However, Pam may choose to sue separately either Duratires or Maurice, or Pam will sue them both in the same action. Since Pam may sue Maurice in anther independent lawsuit, Maurice is not mandatory joinder in the lawsuit between Pam and Duratires. On the other hand, Duratire is allowed to join Maurice as a co-defendant by filing a crossclaim to join Maurice as a co-defendant in this case. As a result, Maurice's intervention into the lawsuit between Pam and Durtires is not mandated <should be mandatory>, since the plaintiff is the master of the lawsuit - he can choose the parties as defendants as he wishes so long as the requirements for a valid action are met. (Take a look at the whole paragraph. Your point is M is not a necessary party but your explanation tends to be repetitive and turning around and around.)

Thus, Maurice is not compulsory joinder in this case.

Motion to dismiss for failure to join Maurice

Under the Rule 12 (f) of Federal Rules of Civil Procedure (FRCP), a party may file a motion to dismiss for failure to join the mandatory joinder, or it can also attach such motion in its answer in order to dismiss the lawsuit if the plaintiff fails to joins a mandatory

Here, since Maurice is not a compulsory joinder under FRCP Rule 19, she is not required to join the pending lawsuit. As a result, the lawsuit against Dura Tires would not be dismissed for failure to join Maurice as a defendant. It will likely be proper to join Maurice by a cross-claim as co-defendant.

Thus, the court properly deny DuratTires' motion to dismiss 2.

FRCP 12b 6

FRCP 12b 6 specifically deals with motions to dismiss for failure to state a claim upon which relief can be granted.

Here, "D advertised that a scientific report declared that its tires will not go flat for the first 7,000 miles of use if driven properly." The condition of the guarantee is "if driven properly." No facts show how P drove. Facts show P "drove 100 miles" only, without indicating what kind of road it is. Whether he drove in a city, the countryside. bumpy road, or drove in an illegal racing is unclear. If P failed to explain the condition of his driving, then D may be able to dismiss the claim according to 12b6.

If P does not clearly state his condition of driving, D may be able to dismiss the motion based on 12b6 but not failure to join M.

As such, the court may have improperly denied D's motion to dismiss.

<For question 2, you can talk about what is discovery; what can be discovered: relevant and in proportion to the need; does not have to be admissible evidence; under what circumstances the parties can compel production. >

motion to compel

Initial disclosures

The parties to the lawsuit must confer as soon as practicable 21 days before the pretrial conference or a scheduled order falls due, and the initial disclosures must occur within 14 days after the parties' conference for the purpose of discussing the disclosure and developing a disclosure plan. In proceeding with the initial disclosure, the parties shall disclose (1) the name, address, telephone, etc, of the person whose testimony supports their claims or defense; (2) the documentary evidence and other real evidence supporting the parties' claim and defense; (3) the computation of the damage; (4) if any, the information of the insurance which cover the liable parties' liabilities.

Here, Pam is free to offer any evidence supporting his claims against Duratires. Therefore, he is not compelled to disclosure any information. <Wrong: The focus here is whether he should be compelled, not whether he is compelled.>

Thus, Pam is allowed not to offer Wynne's statement.

Motion for request of production

Motion for request of production is a discovery method that allows the parties to require another after the parties' conference for the purpose of discussing the disclosure and developing a disclosure plan. In proceeding with the initial disclosure, the parties shall disclose (1) the name, address, telephone, etc, of the person whose testimony supports their claims or defense; (2)

the documentary evidence, and other real evidence supporting the parties claim and defense; (3) the computation of the damage; (4) if any, the information of the insurance.

<These points look irrelevant to the main discussion. And you just brought them up, but you did not explain. If you do not plan to explain, please do not mention it at all. >

Here, Pam is free to offer any evidence supporting his claims against Duratires. Therefore, he is not compelled to disclosure <should be "disclose"> any information.

Thus, Pam is allowed not to offer Wynne's statement.

Motion for request of production

Motion for request of production is a discovery method that allows the parties to require another party or third-party to produce the indicated document.

Discovery

Motion to compel

<You did not explain under what circumstances people can compel: when the statement cannot be obtained elsewhere or without undue burden. >

Here, facts show that W's statement was favorable to P's case. Although it is not favorable to D, D also needs to know in order to prepare for the litigation. But D should try to obtain the statement from W by themselves. If it is unavailable and they have exhausted all other possible means, D can demand from P. If P refuses to provide, then D can file the motion to compel. Facts do not show that D has ever requested the w's statements. If they never request and get declined, they may not file a motion to compel. If they did and P refuses, it would be proper for D to file a motion to compel.

As such, the court properly granted D's motion.

Here, Pam did not produce Wynne's statement in its initial discovery. DuraTires seems to already have known the existence of Wynne's statement. The motion for request of production permits Duratires to request the production of Wynne's statement.

Thus, Duratires is allowed to request Pam to produce Wynne's Statement.

Motion to compel production of the statement

A party is permitted to move to compel production of the required documents or other evidence since the other party fails to do so and the information cannot be obtained in any other available way.

Here, Wynne is not a party to the lawsuit between Pam and Duratires. If Duratires intends to obtain Wynne's statement, it can directly seek Wynne to do so. As a result, obtaining Wynne's statement is not impossible by asking directly. That is a motion to compel the production of Wynne' statement is not necessary. The court can grant Duratires' motion to compel production of the statement from Wynne if Wynne refuses to do so.

Thus, Court's grant for motion to compel the production of the statement from Wynne is likely not proper.

B. motion to compel a physical examination of Pam. Physical examination

A party may move to obtain a physical examination of another party if such party's physical condition is in issue and there is a good cause.

Here, Pam's physical condition after the car accident is in issue, and there is good cause, because its physical condition can determine whether Pam suffered any physical injuries during the car accident. a Negligence action require proof of (1) duty of care, (2) breach of duty; (3) causation, and (4) damage. Pam's physical condition may prove whether there is required damage to support its negligence action. (NO NEED TO TALK ABOUT NEGLIGENCE. This essay is about Civil Procedure.)

Thus, a physical examination for Pam is likely necessary. <You did not pay attention to the facts of the essay: Pam was not physically injured in the accident. P alleged that he suffered property damage and emotional distress as a result of the accident.>

Here, the issue is the property damage and emotional distress because those are the damages P claimed to have. D should request a report of the property damage and P's report from his psychologist. P's physical examination does not appear to carry any importance on the damages suffered by P.

Good cause

If there is good cause, the physical examination may be requested. Here, D did not explain why it wants a physical examination of P. If D thinks that emotional distress would also affect one's physical health, then D would have a good cause to make such a request.

However, without a direct impact on P's physical condition, a physical exam of P does not appear to be needed. Instead, W, the other driver, suffered a minor injury. If D's tires are proved defective, W's injury would be covered and paid for by D. Hence, a physical exam of W should be requested by D.

Thus, D should not compel a physical exam of P but the same exam of W. As such, the court improperly granted D's motions.

Motion to compel a physical examination of Pam

A party is permitted to move to compel a physical examination of a party is proper since that party refuses to do when its physical condition is in issue, and there is a good cause. The motion must be filed before the court in which the cas2eoifs3pending is the party to be examined is a party to the case.

Here, Pam's physical condition is in issue,(NOT an issue)

and there is a good cause. However, Duratires has not demanded Pam to submit first to a physical examination, which means Pam has not yet express the car accident. a Negligence action requires proof of (1) duty of care, (2) breach of duty; (3)

causation, and (4) damage. Pam's physical condition may prove whehter there is required damage to support its negligence action.

Thus, a physical examination for Pam is likely necessary.

A party is permitted to move to compel a physical examination of a party is proper since that party refuses to do so when its physical condition is in issue, and there is a good cause. The motion must be filed before the court in which the case is pending is the party to be examined is a party to the case.

Here, Pam's physical condition is in issue, and there is a good cause. However, Duratires has not demand Pam to submit first to physical examination, which means Pam has not yet expressed its consent or refuse. The court cannot grant the motion to compel a party who has not yet refused to submit its physical examination.

Thus, Court's grant for a motion to compel a physical examination is likely not proper.

Production of Duratires' scientific report

Rule 26 (f) Meet and confer

Rule 26 f states that there would be a conference of two

parties, including P and D, for cooperating and setting out a clear plan for the process of discovery.

Here, P met and conferred with D, but D refused to produce its scientific report. <The heading is Rule 26(f), so the discussion should be whether there is a "meet and confer;" and whether P and D have cooperated and set out a clear plan. But you pointed out D has refused to produce its scientific report. Then your discussion is: P may file a motion to compel. You are not analyzing the rule you stated, and your conclusion has nothing to do with your discussion.>

Thus, P may file a motion to compel, along with arguments in support of the motion, if the report is not privileged, which is going to be discussed below.

Work product doctrine

Work product is a report <does not have to be reported, can be documented, or any correspondences> prepared by a party's counsel in anticipation of the litigation. A party may prevent another party from disclosing the workout.

Here, the scientific report was prepared by Durtires's legal counsel. However, when it is done, <not when it is done, but when it is in the process of production> there was not any litigation between Pam and Duratires. Thus, the scientific report in question is not a work product.

(You get thc right idea, but you can explain more in detail: D's scientific report was made at the direction of its legal counsel. It is likely that the report is made to substantiate what D claimed in the advertisement: "its tires will not go flat for the first 7,000 miles of use if driven properly." So P may argue that the report is not made "in anticipation of litigation" but aiming to support the advertisement. Then D should produce it. >

However, D can also argue that since D advertised that a scientific report declared that its tires will not go flat for the first 7,000 miles, the report made could be aimed to defend D when there is litigation, even though no claims are actually made at the creation of the report. The report was made upon the request of the counsel, not the manufacturers and a legal counsel always concerns the possibility of litigation. Thus, D can also argue the report is a work product so they should not be compelled to produce it.

Thus, Court properly order Durattires to produce its scientific report.

Attorney-client Privilege

Definition

Here, even though the legal counsel directed D to make the report, the report itself was not within the privilege, but the conversation between the counsel and D could be within the privilege. <You did not explain clearly enough. Compare: While the conversation between the counsel and D falls under the Attorney-Client Privilege, the report prepared under the counsel's direction does not.>

Thus, D cannot refuse to produce the report based on the attorney-client privilege. As such, the court properly ordered D to produce the report. <This logic is not correct: D cannot defend himself based on the attorney-client privilege does not necessarily lead to the conclusion that the court properly

ordered D to produce the report. D can defend based on other doctrines such as the work-product doctrine.>

Feb 2023 Evidence Essay

Overall comments

I would suggest you to do more MBEs on the subject of Evidence in order to be familiar with the rules and exceptions, as well as limitations. If you score high on MBEs, you are more likely to spot the nuances between different rules and in different situations.

Furthermore, when there are five sub-questions in an evidence essay, each item should bring up at least one new rule that is not included in the previous item. Please focus on the new rule in each new item. Although relevancy is the element for the admissibility of every item, you can just mention it once in the first item, or for safety, you can discuss it twice but not more than that for the whole essay, in order to save time to discuss other doctrines.

If you have time left, you can always go back to add the analysis of relevance, but from what I heard from my previous tutor, even though you write "relevancy" five times, you would score the point "once" only. Regardless of the truthfulness of what she said, you would not have sufficient time to go through relevancy for every sub-question.

Before you start typing, you have to spot at least one unique aspect of each sub-question. For example, items 4 and 5 are very similar, but item 5 has a prior inconsistent statement and that would be something you need to focus on in sub-question 5.

Besides, your analysis always fails to address the elements included in the definition of the rules, which would be a big mistake. You would never get 65 if you keep doing that. The gatekeeper would not let you pass, no matter how many elements you can recite. That is because it shows that you do not know the methodology of analyzing with IRAC.

Also, you always argue about the wrong thing. Many facts are given in one single essay question. You have to learn how to sort them out and identify the functions of each fact. Please do not wrongly focus on something that is not worth your precious time in the bar exam.

I understand as a full-time worker, you may not have much time to write essays, and you did not seem to think thoroughly at all. Try to practice with analysis from issues in daily life. Make sound arguments. Or you can try to write one essay every three weeks, but each week you write just one part and then you can think more thoroughly. (One week for writing outlines, one week for identifying issues, and one week for sorting out facts.) Otherwise, you just keep practice typing.

Pedro (P) v. Gallery (G)

Photocopy of the advertisement

Relevance

Only relevant evidence is admissible. Evidence must be logically and legally relevant.

Logical Relevance

Evidence is logically relevant when it tends to make a fact of consequence more or less probable than it would be without the evidence. The fact must also be in dispute.

<When you discuss logical relevance, you do not need to talk about the outcome of how the evidence proves the central issue to be or not to be. Just point out it is logically relevant:

Here, Pedro brought fraud and breach of contract action against the Gallery, and Pedro claimed that he was willing to pay $200,000 just because he saw an advertisement bearing the Gallery's logo stating that the painting was "the only painting by a noted 17th-century artist available for sale in the world." If the advertisement does not claim the painting to be "the only painting," Pedro would not pay such a high price. A reproduction of a painting is worth only $10,000. The difference in price between "the only painting" and another copy is $190,000. There is a huge difference between the term promised and what is actually delivered, and that is exactly the central issue of fraud and breach of contract.

Thus, the photocopy of the advertisement is logically relevant.>

Here, the copy of the advertisement is of logical relevance because G's photocopy advertisement is the center of the whole disputed issue in the value of the painting. G's advertisement states the painting is worth $200,00 because it was painted by an artist in the 17th century, and it is the only painting on sale in the world. P bought the painting and found out he was being cheated. After three art dealers appraise the painting, the average value of the painting is $10,000. P relied on G's advertisement, which causes him to be cheated on the purchase. The advertisement is relevant to the dispute.

Thus, there is logical relevance.

Legal Relevance

Evidence is legally relevant if its probative value is not substantially outweighed by the danger of unfair prejudice, confusion to the jury, confusion of the issues, or undue delay/waste of time.

Here, the copy of the advertisement has legal relevance because there is a big difference in the value of the painting after P relied on G's advertisement and bought the painting. <You failed to explain the legal relevance. You explained logical relevance only. You have to explain it would not cause undue prejudice, confusion to the jurors, waste of time, etc. With the copy of the advertisement, the jurors would be clear about the expectations of Pedro, and what the Gallery claims to have, which is much clearer than the testimony by either side. No confusion or undue prejudice would be caused. Furthermore, reading a copy of the advertisement does not cost much time.

Thus, there is legal relevance.>

The advertisement is for the juror to see and decide as evidence on the case. It does not cause confusion, delay in the court proceeding or waste time.

Thus, there is a legal relevance.

Authentication

A document can be authenticated by a witness with personal knowledge, testifying that the document is what it is purported to be. <or other valid ways of authentication.>

Here, a photocopy of the advertisement can be authenticated because P could testify in court that based on his personal knowledge, <It would be easy and simple for Pedro to say the photocopy of the advertisement does or does not show the real context of the original advertisement.> he relied on G's advertisement bought the painting, and lost the painting's value from $200K to $10,000. <Just focus on the elements of authentication; do not keep repeating the same kinds of stuff for every IRACs.> <Furthermore, the advertisement should bear Gallery's logo, meaning the copy should also have the logo. Without evidence to the contrary, the copy is deemed authenticated.>

Thus, there is authentication. <Thus, it is authenticated.>

Business Evidence Rule (Wrong name: it should be the best evidence rule)

Under the Federal Rules of Evidence, if the terms of a writing are material, the original writing must be produced to prove those terms. Under the California Rules of Evidence, secondary evidence of a writing's term is admissible only when the original is unavailable. <You are asked to use FRE, so there is no need to talk too much about CA> A photocopy is sufficient.

Here, the photocopy of the advertisement does not meet the federal rule of evidence because it is a photocopy advertisement. P saw and relied on G's advertisement and bought the painting and caused him to lose the value of the painting. Without the original advertisement, P cannot prove he was being cheated the painting is the only painting in the world and painted by a 17th-century artist.

However, under California's rule of evidence, the photocopy of the advertisement is admissible because the original advertisement is not available to P. P saw G's photocopy of the advertisement. P bought the painting based on the photocopy of the ads, and the ads were admitted into evidence in court.

<It is unclear how the advertisement is posted on newspapers or online. In a digital generation, all copies printed out from the computer are genuine copies, and the "original" could be an online version. It would be more difficult to submit the laptop as the original copy. If the internet connection is broken, there would be nothing for the jurors to see.>

Thus, P does not meet the federal business evidence rule, but he meets the CA rule.

Hearsay

Hearsay is an out-of-court statement offered for the truth of the matter asserted. Hearsay is inadmissible unless an exception or exemption applies.

Hearsay Exemption

<First of all, the ad. is not offered to prove the truth of the statement. The purpose is not to show whether the painting is by the 17th century artist. In fact, it is the opposite. Pedro is trying to show the painting is not what the Gallery claims to be.>

Adopted Admission

A party may admit something made by another person.

Here, there is an adopted admission because P can admit that he saw and relied on the photocopy advertisement and bought the painting from G. P will admit that G told him the painting is a 17th-century painting and is the only painting available for sale in the world.

There is an adopted admission.

<This should be an admission by party opponent:

Here, the opposing party is Gallery and the advertisement bears the logo of Gallery, so what is asserted on it can be deemed the statement by Gallery. Hence, the words on the advertisement would be deemed an admission by the party opponent, which is an exception for hearsay.

As such, the advertisement is admissible because it would not be deemed hearsay; and even it is, it would fall into an exception.

Based on the foregoing discussion, the photocopy of the advertisement should be admitted.>

Conclusion

The Court should admit the photocopy of the advertisement based on relevance, authentication, business evidence, and hearsay exemption.

Value of the painting

Relevance

Supra

Logical Relevance

Supra

Here, the value of the painting is logical relevance because P testified he had three art dealers to appraise the painting. The appraisal information does not match the advertisement form G.<You mean just because the appraisal information is inconsistent with what the ad. claims, so the testimony is logically relevant. But the way you expressed is not clear enough to convey the meaning. > The painting was determined as a replica of the original painting, and it was painted within the last 50 years. All these facts lead to dropping the value of the painting and casing the dispute between P and G.

<Here, the litigation is about fraud and breach of contract, and the real value of the painting is the central issue because if the painting is really worth the price Pedro paid, there would be no fraud or breach of contract.

Thus, P's testimony about the value of the painting is logically relevant.>

Thus, there is a logical relevance.

Legal Relevance

Supra

Here, the painting's value does not meet the legal relevance because the appraised value from the three art dealers is subjective. There is no fact stating that the art dealers are independent of both P and G. The three art dealers could be friends with P and appraise to a lower value for P's advantage against G. That is unfair prejudice against G. Furthermore, there is no background information on these three dealers about their education, experience, and how they came up the appraised value. The court has to sort out the background information on these dealers, which could waste time or delay the court proceeding. Finally, P relied on the average value from the three dealer's appraised value, which is subjective and could lead to confusion for the jury. <You have a good point, but you can express the idea in a clearer and more concise manner.>

<Here, the background or, style or genre of the people making the three appraisals are unknown. If they all belong to the same school or from the same teacher, three appraisals could be redundant and deemed a waste of time.

If they can represent three different generations, and three different genres, then it probably makes sense to include the opinion of the three appraisals. But the appraisals are made by art dealers, which are also merchants. They may not be as neutral as those who are not selling paintings or scholars.

Besides, facts show that he "based his valuation on the average of three appraisals of the painting by art dealers." The value of art is very subjective. If you like it, it can be worth a million dollars; if you do not like it, it could be deemed garbage. Hence, getting an average of these two prices just mentioned means nothing. The average would be half a million dollars. But this dollar amount is not indicative of the market value at all.

Thus, it does not make much sense to get P's valuation when more undue prejudice would be caused. There is no legal relevance>

Thus, the painting's value does not meet the legal relevance.

<When a witness is involved, it is always helpful to talk about personal knowledge.>

<Personal knowledge

A witness is supposed to have sufficient personal knowledge in order to be a competent witness.

Here, P is just a buyer. No facts show that he is an expert in the arts. By simply reading three appraisals of the painting, he is still deemed incompetent to talk about art, especially since art is a specific subject.>

<Hearsay

Definition supra

Here, the litigation is about whether there is fraud and breach of contract, meaning Pedro claims that the real value is less than the price of the painting. Quoting the price given by others would be trying to use the out-of-court statement to prove the truth of the matter asserted. Hence, it is deemed hearsay.

Furthermore, if the three appraisals are valuable information, it would be more appropriate to invite the three parties to the court to talk about their first-hand evaluations rather than having P summarize what they said. When P is trying to show the value of the painting, the price given would be the context of the hearsay, which P is trying to show its truthfulness.

Thus, Pedro's testimony about the value of the painting would be deemed hearsay. As such, it is not admissible.>

<Laypeople vs. Experts

Definition

Art is very subjective, and Pedro's perception of the three appraisals may not be exactly the same as the original context of the appraisals. His interpretation could be different from the people who made the three appraisals. After P read the three appraisals, he is still a layperson. He would not become an expert just because of the information given by the three appraisals.

As laypeople, they can only talk about something in general.

Thus, P's testimony about the value of the painting should not be admitted.>

<Experts

Definition

Here, the appraisals are done by art dealers who are doing business. Their appraisals could be deemed a kind of expert opinion, but not as good as the appraisals by the scholars. Moreover, if the court considers art dealers to be experts, they need to show up in the court and be questioned by the counsel. A layperson is not supposed to repeat words by experts because a layperson may not truly understand what an expert said.

Thus, P's testimony about the value of the painting would not be deemed experts' opinion either. As such, the court should not admit P's testimony.>

Lay Opinion

A lay witness may testify to their opinion when the testimony is rationally based on their own perception, would assist the fact finder in understanding the witness's testimony or assessing an issue of fact, and is not based on scientific, technical, or other specialized knowledge.

P would argue that the $10,000 painting value is based on three art dealer's lay opinions. The dealers are based on their art experiences and help to assess the painting's value. The dealers have no scientific, technical, or special knowledge. Furthermore, he averages out the three values from the three dealers and gives him an unbiased value on the painting. G will counter that there is no information about how the lay witnesses are related to the P. The dealers could just be friends with P and help him out and give subjective opinions on the painting. There is no information about how they came up with the painting value. There is no rational basis to accept the appraisal values from the three dealers.

Thus, the lay opinion will fail.

<You have the wrong focus when we discuss "layperson vs.

Expert, " the focus would be that particular subject needs professional or specific skills or knowledge to explain, and the person does/ does not have such expertise. For example, if the issue is about a heart problem or Coronary Angioplasty, the expert would be a cardiologist or a surgeon. A general doctor may not even be an expert if he usually deals with patients with colds, allergies, coughing. When you explain, you have to point out why you think a certain doctor is or is not an expert on this issue.>

<Here, you are right that the background of the three people making appraisals are unknown and unidentified. But the main focus here is Pedro would repeat the price and other opinions made by these three unidentified people, which would become hearsay; also, P seems to be a buyer only, without qualifications to talk about the paintings to a professional level.>

Conclusion – the court should not accept P's testimony about the painting because it fails to meet the legal relevance requirement.

Age of the painting

Relevance

Supra

<In exam, you do not need to talk about logical and legal relevance in every sub-question. The grader would definitely expect you to talk about something else in other parts. It is not wrong but please do not waste time. Save time to talk about something that would give you points.>

Logical relevance

Supra

Here, Rex's (R) testimony about the age of the painting meets the logical relevance because his testimony shows that G's painting is a fake and was painted within the last 50 years. His testimony totally discredited G's claim that the painting was painted in the 17th century and was the only one on sale in the world. R's testimony is more probable and makes G's painting as fake, and without R's testimony, there would not be a case for P to file against G.

Thus, R's testimony meets the logical relevance.

Legal relevancy

Supra

Here, R's testimony about the painting is legally relevant because G's attorney in the trial cross-examined him. He did not get challenged and discredited for being unfairly prejudiced. He testified that most experts had used his XYZ technique to determine the age of the paintings and did not lead to confusion for the jury. G's attorney did not raise any objection that XYZ's technique is confusing the issue. R was able to testify successfully and was excused and left the courtroom.

Thus, R's testimony meets the legal relevance test.

Expert Opinion

For expert testimony to be admissible, the proffering party must show that the proposed testimony concerns a specialized area about which expert testimony would assist the trier of fact; the witness is a qualified expert; the expert can show a reasonable probability that their opinion is correct; and the opinion is properly factually supported.

Here, R is considered an expert,<too conclusive; please consider different facts.> and his testimony is admissible because his XYZ technique is acceptable and considered specialized in the field for testing the age of painting. The technique proves G's painting is fake and was painted within the last fifty years. R qualifies as an expert because four galleries have hired him to determine the age of the painting, <"Four galleries hire him" is not equivalent to "he is capable;" it is more about reputation. Example: A tutor charging you more does not mean she is more capable; it might mean she is more well-known, or she has invested more in advertising.> so he has impracticable experience in his field. He testified that he used the XYZ technique, the painting was painted within the last fifty years, and he reasonably reached that conclusion. His opinion on XYZ technique is widely used by other experts to test the age of paintings.

<Here, Rex is a chemistry professor. Chemistry is a branch of natural science that deals principally with the properties of substances, the changes they undergo, and the natural laws that describe these changes. He is supposed to

have the knowledge of how things would change over time, so it makes sense to expect him to be able to tell the age of the painting. However, he does not appear to have any knowledge about the history of paintings. What kind of paint did people used 50 years ago? What paint was popular in that generation? Chemistry may not offer him a good answer.

Facts show that Rex "had been retained by four art galleries to determine the age of paintings," showing that the art painting profession appears to recognize his qualifications, but it is unknown whether the four galleries are somehow related. If they have the same coordinator, then four art galleries hiring him would mean only convenience. It may not be indicative of his talent. Thus, he may not be deemed an expert.>

<When science is involved, please talk about Daubert standard><You have to be familiar with the game rules of the bar exam: when some facts appear, certain doctrines would be triggered.>

<Daubert……>

<The "Daubert Standard" provides a systematic framework for a trial court judge to assess the reliability and relevance of expert witness testimony before the jury hears about the testimony. The factors considered include the methods and procedures that may be tested, the known and potential rate of error in these processes; if they have been subjected to peer review by the expert's peers in his or her field, which is acceptance by the same profession.>

<You did not talk about Daubert at all>

Methods and procedures

<Here, facts show that Rex claims that he had tested the XYZ technique on paintings of known ages, and the results corresponded with their known age.

But Rex failed to explain how he did the test. The methods and procedures are unclear.

<Known and potential rate of error

All tests are potentially having errors and some results may deviate from the expected results.

Here, it is unclear about the test's known or potential rate of error.

Thus, the XYZ technique cannot be evaluated by known and potential rates of error. >

<Peer review and Acceptance

Here, Rex testified that the "XYZ technique was reliable" and "used by most experts to determine the age of paintings." Assuming Rex is telling the truth, the XYZ technique has been reviewed by peers through actual usage, and the technique looks acceptable in the profession due to its reliability.>

Furthermore, Rex already testified that the painting had been painted within the past 50 years and was a painted reproduction of the original painting. If Gallery does not want Rex's testimony to be admissible, Gallery should have a motion to suppress his testimony.

Thus, Rex's testimony appears to be admissible.>

Thus, R has given an expert opinion.

Competence

A witness may only testify if they are competent. To be competent, a witness must have personal knowledge of the matter to which they testify, base their testimony on a present recollection of events, be able to communicate directly and swear or affirm that they will tell the truth. In CA, the witness must be able to tell the difference between a truth and a lie.

Here, R is considered a competent witness because four galleries hired him to use the XYZ techniques to test the age of the paintings. He gave his knowledge about how the XYZ techniques were used and reached his conclusion. He used the techniques and his present recollection to conclude that the painting was fake. The painting was painted within the last 50 years, and that is different from G's claim that the painting was painted in the 17th century and is the only one in the world on sale. Finally, he gave his testimony in court. He swore in and agreed to testify his testimony was truth and nothing but the truth. He communicated to the juror based on his findings, was successfully cross-examined by the G's attorney, and was excused and left the courtroom without any controversy. <The above sentences are not explain whether he is competent. You just repeated what had happened.>

G will argue that R should not be considered an expert because he was paid to testify favorably for P. His testimony about the age of the painting is subjective. P will counter that G hires his own expert, Marie, to counter or discredit R's XYZ technique in court. It turned out to be unreliable, <which is going to be discussed below.> R was cross-examined by G's attorney in the courtroom and was excused and left without any fact showing R's testimony was unreliable. Finally, XYZ techniques have been used by most experts to determine the age of the painting, and four galleries hired R himself, so he has lots of experience in using the technique to test the age of the painting. Thus, the court is likely not to accept G's argument.

In CA, R is considered a competent witness because he swore at the beginning of his testimony that he agreed to tell the truth. <Wrong concept: Swearing is a procedure to declare that the person will tell the truth, but it

does not mean he is competent.> It is reasonable to say that he knows the difference between telling the truth and lying in court testimony.

Thus, R has competence as a witness.

In conclusion, R's testimony about the age of the painting should be admitted in court because he has met relevancy, competent, and expert opinion.

<I would conclude: assuming Rex is telling the truth on the witness stand, his conclusion about the age of the painting appears to be reliable, based on the elements of Daubert standard, and he looks competent to determine the age of the painting, assuming the four galleries hired him because of his abilities, not due to other external factors.>

Excerpt from "The Science of dating Work of Art."

Relevance

Supra

Logical Relevance

Supra

Here, the excerpt is logically relevant because Marie (M) testifies to the quoted excerpt from "The Science of Dating Works of Art" publication that the XYZ technique is not reliable for determining the age of the work of art. The quoted excerpt totally contradicts R's testimony. The excerpt makes the XYZ technique more probable than without the excerpt.

Thus, the excerpt has logical relevance.

Legal Relevance

Supra

Here, the excerpt does not meet legal relevance because M is an excerpt in a dating work of art. That is not the same as an expert in dealing with works of painting. She used the excerpt and testified that XYZ is unreliable, but she is not an expert in determining the age of painting. Her opinion is dangerous and could cause the danger of unfair prejudice against R's witness in the case.

Thus, the excerpt does not meet the legal relevance.

Hearsay

Hearsay is an out-of-court statement offered for the truth of the matter asserted. Hearsay is inadmissible unless an exception applies.

Hearsay Exception:

Learned Treatise

<Good definition>

A standard scientific treatise or authoritative work if relied on by an expert direct or called to the attention of an expert on the cross. An expert witness must examine it in treaties before being admitted in court.

<For the learned treatise which is reliable to be introduced, there must be an expert witness on the stand. The learned treaties would not go to the jury, but would be read to the jury only. >

Here, the excerpt does not meet the learned treatise requirement because although M is considered an expert, her excerpt has not been examined directly or cross-examined. An expert witness has not examined the excerpt. <You have a good definition, but your analysis is not explain what you need

to explain. The most important is the reliability of the writing and if there is an expert explaining that.>

Compare:

<Here, the publication "The Science of Dating Works of Art" sounds like a book of authority about science, and Marie testified that this is "generally recognized as a reliable authority." Facts show that both parties stipulated that she is an expert in dating works of art, so there should be no controversy about her qualifications, at least not in this court case. When she claims that the publication is "generally recognized as a reliable authority," it appears to be trustworthy. Marie is also available on the witness stand to explain whatever questions the counsels of both sides may have. The excerpt from that publication asserted that the "XYZ technique is not reliable for determining the age of works of art," which is a central issue in this case. Hence, the implication of this excerpt is valuable to the case.

Nevertheless, as mentioned above, the excerpt would be read to the jury only, and it would not be taken as an exhibit.>

Thus, the court can not admit the excerpt.

Conclusion: The court should not admit the excerpt.

Journal article

Relevance

Logical relevance

Supra

<As mentioned above, there is no need to go through relevance in every part. You will not have enough time.>

Here, the journal article has logical relevance because G offered R's written "journal article," in which R states the XYZ technique is not reliable for determining the age of a work of art. R's written statement in the article causes dispute because it contradicts his testimony that XYZ is reliable and used by most experts to determine the age of the painting. The article journal makes R's testimony more probable for lack of creditability than without it.

Thus, the article has met the logical relevance.

Legal relevance

Supra

Here, the article does not meet legal relevance because R himself wrote the article that the XYZ technique isn't reliable for determining the "age of works of art." R will argue that "work of art" could have many meanings. <This argument is offtrack. I believe you get lost. The focus is the journal article authored by Rex, not "The Science of Dating Works of Art." > The art could be a sculpture, a solid artwork, or an artifact. <Moreover, "…Works of Art" is the name of the publication. If the context is useful and admissible, the name of the book does not matter. You have to be careful about what to argue.> It is not just limited to painting. G introduced the article as trying to confuse the juror or confuse the issue that art is the same as painting. G's introduction to the journal article is not only causing undue delay in the court proceeding but also wasting time on the jurors. This clearly shows that the probative value of R's creditability in the journal article is outweighed by confusion to the jury, confusion of the issue, and undue delay.

Thus, the journal article does not have legal relevance.

Business Evidence Rule

<?What is it? Do you mean the Best Evidence Rule?>

Supra

Here, the journal article meets the FRE best evidence rule because G offered a journal article as evidence written by R. There is no fact stating the article was a copy, so the journal article meets the best evidence rule.

There is no fact stating that the journal article is a copy document. <A journal could be a magazine that would have many copies, so this is not the rule you need to bring up here.> It is likely to say that G offers original journal articles, which meets the FRE requirement. If not, then it is a copy article, and G meets the CA rule as secondary evidence.

Thus, the article meets either the FRE or CA best evidence rule.

Hearsay

Supra

Hearsay Exemption

Prior inconsistent statement<This is the real issue.>

<The unique aspect of the journal is that Rex said something inconsistent with what he said in court before. The importance of the fact "Rex was excused and left the courtroom" in my opinion is: R does not have any chance to explain why there is such an inconsistency. You have to think about the function of each fact before you start writing. Once you start writing, it will be easier for you to get lost.>

A prior inconsistent statement is admissible when the declarant testified and is subject to cross.

Here, the journal article written by R shows he made an inconsistent statement about the XYZ technique in terms of testing the age of a work of art. However, R will counter <This argument does not make sense or sustain because R is gone and he would not be present in the witness stand.> that the "age of works of art" is not the same as testing the "age of painting." As stated in the prior issue, art is not just limited to painting but it could also include artifacts or sculpture. The XYZ technique is not reliable in determining the age of sculpture or artifact, but it is reliable in testing the age of painting. <Wrong logic and wrong analysis>

<You failed to write the key point:

The prior inconsistent statement can be offered for the limited purpose of impeaching Rex if Rex has an opportunity to explain.>

Here, prior inconsistent statements are hearsay exemptions, but the person who made the statement must be given an opportunity to explain. Facts show that Rex left the courtroom. Unless Rex comes back and is called into the witness stand again, the statement from the journal would not be admitted for impeachment.

Thus, Rex's journal article could be admissible for impeachment purposes if Rex is given an opportunity to explain in court.

Thus, there is no inconsistency in the prior statement. <Wrong conclusion>

Conclusion: The journal article should not be admitted in court because there is no prior inconsistency to R's testimony, and it does not meet the legal relevancy requirements. <Wrong conclusion>

July 2022 Contracts

Overall comments:

Each essay has many unclear terms or some acts with ambiguity, which allow you room to discuss and come up with arguments for both sides. You have to take advantage of the unclearness or vagueness to fulfill your purpose.

Before you start typing or writing, you have to know which facts go to which argument. Some facts only belong to argument A, so you should not include that particular fact in argument B.

In this essay, there are two contracts. Both mention FOB. But the FOB does not have much impact on Contract 1 because the risk of loss does not go to the buyer until the shipment has arrived. But FOB is the meat of the discussion in Contract 2 because once the goods are delivered to TruckCo, the risk of loss has passed onto the buyer. That is why Hot has no more obligations, and you have to be clear about that.

1. Did Bath and Scents have a binding contract and if so, did either party breach the contract? If there was a breach of contract, what damages are likely to be recovered, if any? Discuss

<In the exam, no need to retype the whole question. Just write or type headings when you IRAC that point.>

Bath v. Scents

Governing Law – UCC

Contract involving sales of goods.

<You should explain more:

A contract involving the sale of goods, which are tangible commodities, would be governed by UCC, while a contract involving the sale of services or land would be governed by the common law.

Here, the contract between Bath and Scents is about buying and selling candles, which are tangible commodities.

Thus, UCC governs. >

Here, the contract involves selling candles between Bath and Scents. The candle is a type of good. <You failed to briefly explain what goods are in your own definition.>

Thus, the UCC governs the contract.

Merchant

A person who regularly deals with the kinds of goods sold or possesses a special knowledge of the goods sold.

Here, Bath is a retailer selling goods in Betaville. Bath orders 1,000 quantities of candles, showing he has the knowledge and regular deal in selling such big quantities. <Wrong logic: ordering 1000 candles does not show any knowledge of the product. It only shows that Bath knows how to order. >

In addition, Scents is an importer and sent a signed acknowledgment that the shipping boxes have external water damage, but 1000 candles have no damage. This shows Scent has knowledge of selling candles. <Knowledge does not mean merely knowing some isolated facts. Instead, the knowledge should be a professional skill in the quality of candles. Imagine if a person

just gets hired and starts working today, and he is told that the shipping boxes have external water damage. Then does this awareness constitute the knowledge a merchant is supposed to have?>

Thus, both Bath and Scents are both merchants.

<You failed to fully explain why they are merchants. Based on the way you explained, I was not persuaded that they are merchants.>

<Compare: A merchant is a person who deals in goods of the kind or otherwise by his occupation and holds himself out as having knowledge or skill peculiar to the practices or goods involved in the transaction, as opposed to a causal buyer or seller who deals with the goods occasionally or once in a lifetime.

Here, Bath is a retailer located in Betaville selling candles. Bath deals with candles in his business and holds himself out as having knowledge about candles in the eyes of customers, as opposed to a buyer who may buy candles once a year for a birthday cake. Scents is an importer located in Sunville selling 1000 individually wrapped candles to Bath. Scents also deals with candles as part of its business and holds himself out as having skill peculiar to candles.

Thus, both Bath and Scents are merchants. >

<This is the foundation for the UCC 2-207 discussion, so it is important to establish that they are merchants.>

Goods <You can insert this part into the paragraph above.>

Tangible items that are 1) identifiable and 2) movable in the contract.

Here, the 1000 candles arc mentioned in the contract. It is identified that the shipping box has external water damage, but the inside content (1000 candles) has no damage. <You use these facts in the wrong spot. That goes to the discussion of UCC 2-207>

The candles are sold from Scent to Bath and they are movable when Scent transports them on a TruckCo carrier.

Thus, the goods are 1,000 candles.

<This IRAC does not have much value, even if it is not wrong. Whether the candles are good is not an issue, so it is not worth an IRAC for it. In contrast, if the goods are something arguably intangible or also involve services, then it is worths an IRAC. For example, if the goods are small puppies, then you can explain even though puppies are live animals, they are deemed goods in this transaction because……>

Contract formation – needs offer, acceptance, consideration, and no formation defense.

Offer

Offer intent to form an agreement, define, and certain and communicate to the offeree.

Here, Bath sent Scents a signed purchase offer to buy 1000 individually wrapped candles; she is an offeror and intends to buy 1000 individually wrapped candles. The signed offer specifically states to purchase 1000 individually wrapped candles at a price of $10,000, Free on board (FOB) Betaville. This shows there is an agreement fully defined. Scent received Bath's offer and responded promptly, and this shows that the offer has been communicated to the offeree.

Thus, there is a valid offer.

Acceptance

Assent to the terms of the offer and communicate acceptance back to the offeror.

Here, Scents quickly sent a signed acceptance back to Bath, including a statement that there is external water damage on the exterior boxes, but there is no damage inside content. <This point should be reserved to UCC 2-207>

Because Scent sent a signed acknowledgment, the information has been communicated back to Bath.

Bath would argue that he has not responded to the acknowledgment. Because there were no responds from him, he never accepted the 1000-candle shipment, which had exterior damage in exterior boxes. Furthermore, Scent's signed acknowledge has no express warranty or disclaimer. Any buyer would not accept a shipment that has exterior damage boxes, especially if he might sell the whole 1000 candles to his customers, and his customer would not accept exterior box water damage. He will be stuck with the candles that nobody wants. Since there is no express warranty or disclaimer, Bath is not responsible for accepting it.

Battle of Form <Battle of form is a topic when we studied in-laws. but when we use IRACs in an essay, that would not help. You can simply say UCC 2-207. Imagine if I start a heading named legal dispute, then I conclude: Thus, there is a legal dispute. Then how is it going to benefit the solution to the problem?>

<Battle of the form should be discussed in acceptance. According to the common law, the mirror image rule applies, but UCC Article 2 changes that.

Since goods are involved here, UCC 2-207 applies instead of the mirror image rule.>

<Then discuss if the following exist:

The additional terms are to be construed as proposals for addition to the contract. Between merchants such terms become part of the contract unless:

the offer expressly limits acceptance to the terms of the offer;(NO here: "No other express

warranties or disclaimers were stated in the offer or acknowledgment.")

they materially alter it (The box is just a protection or a mode of storage, so not material.) or

notification of objection to them has already been given or is given within a reasonable time after notice of them is received.><No notification or response is given by Bath.>

Additional terms become a UCC contract when both parties must be merchants, new terms do not materially alter the agreement, have no express limitation, and do not object within 10 days.

Here, Scents would rebut that Bath is a retailer selling goods to retail customers, and Scents is an importer selling goods to retail store customers, so they are both merchants. The 1000 candles are individually wrapped, and no damage at all when shipping inside the boxes. The exterior boxes have damage, but it is not material to alter the agreement. The agreement has no express limitation, like a disclaimer or express warranty. No Bath rejected his signed acknowledgment within 10 days after Scent sent the acceptance.

Thus, there is a battle of form.

Scents has a stronger rebuttal argument using the battle of form to argue no acceptance defense from Bath.

Thus, there is a valid acceptance from Bath.

<Use a separate IRAC -UCC 2-207>

Consideration

Bargain for exchange and legally sufficient in value

Here, Scent agrees to sell 1000 candles to Bath. Bath agrees to buy the candles for $10,000. The price is $10 per candle and that is legally sufficient for the candle price.

Thus, there is a valid consideration.

Lack of Defense Formation <should be lack of defense to the formation>

Statute of Fraud

Contract for selling goods over $500 must be in writing.

The contract is for selling $10000 in goods, so it is over $500. When Scent signs Bath's order, the signature shows it was done in writing. If Bath uses a statute of fraud as a defense, he will not be successful.

Thus, the statute of fraud is not a valid defense. <SOF is a valid defense in general, but it does not apply here.>

<Compare: Here, Bath sent a signed offer to Scents, and Scents sent Bath a signed acknowledgment, specifying the price ($10 each= $10,000/1000) and quantity (1000), and the type of goods (individually wrapped candles), so the requirement of writing is fulfilled.

Thus, SOF is met. It is not going to be a defense for the formation of the contract between Bath and Scents.

Perfect tender rule <I would use perfect tender rule vs. substantial performance as a heading.>

<Compare: For contracts governed by the common law, substantial performance is sufficient to avoid being accused of breach of contract, but for contracts governed by UCC, the performance must be perfectly tendered. >

Here, according to the contract between Bath and Scents, 1000 individually wrapped candles have to be delivered to Bath. To be precise, the products at issue are individually wrapped candles instead of candles. In other words, the wrapping has to be intact when the goods are delivered in order to fulfill the perfect tender rule.

Bath may claim that the shipment has to be "perfect" according to the perfect tender rule. But Scents may argue that the shipment is not the product at issue, but the "individually wrapped candles." As mentioned above, only the "shipping boxes showed signs of water damage," while "all candles and individual wrapping were undamaged." From the perspective of Scents, nothing is damaged. The candles and the individual wrapping are still "perfect."

<Add:

Right to reject

Buyers have right to reject the shipment after inspecting the goods within a reasonable amount of time if the goods are found defective or not in compliance with the request made by the buyer.

Here, Bath's employees never open any boxes. So, no inspection of the actual goods is even done by the buyer. Most importantly, what Bath ordered were 1000 individually wrapped candles, not the shipping boxes. When Bath's employees noticed the signs of water damage, they were merely suspicious of damage inside. They do not find real damages to the goods ordered by Bath or failed to try to find if there are damages of the goods.

While the buyer has right to reject defective goods, Bath's employees fail to finish a legitimate inspection procedure. As such, Bath may not have good-faith or legitimate reasons to reject the goods.>

<You may discuss parol evidence rule here about the meaning of "some.">

Parol Evidence Rule

As discussed above in UCC 2-207, the term about some shipping boxes with external water damage is deemed part of the contract. As such, Bath's employees are not allowed to reject the shipment just because of the shipping boxes, which they think are suspicious. They are not sure what their boss has exactly agreed to, regardless of whether Bath's lack of response means agreement or ignorance.

On the other hand, assuming Bath has read the additional term, he may still rebut that the additional term specified "some shipping boxes" only, while Bath's employees find one-quarter of the shipping boxes showed signs of water damage. A 25 percent of shipping boxes can be deemed a big portion, even though it is not a majority, and Bath and Scents may have different interpretations of what "some" means.>

Goods delivered must comply with ALL the contact terms (including delivery term); 2) The Smallest non-conformity is a breach, and the buyer may reject all or a portion of the goods.

Here, Scents timely delivers the 1,000 candles using TruckCo. Each of the candle boxes contains individually wrapped candles.

On the other hand, Bath would argue that his employees noticed that one-quarter of the shipment of the boxes contained water damage. In Scent's signed acknowledgment, he states that "some of the boxes have external water damages." <This goes to UCC 2-207 discussion> However, one-quarter of the shipment boxes have water damage, and that is a material breach. Scents would rebut that he did disclose some of the shipments have exterior water damage. In his view, one-quarter of the shipment with water damages is the same as "some" of the shipment. <good that spots the contrast between one-quarter and some>

The water damages are not considered even with the smallest non-conformity in the contract because he has fully disclosed the issue in the signed acknowledgment. Besides, when the goods arrived at Bath place, the employee acted in bad faith, <Not bad faith, but unreasonable; it is also understandable when regular people see a damaged box and infer the products are damaged. Bad faith would be an unfair description. Please do not twist the facts to fit the words in concepts or doctrines when they, in fact, do not apply.> did not even open the boxes to inspect any other damage to the candles and promptly rejected the whole shipment. Scent has complied with all the contract terms by shipping the goods to Bath on time and with no deviation. It seems like Scents have a valid argument.

Thus, there is no perfect tender defense.

There is a valid contract formation between Bath and Scents.

Major Breach <No need; this is not governed by the common law, and the standard is not substantial performance.>

A party does not render substantial performance. <incomplete and asymmetric definition: A major breach is an act, while a party is a person or a corporation.>

When the shipment arrived at Bath's place, his employee did not open any boxes to see if there was any damage to the candles and immediately notified Scents, rejected the shipment, and refused the payment. <The main point is failing to inspect.>

Not accepting the shipment and not going to pay the $10,000 is a substantial non-performance.

Thus, there was a major breach of contract by Bath.

Incidental Damages - $400 freight cost to deliver to Bath.

The damage involves shipping for storage costs.

<Compare: Incidental damages are the cost dealing with the breach.

Here, the $400 is used to ship the original shipment, which is part of the cost of the transaction, so it would not be deemed damaged. Had the transaction gone through without problems, Scents would have had to pay it anyway. However, after the shipment is rejected by Bath, Scents paid $500 to ship the candles back to Sunville, and this $500 is the cost to deal with the breach.

Thus, $500 would be the incidental cost incurred by Scents.>

Here, the $400 is the freight cost for shipping from Scents to Bath. Because there is no sign acknowledgment for charging freight cost separately from the $10,000 candle price, it is reasonable to infer that the $10,000 in the signed acknowledgment includes the freight cost to ship the goods to Bath. The $400 incidental damage is not damage that Scent can recover.

Thus, Scent cannot recover the $400 incidental damage.

<The $400 is not deemed incidental damage. That is the shipping cost of the original transaction.>

Incidental Damage - $500 shipping the candle back

Supra

Here, the $500 is the freight cost for shipping back from Bath to Scent. Because Bath employees did not even bother to open the boxes to inspect the candles, that is bad faith. Scent is entitled to recover the freight cost.

Thus, Scent cannot recover the $500 incidental damage.

Mitigating damages

The damage party has a duty to mitigate the foreseeable damage.

Here, as soon as Scent received notice from Bath that Bath was not going to pay for the $10,000 candles, he quickly notified Bath that he intended to resell his candles by soliciting bids from all his customers. He eventually gets the highest bid from one of his customers, Redemption for $9,000, <No value; you just repeated the description, not deemed analysis.>

<Compare: Scents also sues Bath, showing that Scents does not agree that Bath should have rejected the shipment. However, Scents does not just sit there doing nothing and sue. Instead, Scents has fulfilled its duty of mitigation by soliciting bids from other customers and trying to get the best deal for reselling the candles. Even though the price he gets is still less than what Scents should have received from Bath, the loss would be a $1000 difference in price only.

Scents may have had a choice of curing the shipment or products within a reasonable amount of time, but Scents chose not to do it, and he made it clear to bath by telling Bath that Scents intended to resell the candles before the actual sale. That is a clear communication to bath that Scents does not intend to cure the problem and reship them to Bath; or if Bath would like to revoke his employee's rejection, he can do it when he is notified. But no facts show Bath would like to make any revocation of the rejection. That means Scents can simply resell them and try to seek damages from Bath.>

FOB Sunville. Scent foresees that damage when Bath is not going to pay for the candles, and he mitigates his damage down to $1,000 ($10,000 - $9,000). There is no fact where Redemption is located. But Scent did a good job by securing a shipping term, FOB Sunville, to limit his risk of loss to the city he is operating.

Expectational Damages <Expectation damages, not expectational>

The expectational benefit or profit from the contract.

Here, Scent can recover the profit he is expecting to get from the contact with Bath.

<The candles are resold. Unless the profit he gets from others is less than what he expects to get from Bath, there is no more expected profit for damages. However, the $400 shipping cost can be offset from the original profit from Bath if the transaction goes smoothly, but not when Bath refuses to pay.>

<One thing you failed to discuss:

Scents are located in Sunville, and the contract with Redemption Candles (contract 2) is FOB Sunville, while contract 1 is FOB Betaville, so the shipping cost for contract 1 would be higher than contract 2. In other words, the savings in shipping cost in contract 2 have to be deducted from the shipping cost in contract 1 in order to be sought as damages.>

Thus, there is an expectational damage <should be expectation damage> for Scent.

Countersue from Bath against Scent for expectational damage $2,000 ($12,000 - $10,000)

Since Bath breaches the contract, he cannot recover the expectational damage against Scent.

Thus, there is no expectational damage for Bath.

Conclusion <When the heading is conclusion, the first two words of the following paragraph should not be "in conclusion." It sounds redundant.>

In conclusion, there is a binding contract between Bath and Scents. Bath breaches the contract. Scents can recover $500 in incidental damage and expectational damages. There is no damage that can be recovered from Bath against Scient<Too conclusive>

<You should list both sides' amount of damages trying to seek, and then say which side is more likely to prevail.>

<Compare:

Bath can try to reorder the candles from Hot and recover the damages, including the difference in prices, from Scents; and Scents can resell the candles and try to recover the difference in profit, deduct the cost saved and add the cost spent from Bath. ______is more likely to prevail because...>

2. Has Bath or Hot breached their contract? If so, what damages are likely to be recovered, if any? Discuss.

Hot v. Bath

Valid contact - a valid contract has an offer, acceptance, consideration, and no defense formation. <No need to talk about that. You already discussed above, and the main point for Q2 is FOB>

Here, a valid written offer is entered between Bath and Hot Candles, so it is reasonable to say that all the valid contact elements are met. Each of the parties is expected to perform as Hot agrees to sell 1,000 candles to Bath. Bath agrees to pay $12,000 for the goods.

Thus, there is a valid contract. <Fact pattern already said "valid," and the main elements of a contract are discussed in contract 1, so there is no need to further discuss here. You would not have points for twice.>

Major Breach by Bath

Supra

Here, Bath is substantially not going to perform his duty by not paying the $12,000 worth of candles because the candles were melted when TruckCo's truck was hit by lighting in a store.

Risk of Loss – FOB Hatville <That is the main point>

The seller's risk of loss has passed to the buyer once the goods are loaded on a common carrier's truck.

Hot would argue that his business is in Hatville. Once the candles are loaded in TruckCo's truck in Hatville, the risk of loss has passed to Bath in Hatville.

It is unfortunate that the truck was hit by lighting and all the candles were melted, but he is not responsible for the loss once the truck leaves Hatville. Bath would counter the FOB Hatville means the risk of loss is with Hot until the truck leaves Hatville City Limit. (Once the products are officially placed on the carrier, the risk of loss will be transferred.)

If the contract states FOB, Hot's warehouse, then Hot is not liable for the loss. Furthermore, the truck was in transit to Bath place in Betaville. The truck could be hit by lighting while it is still within Hatville city limits, so Hot should bear the risk of loss. <"In transit" means on the way of transporting. If people or things are in transit, they are traveling or being taken from one place to another. Synonyms: en route, on the way, on the road, on the move. The risk of loss is transferred already.> It seems like Bath has a valid argument here. <Not valid at all>

Thus, Bath has a valid defense for the risk of loss.

There is no major breach by Bath.

Major Breach by Hot

Supra

Here, Hot refuses to send replacement candles after TruckCo's truck got hit by lighting, and all the candles were melted. Not sending a replacement is a substantial non-performance of the valid contract between Hot and Bath.

Thus, there is a major breach of contract by Hot.<No: the contract is FOB Hatville; Hot has no obligation to send a replacement>

Expectational Damage <should be expectation damage>

Supra

Bath can recover from the profit he is expecting from the 1,000 candles from Hot.

In Conclusion

Bath did not breach the contract. Hot breach the contract. Bath is entitled to expectational damages.

<Q2 asks about what damages are likely to be recovered, while there is no identification of parties. I would also discuss TruckCo. When you answer an essay question, each party mentioned plays a certain role. Please do not ignore anyone, even though the parties are not identified. Everyone's act has an impact; if you think there is no impact, please explain why.>

Indemnification

Definition

Here, Bath may try to indemnify the loss from TruckCo, which may have its insurance to cover the loss of shipment. But TruckCo may also rebut that the loss is due to the acts of God, including lightning, so the insurance may not cover.

Thus, Bath may not be able to recover from TruckCo.

July 2022 Constitutional Laws

Overall comments:

Constitutional laws seem to be one of your weakest subjects. Some of your arguments are offtrack. Please do more MBES to solidify your understanding of the doctrines or rules. I believe you do not understand most of the rules. Please read your previous textbooks or outlines to find

out what the rules mean, not just literally, but also how to apply them to different situations.

The rule by D is unreasonable and arbitrary, even though combating gang violence is necessary and legitimate. The important facts include "P has never been associated with any gang." But P was suspended simply because her wrist has a dove, while the W gang symbol includes birds. Dove is one kind of birds but the birds used by W could be different. If P uses white Dove and W uses black raven, it does not make sense to generalize P's Dove as a symbol of W. The compelling government interest here is to deter the violence caused by confrontations between W and E. That is the root cause of the gang violence, not the drawing of any birds. W and E would not fight just because they see something similar to a bird, but probably something W and E are actually fighting for. D has wrongfully focused on the dove tattoo. "No tattoo" does not mean "no violence."

Regarding to the certainty of the local law enforcement officials, they said that "it sounded like a Westside gang symbol." Just because the phrase "sounded like," a student with no actual connection with gangs was suspended. How legitimate was this decision? You seem to fail to realize the unreasonable nature of the decision.

Regarding the rule made by D, it was overbroad, vague and content-based. You have to first discuss the problems of the rule itself, and the unreasonableness of the decision by the D.

Moreover, you did not fully discuss the 14th Amendment: "substantive" and "procedural." For "substantive," you have to discuss the strict scrutiny, intermediate and rational test (SS applies to free speech but education is not fundamental, so another test will apply.) For

"procedural," there is no notice or hearing before the 10-day suspension takes place.

I am not sure whether you have realized that your standpoint is inconsistent: One time, you blamed P for not covering the tattoo or having it removed, but another time, you blamed D for suspending P due to P's refusal.

Please take a look at the suggested answer released by the State Bar. I do not think you understand this aspect.

<u>Paloma (P) v. District (D)</u>

Paloma (P) argument in support of her First and Fourteen Amendments.

Freedom of Speech under 1st Amendment

State Action - State action requires government involvement with the challenged action.

Here, D is a public school district that is a part of local government. <You did not explain it well. I would say the public school is funded by the government, as opposed to private schools funded and fully controlled by private individuals or organizations. A public school has to abide by rules set by the government. > It involves reducing gang violence in its district by involving and consulting with local law enforcement to adopt an action with a school rule for all high school students to follow " –No student shall wear any label, insignia, words, colors, signs or symbols that reflect gain-related activities. Students violating the policy will be immediately suspended or expelled from school." This new rule is challenging students from wearing gang-related insignia on school campuses. <The above big chunk of facts does not explaining why the state act is included. Also, there is no need to mention the big chunk of facts.>

Furthermore, when D found out P had a dove tattoo, it communicated with local law enforcement officials and determined the tattoo sounded like a street gang symbol. D placed an action on P by putting her on a 10-day suspension because she refused to wear long sleeves to cover the tattoo or have it removed.<What they did and how they reacted do not explain why it is a state action. > <What matters here is P was suspended for ten days of school after she refused the request of the school district, which is funded and controlled by the government.>

Thus, there is a state action.

Symbolic Speech - Freedom to communicate an idea by use of a symbol or communicative conduct

Here, there is a symbolic speech because P has a small tattoo of a dove on one of her wrists. She wants other people to see her wrist and know she is a peaceful person. The dove tattoo is her way of communicating her ideas to others.<This is a symbolic speech. But you failed to express it clearly. As opposed to verbal speech, symbolic speech conveys a message by symbols, marks, and drawings instead of words. Here, P uses the dove to self-express that she is a peaceful person, without saying anything. People are supposed to perceive her message merely by looking at the dove.

Thus, the dove is deemed a kind of symbolic speech.>

Thus, the dove tattoo is a symbolic speech.

<Your analysis of content-based and content-neutral does not make sense as a whole. Either one would be “no." But you say both exist.>

Content-based - Regulations restrict speech based on its subject matter or its viewpoint.

<When you copy the facts given, I would think you do not understand at all: You do not have to quote the exact words. Just explain the gist: Why it is content-based: It is content-based because the context or the messages of what students wear is controlled by the school district, which reflects gang-related activities.>

Here, there is a content base because D puts restrictive speech like no student can wear any label, insignia, signs, or symbols that reflect gang-related activities. D and the local police officials viewed the dove tattoo sounds like a Westside gang symbol. D place this regulation or restrictive speech to reduce gang violence.

Thus, there is a content base.

Content Neutral - Content-neutral regulations do not regulate a specific topic.

<Contradictory: content-based and content-neutral would not co-exist. I do not understand what you are talking about.>

Here, there is a content-neutral because D's rule regulates bird tattoos that could be symbolized a gang member. That regulation is a specific topic to reduce gang violence in D's district.

<If the restriction is not wearing any accessories, then it may be content-neutral.>

Thus, there is a content-neutral

<Strict scrutiny test should be discussed when you talk about the 14th Amendment.>

Strict scrutiny - to satisfy strict scrutiny, the government must prove that the law is narrowly tailored to meet a necessary and compelling government interest.

<Two elements are required to prove:

Narrowly tailored to meet a compelling government interest.>

Here, there is strict scrutiny because D, a government-run public school district, is trying to reduce gang violence in its high schools. It is necessary to protect student's life from gang violence. Saving lives on the school campuses and preventing the school district from getting lawsuits from victim students of gang violence is compelling school interest. <You did not explain why it is compelling. You just talked about it but failed to hit the main reason.><I would say that gang-related activities might include fighting, killing people, and selling drugs, and protecting students from these illegal activities is important because students are important people in society in the future. They would affect the well-being of the whole society, the economy and the long-term development of the State. If students are associated with the gangs, the next generation would be full of gangs. The more the number of gangs, the more difficult it would be for the government to control or combat them>

<Too early to conclude: You did not explain whether it is a tight fit. Obviously, it is not narrowly tailored.>

Thus, D has met the strict scrutiny test.

<The rule prohibiting the wearing of labels, insignia, words, etc stems from the conclusion drawn by the District that "most violence results from confrontations between two gangs," the W and the E, and the W's gang symbol includes birds. First of all, violence can take place for any reason, such as competition of drug business. It would not have to be confined by a

symbol. Whether the symbol exists would not increase or decrease violence. Secondly, W's gang symbol includes birds, and there are so many types of birds. The birds used by W may not resemble a dove at all. The birds could be owls, parrots or quelea. There are so many possibilities of birds so the dove on P's wrist is not equivalent to the birds which are chosen by W. Prohibiting the dove means nothing to combat the gang violence; thirdly, the facts do not say what symbol E uses. If E's symbol is a hamburger, it would be ridiculous for the school district to stop students from eating hamburgers. Based on the foregoing discussion, the restriction is not relevant to the goal of combating gang violence at all, more than falling short of the standard "tight fit." >

<Also, you should know there are three standards of tests: SS, intermediate, rational, and free speech is the fundamental right, so SS applies>

<In my opinion, the following discussion is unnecessary. The W's symbol includes birds, but also something else. It could be birds in a garden, birds plus dogs, birds flying on top of a pond. How can the above symbols lead to imminent lawless action? Very unlikely. Unless birds are instead command for W to kill people, then it could be described as inciting imminent lawless action.>

Unprotected or less protected speech - Speech that is unprotected includes (1) inciting imminent lawless action, (2) fighting words, (3) obscenity, (4) defamatory speech, or (5) commercial speech that is either misleading or fraudulent or promotes illegal activity.

Here, the dove tattoo on P's wrist is an unprotected speech because local law enforcement or police officials have determined the Westsider gang symbol includes birds. If P shows her dove tattoo to others, she could instigate other gang members, like Eastsider, to have illegal or lawless action, which could lead to violence, and someone could be injured or die in the gang violence. <no need>

<The birds are only representing W, but this symbol is not exclusive to W, and is not proof for involvement with gang activities. Dove can also mean different things for different people. So the restriction on the dove has almost nothing to do with combating gang violence>

P would argue that she has never associated with any gangs, including Westsider or Eastsider. Beside it was a small dove tattoo on one of her wrists and could hardly be seen. <Hardly to be seen is not an argument. If the school allows it because it is hard to be seen, it is still a suppression of free speech because they ignore it just because almost nobody sees it. It is still a form of prohibition.> She has the right to make her protected speech that she is a peaceful person. <Please read the above sentence. No logic: Can she make the speech just because she is a peaceful person? Anyone can make a protected speech, regardless of the personality.> D should not suspend her for 10 days of school because she refused to cover with a long sleeve or have it removed. <This is not an argument; suspension for 10 days is a kind of penalty; what you need to argue is whether the dove constitutes a problem, and how to penalize is not something you should argue; just like in court, you are trying to defend yourself; claiming that you are not guilty; but you are not arguing whether you should pay the fine or go to jail.>

D would counter the argument any rival gang members would interpret the dove tattoo as a symbol of Westside gang members. The rival gang member would immediately interpret P as a Westsider gang member, leading to immediate violence. She or anyone associated at the time could be in danger, leading to violence and death. <what would lead to death is violence, not the dove>

D has a better argument.

Thus, the dove tattoo is an unprotected speech.

Vagueness - A law is void for vagueness when it fails to give people reasonable notice of what is prohibited.

<I think you do not understand what is vagueness. The definition is not correct. It just means the rule fails to define what is prohibited. The government would not give anyone a notice when a law is made. If you violate a rule because you do not know it, you are still guilty.>

Here, the rule is not vagueness because the rule is not a law.

<This is not a reason. Whether it is a rule or a law, P is suspended because of it. > D has adopted the rule for all high school students. P had been given a chance to either remove the tattoo or wear a long-sleeved shirt to cover the tattoo before she got her suspension. She was given reasonable notice before she got her punishment. <The point is not about the notice. The point is the rule does not allow students to wear any label reflecting gang-related activity, which is vague. It is unclear what can be deemed to reflect gang-related activities. If gangs like to fight with folded wooden chairs, it does not mean students cannot sit on wooden chairs or wear anything showing the pictures of chairs.>

Thus, there is no vagueness for P. <This conclusion clearly shows that you misunderstood vagueness. The vagueness is about the literal meaning of the rule, not how much P would understand. When you explain vagueness, try to explain with the opposite word: Is it clear enough in several aspects?>

Overbreadth - A law is overbroad when it prohibits both protected and unprotected speech, regulating substantially more speech than necessary. <A regulation of speech is unconstitutionally overbroad if it regulates a substantial amount of constitutionally protected expression, as opposed to

unprotected speech. You can explain more about what unprotected speech is here.>

<Your focus should be the restriction should not exist because the dove is a kind of protected speech.>

Here, there is no overbreadth because D's rule is not a law. However, having a dove tattoo is symbolic speech and is a protected speech. The protective speech does not apply to school rules when a bird tattoo could lead to confrontation and might cause death due to gang violence. Having a dove tattoo in a school with different gang members running around on campus and the tattoo could lead other gang member students to commit violence or any lawless activity, then it is unprotected speech. <The dove could lead to gang members running around on campus. This is groundless.>

Thus, there is no overbreadth in D's rule.

Equal Protection Clause of the 14th Amendment

Equal Protection Clause - Under the 14th Amendment Equal Protection Clause, no state shall deny to any person within its jurisdiction the equal protection of the laws. The Equal Protection Clause protects against state discrimination based on an individual's classification or whether a fundamental right is implicated.

<Under the 14th Amendment procedural Due Process Clause, no person shall be deprived of life, liberty, or property without due process of the law.><You have to talk about substantial and procedural.>

Here, there is no equal protection clause under the 14th Amendment <What do you mean by no equal protection clause? Do you mean it does not apply? Please use the appropriate wording.> because D's newly adopted school rules do not discriminate against P or people with bird tattoos. D offered P to wear a long sleeve to cover the tattoo to avoid being mistakenly identified as a Westsider gang member, which could lead to violence against her personally or toward other students on campus. In addition, the rule applies to all high schools on campus and is not against her personally or people with bird tattoos on their bodies.

Thus, the equal protection clause under the 14th Amendment is not violated.

Intermediate Scrutiny - Requires the gov. to prove that the classification is substantially related to important government interest.

<You appear to not understand the three levels of the test. D does not "show" any scrutiny, but the level of scrutiny applies to different issues. SS applies to fundamental rights such as free speech; for another two levels, please check the book of Mary. >

Here, D shows intermediate scrutiny because the government is interested in protecting all the students in the district from gang violence. The school has a duty to ensure the students come to campus to study and get home safely and are not victims of gang violence on the school campus. So, classifying students with bird tattoos on their bodies as wearing long sleeves to cover the tattoos or remove them is necessary to achieve important government interest to protect student's safety on campus.

Conclusion – P can argue symbolic speech, vagueness, and overbreadth under the 1st Amendment. She can also argue equal protection under the 14th Amendment, but they will all fail.

District (D) argument in support of the motion to dismiss

P is no longer a high school student- <this is about mootness><You have to explain even when P is no longer a high school student, the situation is capable of repetition, so it is not moot.>

Standing - An individual must have standing to bring a claim. An individual has standing when they suffer an injury. In fact, their injury is caused by the conduct complained of, and the injury is redressable.

Injury in Fact - There is an injury in fact when the plaintiff can show they have been or will be directly and personally injured by the allegedly unlawful government action that affects their rights under the Constitution or federal law.

Here, there is no injury in fact, because P is not injured by D's rule. P would argue that she was placed on a 10-day suspension. However, that argument will fail because D has given P a chance to either wear a long-sleeved shirt to cover the dove tattoo or have it removed. <Wrong concept: When D allows P to wear a long-sleeved shirt to cover the dove or have it removed, it is still suppressing free speech. When P chose not to comply with that, and P was suspended, there was still injury-in-fact. The option given by D is not going to negate the injury-in-fact. > D declined to comply, and she deserves to get her punishment.

Furthermore, D would counter that getting 10 days suspension is much better than being identified as a gang member and could get her injured or killed in school violence. <It makes no sense. No evidence shows that having the dove could cause gang members to hurt P. The restriction by D is arbitrary, but you failed to realize that.>

Thus, there is injury, in fact, on P.

Redressability - There is redressability when a decision in the plaintiff's favor is capable of relieving their grievance.

<Redressability means that the court will actually be capable of doing something to correct or make up for the plaintiff's injury.

Here, P had already graduated, and the ten-day suspcnsion was over, but a decision in P's favor is still capable of making up P's injury, at least emotionally. D can issue a letter of apology to P. Moreover, other students in similar situations would know what is recognized by the court.>

Here, there is no redressability because P got her 10-day suspension, and there is no relief from her grief because she continues to complete high school and go to college.

Thus, there is no redressability. <Incorrect>

Causation - There is causation when there is a causal connection between the injury and the conduct complained of.

Here, there is no causation because P suffered no injury, as discussed above. The 10-day suspension is not an injury because she declined to follow D's rule, which is imposed on all high school students, not just her. <NO. You seem to stand on the side of the school district from the beginning and blame P for not following the rules and think that P is not harmed.>

Thus, there is no causation. <there is causation because the rule by D caused the 10-day suspension.>

Mootness - A real controversy must exist at all stages of review. If the matter has already been resolved, the case is moot unless (a) the controversy is capable of repetition but evades review, (b) a defendant voluntarily ceases a practice but is free to resume it, or (c) it is a class action suit, and the class representative has settled their claim, or their claim is deemed moot for reasons that don't apply to other members of the class. <No need to bring up the class action because no facts trigger that.>

Here, there is no mootness because P 's controversy (dove tattoo) is no longer at the current stage of review in D's school district for current students. She is not a student in D's school anymore, and her controversy no longer exists.

<You do not understand what mootness is and how it applies here: Mootness means the controversy no longer exists. Here, P has graduated. She is no longer a high school student. But whether she should be suspended for 10 days at the time she was still at the high school remains unresolved. If the suspension is deemed wrong, she could seek at least an apology. >

D has now redefined "gang-related activities" in its rule consistent with State X's criminal code

<What does not mean by redefining "gang-related activities" in its rule consistent with State X's criminal code? That means the definition is aligned with the government's requirements. Hopefully, it would be constitutional. If the criminal code of the State is unconstitutional, people may have already opposed that. However, it is possible that D redefined it just because of the declaratory relief action, and D can change it anytime D likes. Thus, the act of redefining gang-related activities is insufficient to dismiss P's lawsuit as moot. The decision of the court to determine the correctness or incorrectness of the 10-day suspension is still needed.>

Vagueness - A law is void for vagueness when it fails to give people reasonable notice of what is prohibited.

Here, there is a vagueness because D's rule has redefined "gang-related activities" that are consistent with State X's criminal code. The rule is considered as a law right now. P would argue that the rule describing "any label, insignia, words, colors, signs or symbols" is very vague. Nothing in the law states dove tattoo is a gang symbol, and it could lead to many different interpretations. P has a valid argument. <What you wrote above has nothing to do with the topic-redefining.>

Thus, there is a vagueness.

<The following discussion is also unrelated to redefining "gang-related activities." Clarify what the act means before you squeeze something from your mind. >

Overbreadth - A law is overbroad when it prohibits both protected and unprotected speech, regulating substantially more speech than necessary.

Here, D's rule is consistent with State X's criminal code (law). P's tattoo symbolizes she is a peaceful person. Her symbolized speech is protected by the First Amendment.

Thus, there is an overbreadth.

<The following point should go up to the First Amendment.>

Unfetter discretion <should be unfettered discretion> - A regulation cannot give officials broad discretion over speech; there must be defined standards for applying the law

Here, there is an unfetter discretion because when D learns about P's tattoo, and not sure if the dove tattoo is considered a gang symbol. D checked with eh local law enforcement and determined it "sounded" like a Westside gang symbol. When law enforcement officials use the word "sound," they are not 100% sure, and there is no standard to define a dove tattoo as a gang symbol.

In the end, there is an unfettered discretion.

Thus, P will succeed in her second motion about "gang-related activities."

<You failed to explain what is a dcclaratory relief: Declaratory relief refers to a judgment of a court that determines the rights of parties without ordering anything be done or awarding damages.>

<You failed to discuss Sovereign immunity: Citizens can sue the government if what they demand is not monetary compensation.>

Conclusion – D can support the argument to dismiss P's motion because she is no longer a high school student. However, the D cannot dismiss the redefined "gang-related activities" that are consistent with the State's criminal code.

<You failed to explain in the right direction, so your conclusion is also meaningless. The question is, "Will either or both of D's arguments in support of its motion to dismiss P's lawsuit be successful?" The conclusion would be both of D's arguments in support of D's motion to dismiss are not going to be successful.>

<u>Feb 2022 Torts</u>

<u>Overall comments:</u>

You do not understand the rules very well, and you do not apply them properly either.

Try to take the scenario as a real case, or imagine you are Pedro, then your analysis would come more naturally. Think broadly from different perspectives before you start writing.

Remember to use the exact words of different elements to explain and conclude whether such a rule applies.

When you explain both public nuisance and private nuisance, you have to explain the main difference between these two: the former is for most of the people there, or at least a big group, while the latter means the individual's use and enjoyment is unreasonably and substantially affected.

When you do IRAC, for the rule part, you have to define the rule first with keywords stating the elements, then talk about what facts are relevant and irrelevant to establish certain accusations. Then you can talk about the defendant's defense and then what the plaintiff would rebut.

For example, in public nuisance, you have to define it first and then explain why the facts given constitute public nuisance. Then you might say even though the neighbors are unable to solve the problem and give up pursuing, or plan to tolerate the problem is irrelevant to regard it as a public nuisance. In other words, not fighting for the problem does not mean that is not a problem. Then, you can talk about the possible arguments Diana may have, then how Pedro can rebut.

You also failed to emphasize the differences between TRO, preliminary injunction and permanent injunction:

TRO is ex-parte; preliminary is a kind of injunction before the trial is held, and permanent is going to be effective forever. You need to have the corresponding analysis according to different elements of the rule. If time is limited, you can just talk about TRO and permanent injunction.

Although there are many rules for you to write about, please do not write like a chart, not in terms of the appearance, but its depth. Even though you did not draw a chart, the way you analyzed it is just like a chart: Stating the words on the face without explaining the details and how the rules apply to the situation given.

When you analyze, besides big points, you also need to pay attention to small points, keywords of other sentences, and descriptions of the whole scenario. They would help you to analyze comprehensively with more details and make more senses, too.

Some sentences you wrote do not contribute any values to the discussion and the conclusion. It merely repeats or paraphrases what the facts have already told you.

Student's Essay:

What claims may Pedro reasonably assert against Diana?

Public nuisance - Defendant unreasonable and substantial interference, health, safety, or property of the community

<You are not analyzing or explaining why it is a public nuisance. Instead, you almost repeated or paraphrased what the fact pattern said.>

Here, after Pedro finds out his house is affected by Diana's rock concerts due to noise and vibration to his house, he asks his neighbors if they are experiencing the same issue. <The above sentence has no value. Your task is to explain and analyze whether Diana's rock concerts constitute a public nuisance, so you have to focus on the nature of the concerts plus their impact on residents' lives. The communications between Pedro and his neighbors are not important. >The neighbors told him that they had complained to Diana about the same issue but had no success. <No value> The noise and vibration affect the whole community near Diana's open-air theater. (Too generalized: "Pedro later learned that his neighbors complained to Diana about the noise and vibration, that they were unsuccessful in obtaining relief, and that they decided to live with it in the end. " No one says the whole community, only "neighbors," could be three or thirty or three hundred people. But that would be a substantial amount of people. The definition of public nuisance does not say "everyone" has to be affected either. Just a large enough group to be arguable to be deemed "public" would be fine.)

<Compare: Here, Pedro thinks that his new house is "a perfect place to raise a family." That means it is desirable to live, enjoy life or have children. Even though the house is "adjacent to the theater," it means noises, but it also means convenience to basic living because around the theater, there must be food, drinks and some basic necessities.

However, Pedro appears to be unable to have a normal life because "he could feel the floor shake and could not have a normal conversation because of the loud noise." Suppose the house owner cannot talk inside the house, that constitutes "unreasonable and substantial interference" because family life includes verbal communication. Although communication can be done through writing, it would be a barrier and also ridiculous if Pedro could not talk to his family members inside his own house. It also affects mental health, which is a criterion of public nuisance. The noise does not only Pedro but his neighbors, which is indicated by the fact that "his neighbors complained to Diana about the noise and vibration." It is irrelevant that the neighbors "were unsuccessful in obtaining relief" and "they decided to live with it in the end." That just indicates that they failed to spend enough effort or did not succeed in combating the problem, but in fact, they are irritated by the noise. Vibration is sufficient to regard the problem as a "public nuisance" when everyone there feels the same way, not just Pedro.

Thus, there is a public nuisance. >

Defense: Meeting Zoning requirements <This is a defense to variance, not nuisance.>

Diana would argue that prior to building the open-air theater, she had gone to the local city hall and submitted the structure building print to meet the zoning requirements before allowing Diana to build the structure. It seems like Diana has a valid argument.

Thus, there is the meeting of zoning requirements.

Bring economic opportunity to the community <This should be a factor to weigh when the judge considers permanent injunction>

Diana would argue that her theater employs 200 people and is the focus of the city's cultural scene. The revenue generated from the entertainment venue is enough to cover the operating costs. She does not need any funding from the city. As a matter of fact, the revenue from the entertainment event brings economic benefits to the city. It appears that Diana has a valid economic opportunity defense. <You are trying to argue being able to cover the cost of operation and not need to use government funding would justify the disruption in residents' lives? That would not work. >

Thus, there is an economic opportunity defense.

Assumption of the Risk Defense – Plaintiff assumes the knowing risk <This defense is for negligence or strict liability>

Diana would argue that at the time her entertainment theater was built, it was at the edge of the city. As the population grows, more houses are built around the theater. When the people bought their houses around the theater, they knew any entertainment event could bring noise and vibration to their houses, and they were willing to take that risk and bought the houses. Diana has a valid assumption of risk defense.

Thus, there is an assumption of risk defense.

Private nuisance - Substantial unreasonable interference with another person's use or enjoyment of property

Here, right after Pedro moved to his dream house, he heard noise and vibration coming from Diana's open outdoor multi-use entertainment venue. The venue runs seven days a week: local dance companies run on the weekend, and rock concerts run on the weekend. When there is an event, the music creates vibration and affects Pedro's house, and that is unreasonable interference. The noise from the rock concerts causes the vibration, and Pedro can feel his house floor shaking, which prevents him from enjoying living on his property. <You failed to explain the "private" aspect here. Please use the words "use" and "enjoyment."><Please also pay attention: the rock concert was held on the weekend only, which means there are five days of quietness when the local dance companies use the space. You have to explain if 5 days of quietness and 2 days of noise still constitute substantial and unreasonable interference. You have to go both ways and then choose a side.>

<Compare: Facts show that Pedro thought that the new house was a perfect place to raise a family, which means he may want to enjoy his family life in this house, including family gatherings, dinner, conversation, etc. But he cannot even talk in the house on the weekend when the rock concert is held, then his need to "raise a family" would be substantially and unreasonably affected.

But Diana may argue that the rock concert is held only on the weekend, which means there are at least five days out of seven days in a week Pedro would be able to talk at home. In terms of ratio, 5 out of 7 is about 70 percent. In other words, for 70 percent of the time, Pedro can still raise his family without any interruption.

Pedro may also rebut he has to work during the week and the weekend could be the only time he can spend time with family, so a noisy weekend could completely deprive him of his family life.

When Pedro is unable to have a normal conversation on the weekend, his "enjoyment" is definitely jeopardized, even though he can still "use" the space.

Thus, private nuisance is more likely to be established when his enjoyment of the property is deprived.>

Coming to the nuisance – The plaintiff is aware of the nuisance and assumes the risk. <it is about the sequence of coming, and coming later does not mean the latecomer has to accept all nuisances made by the antecedents>

Diana would argue that prior to Pedro moving to his new house, he was well aware of her open-air theater. The theater is an open-air structure and provides outdoor multi-use entertainment at the location for thirty years. Every time there is a music event, its noise could affect the surrounding neighbors. The noise could lead to vibration in the standing structures. Pedro could check the theater venue and see it has dance events on the weekdays and rock concerts on the weekends, but he did not do it. Furthermore, he knew about the theater before he bought his house. The venue would show that there are rock concerts on the weekend. The rock concert is just loud, and there is not much she could do about it. Pedro was taking his chance. He thought his new house was perfect for raising his family and bought the house anyway, so he is assuming the risk of getting noise coming from the theater and vibration on his house. It appears that Diana has a valid argument. <This is not the point of coming to the nuisance. It means the sequence of arrival does not matter. You come first does not mean people come after you have to tolerate your problems.>

<Compare: The theater was built 30 years ago, and Pedro knew about the theater when he bought his house, but it does not mean Pedro has the obligation to tolerate any problems caused by the theater just because they came first and existed there for a long time. No privilege would be given to

any users merely with higher "seniority." It would also be unfair to expect people who come later to tolerate the noise created by those who came first.

Thus, the defense of coming to the nuisance would not work.>

Thus, there is a coming to the nuisance defense. < Not a valid defense>

Mitigating the damage – The defendant has a duty to mitigate the damage to the plaintiff <The term mitigation is not the best or even inappropriate. It is used for the Plaintiff when they sue for damages in negligence or breach of contract. They have an obligation to mitigate damages even though they are not the party making mistakes. The acts taken by the Defendant to pay for the damages incurred by the plaintiff are known as remedies.>

Here, Diana could argue that she told Pedro after he approached her that she had taken mitigating damages about the noise and vibration issues, such as stopping all concerts by 11 p.m. and setting a maximum noise level when the events are taking place. In addition, she even went to Pedro's house to see if there is a need for sound-deadening materials might be needed for Pedro's house. <Save this fact for the defense for trespass to Land> She has done everything she could possibly do to mitigate the noise and vibration issue. Diana has a valid argument for trying to mitigate the damage.

Thus, there is a mitigating the damage defense. <NO>

Intentional Infliction of Emotional Distress – Defendant intentionally inflicts extreme and outrageous conduct causing severe emotional distress on the plaintiff <This argument may not be needed because the noise exists because of the concert. I think IIED goes too far. If Diana intentionally does something solely to disturb Pedro, the IIED may exist>

Here, Diana's entertainment theater has been at the location and performing entertainment events prior to Pedro moving to his house, so there is no intent showing that Diana wants to causc distress to Pedro. The dance events and rock concerts are acceptable to their fans, and some people may not like it, so they are not outrageous contacts. There is no sign of severe emotional distress to Pedro.

Thus, there is no intentional infliction of emotional distress.

Trespass to land – intentionally enter the land of another without consent.

Here, Diana wants to relieve Pedro of some discomfort, so she intentionally goes to his house to see if the house could install sound-deadening materials. She let herself into Pedro's backyard (land), took some measurements, and left without disturbing anything. All these were done without telling Pedro (without consent). <This paragraph should mainly talk about what could constitute trespass to land, then the next paragraph, which would be about Diana's defenses, you can talk about measurements.>

<The last paragraph is the analysis, then the next paragraph would be the defense for Diana. Then, you have to say which side's argument is more likely to prevail. But do not use the word "argue" again to avoid confusion. I would use "rebut." Do not let the grader think that you are turning around and around. >

<The structure would be like this:

Diana went to Pedro's house without the consent of Pedro, which constitutes trespass to land (You can also talk about intent, act, causation.). The fact that nothing is damaged or disturbed is irrelevant as long as Diana entered it without permission from Pedro. (the above is about definition) Diana may argue that she simply went into Pedro's backyard to take some measurements solely for the purpose of installing sound-deadening materials, which is for the health and well-being of Pedro. (the above is about defense) However, Pedro may also rebut that measurement is not something urgent to justify her act of trespass to land (the above is talking about: the defensc fails), and the elements of trespass to land do not include bad faith. In other words, entering the land without Pedro's permission but for Pedro's health is also sufficient to establish trespass to the land. (Still, trespass to land even though a good point is included.)

Hence, Diana has trespass to the land of Pedro.

However, Diana would argue that she mistakenly forgot to tell Pedro that she was coming. It was a mistake on her part, so there is no intent. If she has the intent to trespass on Pedro's house, then she would not try to go to Pedro's house and take the measurement and try to relieve Pedro's discomforts. It seems like Diana has a valid argument. <NO: mistake is not a valid defense. Only emergency.>

<extra point to add: Facts show that Diana "forgot to tell Pedro that she was coming." Actually, Diana does not only have to tell Pedro that she was coming but also has to get his permission or consent. Merely telling him is still insufficient to get away with trespass to land.>(Every word is important for argument. You have to be familiarized with the keywords of the rule. When the words given are different in degrees, just point that out to the grader: Hey, I know the difference!)

Thus, there is no trespass to land.

Conclusion:

Pedro can assert trespass to land, private nuisance, and public nuisance claims.

What remedies may Pedro reasonably seek? Discuss

Remedies –

Legal remedy

General Damage - The plaintiff can recover a monetary award from pain and suffering

Here, Pedro can claim that he is listening to the noises coming from the entertainment theater seven days a week. Worst of all the rock concert has extremely loud music over the weekend. While listening to the noises, he is feeling his house is vibrating and shaking. He is afraid his house might collapse on him from the vibration, which leads to his suffering from a nervous breakdown.<This paragraph has no added value. You waste time typing so many sentences, but no new point or analysis is added. You can simply write: as mentioned above, Pedro suffers because of the noise. He may need to see the doctor for further evaluation. He would be able to recover the money he spent on the diagnosis and the treatment caused by the noise.>

If Pedro could show that he has a medical evaluation report showing he has been mentally suffering from a nervous breakdown, then he is eligible to claim the damage. <He can claim the payment for medical treatment.>

Thus, Pedro has a claim for the general damage.

Equitable remedy

Temporary restraining order - to preserve the status quo for a short time, pending further litigation regarding a preliminary injunction.

Here, Pedro could ask the court to put an injunction against Diana from allowing her entertainment to have any effect until the court makes the ruling. While waiting for the injunction ruling, he does not have to hear the noise and feel the vibration in his house. <TRO is ok, but you failed to explain what "status quo" the TRO is aimed to protect.> < Facts show that Pedro was horrified by the noise and vibration coming from the theater during rock concerts, which would affect his mental health and make him sick or nervous. Before the court has a ruling or finds long-term solutions, a TRO can be used to avoid further harm to his health instead of maintaining the status quo of big noises.><Do not just recite the rule, but you have to think which part of facts goes to which element of the rule.>

Thus, Pedro can claim a temporary restraining order remedy.

Preliminary injunction - The court orders one to perform an act or stop performing an act pending trial. < legal damage is inadequate; enforcement is feasible; balance of harms and equities >

Here, Pedro can sue Diana in court to stop the entertainment event in her theater pending the trial outcome. <Not an analysis>

<compare: Money damages would be insufficient here because merely paying money is not going to get rid of the horror suffered by Pedro...>

<Enforcement is feasible because it just means the rock concert has to be banned. The injunction is not asking Diana to take an act that would lead to involuntary servitude, but merely stop holding the concerts.>

<Balance would require more explanations:

Pedro can argue when the theater was built, its location was near the edge of the city, and housing was included later in the development, meaning the impact on the residential area was not taken into consideration at the beginning. But when housing was included, the impact on people would become an important factor to consider.

Facts show that "revenue from the rock concerts funds most of the operating costs of the venue," which would be the strongest argument Diana has. "Diana explained that the facility could not survive economically without rock concerts and that rock concerts were, by their nature, loud. " If the rock concert is banned, 200 people would lose their jobs. However, the revenue cannot be generated at the expense of residents' health. If everyone has severe health problems because of that, the impact on their health or lives cannot be compared.

Moreover, facts show that the theater is built to "provide an outdoor multi-use entertainment venue, " meaning holding rock concerts is not the only possibility. There must be other ways of providing the same amount of job opportunities without creating noise. Other solutions may be available, for example, holding other concerts such as Jazz would reduce the harm, playing popular movies. Diana claims that the facility could not survive without rock concerts, but no facts show that she has ever tried looking for alternatives. >

Thus, Pedro can claim a preliminary injunction.

Permanent injunction - A court orders one to perform an act or stop performing an act after holding a full trial on merit.

Here, if Pedro wins the sue against Diana in court (final trial on merit), he can order Diana to stop having performances at the entertainment theater, so he would not have to listen to the noise and feel his house shaking seven days a week.

Thus, Pedro can seek a permanent injunction.

<A permanent injunction is possible. The city expanded the development to include housing for a theater, which was built 30 years ago. That means what was allowed 30 years ago has to somehow adjust in order not to violate the right of other property users. >

Defense: Mitigating Damage

Supra

Conclusion: Pedro can have general damage, temporary restraining order, preliminary injunction, and permanent injunction remedies against Diana.

<Trespass to land -Nominal damages -just to show Pedro's legal rights are violated.

Nothing is disturbed or damaged in the property of Pedro, so $1 can be paid by Diana to merely show that Pedro's property is being trespassed. It can also deter future trespass. If nothing happens after Diana has trespassed on the land, it will encourage her to come again in the future.>

Section 4

For CA Bar Exam takers and repeaters

Advice for Performance Test (PT)

Handling Approach

PT is similar to a respectful break-up speech for your lover

The way we use the facts in the library to justify the conclusion we are supposed to reach is similar to the methodology of preparing a respectful break-up speech for your girlfriend or boyfriend. Almost everyone has this experience, so it would not be difficult to imagine.

Goal-oriented approach - Breaking up with your lover

Here, your goal is to break up with him or her, regardless of what he or she says and whatever sweet memories you have brought up in your head. You have already made up your mind, so you would not be swayed by any words or acts.

Start by saying something you value him or her

You can start by saying something you value him or her. He or she must have done a lot for you, and you value the days you two spent together. Nevertheless, the relationship between the two of you does not work: "We are pursuing different goals for our future. I do not see a future for us as a married couple, although I enjoyed the time we spent together." Even when he or she tries to make reasonable efforts to save the relationship, the problems will not be resolved.

Rebut all arguments he or she is going to raise

Then, he or she may say something to try to change your mind. Certainly, you will rebut all arguments with strong and compelling reasons because you have already made up your mind, meaning you already weighed the harm against the benefit. When you prepare your counterarguments, your standpoint will not be swayed by what he or she said. The purpose of your counterargument is simply letting him/her know that the relationship is not going to work anymore, and you must end it.

Ending: You apologize if this hurts her/him

Here, you would wish him or her the best: "Hope you would find a better match. "

Applying to PT

You would adjust the ending according to the task given. You might want to make a conclusion highlighting your standpoint or your request to the court.

Sorting out information

Get the big picture first before you might be misled or distracted

Always stay focused on your own task. Be open-minded to learn more information, but you have to take control.

Example: When a police officer comes to the scene after fighting took place

Two police officers came to a coffee shop where fierce fighting just took place. When the officers walked into the coffee shop, they saw blood stains on the floor, overturned tables and chairs, two men staring at each other, and each of them being surrounded by a few people, stopping the two from approaching each other. For the two men being surrounded, one of them has his shirt torn, and another one has messy hair.

Looking at the side, there is a pretty young lady in a pink dress sitting in the corner. Three teenagers standing or sitting at different positions carry their smart phones. Five other customers are working on their own laptops.

Two of the employees, and the manager at the counter stop selling coffee to the customers and get ready to answer the questions for the officers.

Question:

If the police officers want to know what just happened, whom they should talk to first?

Probably the employees or the manager of the coffee shop for an overview of the incident. Assuming they are strangers to each other, they would have no motivation to lie to anyone. If the manager or employees know any customers or they are related, that fact would complicate the situation.

For the two men appear to have participated in the fighting, probably the police can wait till the end for questioning. That is because the men are likely to point their fingers at each other. By merely hearing either side, the story must be subjective and one-sided.

For the teenagers with smart phones, the police may request possible videos from them if they capture the occurrence of fighting, which would be objective evidence. But in order to show the full picture of the story, videos from different perspectives may be required.

The pretty young lady in a pink dress sitting at the corner could be irrelevant, or she might see part of the fighting, or she could even be the main cause of the fighting between the two men. Depending on who she is, the police can use her version to collaborate with the other versions given by others.

For the five customers working on their laptops, their focus could be on their own tasks, but when the fighting took place, they could be distracted by the acts and sound of fighting, and at least the laptop users would have to take a look at the fighters to check if the fight would harm them unintentionally. The descriptions made by the laptop users may not be the full picture but could be used to "fill in the blanks" when there are unknowns in the whole story and when there are blind spots in the video.

Assuming the two men fought due to the pretty young lady in the pink dress, her testimony may be too subjective; or if there is a love relationship among the three and the lady dates the two men, her story could be biased, especially if she likes either one more than another.

Relevancy Illusion

When we read the big stack of information of the "File" and the "Library," we have to look for something relevant to our task, but there is "real relevancy" and "fake relevancy," which I would name the false belief to be a "relevancy illusion." Some information looks relevant because its context is somehow similar to the theme of our task or have identical keywords in some sentences, but they are not actually needed to complete our task, or they are unhelpful for we need to explain.

Example: Astronomy

For example, if the task is to handle a litigation about a big project of astronomy, then there could be some information about the defendant's education background in the subject of astronomy. The keyword "astronomy" can be misleading to make you believe that this section about his education background should be typed into your piece of writing, but in fact, the litigation is about broken pieces of a few expensive telescopes at the exhibition venue. The education background on the subject of astronomy does not seem to help the amount of money compensation as remedies unless some other facts are provided to show the connection.

"Walking around the garden"

In Chinese, we call the trick of not directly answering a question "walking around the garden." It means the responding words appear to be responding to the theme or the question, but in fact, those words merely guide you to another wrong direction, and the party delivering those words is trying to evade the main issue. The importance of being aware of this trick is not to select useless information in your own piece of writing. It would waste your time and effort in typing and also sap your energy in addressing the main issue of the task.

Example: Borrowing money from another person

When you want to borrow money from a former co-worker……you might instantly understand what "relevancy illusion" is.

You want to borrow $5000 from your former colleague Fanny; then she told you that she has $5000 in her account of the Certificate of Deposit, which is going to mature in ten more months. Early withdrawal may cost a $100 penalty. Then you said you would not mind paying that $100 penalty for her if she is willing to lend you the $5000, and she can also pay her interest. Then she told you her husband plans to use the sum of money to buy an item of new furniture.

Question:

Are you going to recommend any low-priced furnitures to her?

My advice:

If I were you, I would just walk away from Fanny. You can tell whatever she is going to say. It would be another way of saying "no." If the $100 penalty is the only hurdle, that would not be a problem because you can pay the penalty for her; but then, she would tell you more of her or her husband's "plans" which would need the $5000. You can conclude that they would rather store the $5000 cash inside the drawer of their night stand without earning any interest rather than lending it to you.

Stayed focused on your goal

If you stay focused on your goal of borrowing money, your main task would be finding out if Fanny is willing to lend you money. If there are real barriers for her to lend you money, you can try to overcome them, but do not get dominated or misled into another wrong direction by words of fake relevancy. If the real reason is purchasing a piece of new furniture, then finding a piece of low-priced furniture for her would help; but if you really do so, then she might tell you that her husband's mother needs money to pay for her big hospital bill, or her grandmother, who already died a decade ago, "died again" recently, so she would need the amount of money to pay for a funeral which is not going to happen.

Takeaway from the above discussion

You have to put the control into your own hands.

Conclusion

In a nutshell, do not let those information with "fake relevancy" sidetrack you from writing your own masterpiece under time stress.

Categorization

Determine the function of every fact in PT before you start typing

When you read the facts, please quickly decide if the particular piece of fact is for supporting or rebutting your standpoint or comparing and contrasting with the instant case. Once you put the facts into the right category and mark them with legible symbols, the most difficult part is already done. Then, your last step would be typing only. That is also why reading the "Library" first is important: If you read the facts first, there are no ways for you to categorize the facts because they could mean anything or nothing. (More about the sequence of reading will be discussed below.)

Example: Drinking beer after a crash

This is a statement made by a witness:

"The driver drinks two cans of beer after the car crash."

Question:

What does it mean? Is he thirsty?

Or he is nervous, so he needs to drink a lot of alcohol to calm himself down?

Or he loves beer very much, so he would drink it for all happy and unhappy incidents?

But if the Library tells you the following rules:

“After traffic crashes, all drivers, regardless of whose faults led to the crashes, need to take the test to verify if their alcohol content is above what the law allows.”

“If a driver drinks alcohol after the crash, and there is no way to determine whether the driver drinks it before or after the crash, then the result of alcohol test would not be admissible in court."

If we read these two rules first, we would know why the driver keeps drinking alcohol after the crash: That is because the act of drinking after the crash would negate the admissibility of the blood alcohol concentration test result. As such, the test would become useless because it would be unable to distinguish when he consumed the alcohol before or after the crash. The alcohol content in his blood would not accurately show the time he swallowed the beer. In other words, the result would be unable to prove his act of DUI.

Some other facts could change the likelihood of prevailing the case.

Fact 1:

If someone celebrating her birthday in a bar videotaped a scenario capturing the moment the driver was drinking beer, and the exact time was also shown in the video, then whether the test result is admissible could be irrelevant.

The video appears to be stronger evidence of his alcohol intake before the crash.

Counter-argument

But the driver could argue that the video shows that he was drinking something similar to beer, but in fact, no one can tell exactly what it was.

People think that the liquid is beer just because they connect the bar scenario with the car crash.

Fact 2:

The driver was leaving the bar with unequal steps, which was shown in the surveillance video outside the bar.

That shows he was not sober when he left the bar and before he started driving.

Counter-argument

But the driver could argue that was just an impression without concrete evidence.

Conclusion

The same fact can be interpreted in different ways. Whatever your standpoint is, you need to correctly categorize them, use it for the biggest impact and fulfill your own purpose.

Categorize information when you first read it.

Do not spend double the amount of time to categorize the information given in a PT: Just categorize the information when you first read it.

Meet and scan and judge vs. Read and categorize and judge

Example: Meeting new faces in a party

Imagine when you meet a new person in a party......how would you categorize the new face?

Rules of making a friend:

We always have some hidden rules in our mind about what kind of people we want to befriend, which we may not consciously realize it.

Scanning new faces

Whoever appears in front of us, we promptly scan the person for different characteristics, such as occupations, hobbies, personalities, moral characters or whether they have the potential to become our clients if we are insurance agents or financial advisors. If they do not have any potential or merits or may even give us trouble due to the nature of their jobs, such as growing or selling marijuana, we may not want to spend any more time on these people at the party.

Are the new acquaintances telling you the truth?

For people whom you first met in a party, they might not tell you the truth, which is normal because people might want to protect themselves from strangers. Nevertheless, you can also know the real aspects of them by observing how they look, how they act, or what they say.

Example: "Causal" in clothing

If someone claims that she is very "causal" in clothing, but according to your own observation, she wears a lot of famous brands with limited editions, then you would know that she is either lying or how she perceives herself to be is substantially different from how she is being perceived by others.

Example: Very "generous" about money?

Or if someone tells you, he is very "generous" about money. However, according to your observation, he squeezed himself awkwardly into the dancing pool merely to look for a coin dropping out from his pocket, when everyone was dancing elegantly. Then would you believe in his words?

Making a judgment

As a mature adult, you would not completely trust what a person tells you. You would have your own judgment to determine whether what he said is real or fake, or he subjectively claims that is true, but you do not think so. Your head has a kind of mechanism that translates the messages received immediately when you hear them, and then you categorize them as real or fake; reliable or untrustworthy.

Meet and scan and judge vs. Read and categorize and judge.

Combination of meet and scan and judge

When you describe the new faces to a third party after the gathering, you would also apply the method of "meet and scan and judge."

After the party

The party is over, and you are home now. You might share your feelings with your spouse, or your close friend by text messages. You would tell them you just met a new person and what you think about this person. Your comments on this new person would be supported by what you observed, and also what the person said or how she acted.

Support your standpoint by quotations

Your loved ones or friends may also challenge your judgment and ask you for more information to support your standpoint. Then, you have to recall something the new person said by making quotations of what was said exactly. For example, you emphasized that the man you met tonight would be a good boyfriend for you or your future husband. Then your mother might question you: what did you see, what did he say, or what did he do? Hence, your task would be to quote what he said, or describe what he did in the party.

Finding the similarities and differences of friends and non-friends

If the new person is not a good choice of friends for you, please come up with a rational reason:

You need to compare her to some of your good friends by pointing out that although one of your good friends has an identical problem or shortcoming, you conclude that this new person is not a good fit to your group of friends because of some reasons; or in contrast, you would try to differentiate your current friends from this new face even though they have something similar. For example, this new face and one of your high school friends also went to jail for a year, but you still think that your high school friend deserves to be your friend. That is because your friend was prosecuted for harming someone when his mother's safety was threatened, and his motivation was to protect the safety of his parent, while the new face you met at the party went to jail because of selling drugs for easy money to travel to Europe.

Applying to PT

That is the mechanism you need for PT:

Read and categorize and judge at the same time.

<u>The required speed of your own mechanism</u>

You have to be able to make such a decision quickly: Once you know the elements or criteria or the standard, you would be able to categorize those facts and then make a quick judgment on which side to take and also argue on the points and analyze the facts given in a sensible manner.

<u>Finding the similarities and differences from cases in PT</u>

<u>Example: Trying to save your job in the layoff</u>

Imagine if your boss is planning to layoff ten people in your company.

Emphasizing where you graduated from

You know that your boss has preferences for graduates from Oxford, Cambridge, Harvard, and Yale University. If you are one of these graduates, emphasizing or reminding your boss that you are one of them is a way to save your job.

Emphasizing that you are versatile

If your boss dislikes people who are only good at studying and know nothing else, then you would like to emphasize that you are also good at playing sports or other extra-curricular activities. You have to explicitly and implicitly indicate that you are not a bookworm.

Example: Application for jobs

Scenario: You graduated in the same year as other violent demonstrators

If you are applying for a job position in a certain company, but you know the boss dislikes the graduates in a certain year because over half of the graduates in that year have participated in a big demonstration with violence causing extensive damage to many buildings. If you also graduated in that year, you would need to differentiate yourself from those graduates in order to be selected. If the demonstration lasts for one week, you might want to emphasize that you were out of town for two weeks when the demonstration happened, Or if you participated in this demonstration, you would like to emphasize that you only sat down on the ground peacefully without doing any destructive acts.

Applying to PT

Compare and Contrast

Finding similarities of your case to the favorable cases, and distinguishing your case from the unfavorable cases. The similarities you find in the favorable case are the same reasons why the case has become favorable to your own case, and the differences you find in the unfavorable case have to be the reason for making that case unfavorable, but your own case does not have the same problem. In other words, your case is still optimistic because it does not have that negative features.

Sequence of reading

Read the "Library" before the "File"

The Library would tell you the main rules you need to be based on, and the File would tell you the facts in the scenario. The rules would determine the standard for you to analyze and whether your client is likely to win, while which facts are more important depends on the elements of the given rules.

Example: Felony criminal record over ten years

For example, if the rule says, "the felony criminal record over 10 years of the defendant would not count in one's criminal history unless death is involved," then you would know you have to differentiate the old felony record from the recent ones; and if death is involved, you would know it counts, regardless of when it happened. If you do not know this rule before reading the File, all felony criminal records could mean the same to you.

If you work in the wrong sequence

If you read the File first, you must go back to the File again to pick relevant facts after you read the Library. Then you would eventually spend more time, which can be saved for analysis and comparison.

Create your own symbols

When you do a PT, you need to create your own symbols to be markings on the paper, and you must be familiar with those symbols, meaning doing enough practice to make sure you know what those symbols represent under time pressure.

R1, R2; F1R1, F2R1;CCR2

For myself, I would first grab the big rules and then mark R1, R2, meaning Rule 1 and Rule 2. For facts matching Rule 1, or can be F1R1, and F2R1, meaning fact 1 under rule 1, and fact 2 under rule 1; for cases for comparison, I would mark CCR2, meaning compare and contrast for rule 2.

Going up and down in your own typing area

After you have marked all symbols, when you type, there would be a lot of going up and down the keyboard screen or turning the pages of file and library. I would suggest you go up and down in your own typing area rather than the File and Library. That is because the File and the Library together may have about 15-20 pages, but your own typing version, I believe it would be approximately six to eight pages in total, and when you first start, it would be a few pages only. Hence, it would be easier for you to go up and down in your own version rather than the File and the Library.

Do not insist on finishing typing one rule before another rule.

For example, for the second page of the library, you may have R2, CCR1 and F2R1. If you insist on finishing typing R1 before you go to R2, you would have to turn over the pages of the library to find R1, F1R1 and CCR1. That would waste a lot of time and energy. Then, you would have to do the same thing for R2. I would feel dizzy and would not know what I was doing if I did it in such a dumb way.

Follow the sequence of the pages after symbols are marked.

If you follow all symbols you marked on page 2 of the library, you will type all the rules, relevant facts, cases comparison and contrast in the corresponding position of your typing version; and then go to page 3 of the library, type the facts and rules in the right spot according to what your symbols tell you. Then, after you finish typing all rules and facts in both Library and File, you can make little adjustments and analysis in your own typing version. When you adjust and analyze, you can also move around facts or rules which are placed in the wrong position, and also add words or sentences to connect paragraphs to make the context logically flow.

Read the facts of other cases only after you know what you need to compare in your own case

The facts of other cases are useful only when you know the particular facts of your own case. If you are not even clear about the facts in your case, you are more likely to be confused by reading two more other cases.

Example: Feb 2023 PT

In the Feb 2023 PT, you have to show that the defendant was not in severe pain as the defendant in another case. So what you need to compare would be: what medical treatments both are receiving; how much time has passed after the surgeries or the injuries took place.

Also, you know that the elements of the rule include the aggressiveness of the police officer, so you have to compare how the officer treated the defendant in your case, and how other detectives treat the defendant or the accused in other cases.

Outline

Most of the PT Outline should be in your head

Do not write an over-detailed outline for PT in the real exam. Do not write them on paper if it would take you more than ten minutes. The main outline should be naturally in your head, with markings on paper in the File and Library to remind yourself what to type if you have done enough practice.

Just spend five minutes in writing an outline

You might spend five minutes writing the outline in a legible manner. If there are any long quotations, write the first word and the last word on the paper, but type the whole quotation in the typing area in your laptop.

Markings would form a roadmap for you in the real exam

Instead of writing a long and detailed outline, simply make markings on the File and the Library, and then they would be a roadmap for yourself to type in the right sequence with your own analysis and thoughts.

Type your generalizations and comments and then you can include the facts later.

When you read the Library, you would know what elements in the rules you need to prove; While you read the File, you can also write or type your own generalizations and comments, such as different adjectives to generalize your impressions on these facts, and then support these adjectives by quoting the facts you find in the Library. Do not worry about possible changes you may want to make later. You can always add words or adjust your standpoint. If you later find that you want to change your standpoint but may not have enough time to find out the wrong sentence in your eight-page piece, you can simply say: as mentioned above……however, based on……that may not work because……Hence, the outcome would be…or the best choice for my client would be……instead of……

Your goal is to persuade the judge to rule in your favor

These adjectives are all aimed to persuade the judge to rule in your favor: if you are representing the defendant, you have to prove that he is likely to be innocent; if you are the Prosecutor, you have to prove that the defendant is making up facts or twisting the facts for self-serving purposes.

Attitude and Judgment

Remain doubtful of the assertions on the documents from the opposing counsel

When one of the documents in the PT is from the opposing counsel, the statements in that document would be deemed assertions by the opposing party only. That means the description would be what they claim to be true. In other words, when you analyze, you need to express doubt on these assertions. You should not say it could be falsified if you do not have enough facts to support it, but you can say something like: assuming the opposing party is telling the truth, more evidences are still required to verify that argument. The most important point is not to be conclusive on what they claim to be true.

If their assertions are inconsistent with your client's assertions……

Even if the assertions made by the opposing counsel are inconsistent with what your client said, you cannot accuse the opposing counsel of making falsified statements unless there are compelling evidences. You may argue like this: Based on the current evidence we have, my client is more likely to tell the truth because……

Pointing out missing facts

When you find missing facts or something unclear, please point that out in your writing. That is because the missing facts are likely to be intentionally made by the exam writer. They would like to see you are able to spot that. You can say something like: "An investigation would be needed to find out if……" Or

"Without knowing more about……we cannot……"

Presentation

Example: Handling an application for the Government department

Scenario:

"You are working for a government department handling applications. Applicants are required to submit records A, B and C as supporting documents. Client Sarah did not submit these supporting documents and her application was denied."

Sarah appeals and tells you the following:

"I moved three times after I came to this country. Many of my records were burnt in a fire ten years ago. Some documents are still stored in a big box, but it is placed at a high level in my storage room. With my current disability problems, I cannot access them."

Sarah's request

Sarah asks if you can grant her an exception or if there are any other alternatives. You need to get instructions from your immediate supervisor.

Question 1

Does your supervisor care about how many times she moved? Does your supervisor care about when the fire happened, or how the documents were destroyed? Does your supervisor care about where Sarah put her documents at home?

Question 2:

Are you going to repeat the whole description by Sarah to your supervisor? What does your supervisor need to know?

My advice:

You can simply tell your supervisor:

"Sarah's documents could be lost, burned in a fire or placed at a spot inaccessible to her now. Is it possible for us to grant her an exception, or can she just write a declaration and make a verbal statement under oath to verify the truthfulness of the information she claims in the application form?"

Add details after the main structure is made

If your supervisor asks you for more details, then you can throw in more facts, including moving three times, documents burned in a fire that happened five years ago, and her disability prevented her from accessing the box at a high level.

That is also what you can do in your analysis of PT after you have finished laying out the main structure of the writing.

You can generalize when you run out of time to look for the details or forget the numbers

If you are running out of time, you can just write something like "the documents are lost due to multiple times of moving, or may be burned in a fire that happened years ago, or may be placed at a spot too high for her to reach. " Even though not all details are included, the main messages are relayed.

Fact to fact comparison

Example: Shopping for a dress

Which dress to purchase

If you plan to buy a dress with pockets on the side, a belt and in a solid color for a work event, you may pick one you like at first sight and then compare that to other dresses you are going to see in the store, in order to confirm which dress to purchase.

Do not go offtrack

When pockets on the side, with a belt and in solid color are the elements, you would compare these three among the dresses available in the store. If you suddenly decide to pick a dress without a belt or in a leopard pattern, you are totally offtrack.

Belt to belt; color to color

It is also possible that some dresses have belts and in solid color but do not have any pockets. Then you would compare the belt to belt and color to color: For the belt itself, you can compare its color, material and the buckle; for the color of the dresses, you can compare if it is too dark or too light; or if it is likely to bring up energetic, healthy or frail feelings.

Comparing the positions of the pockets

For the dresses without pockets on the side, you can still compare if the pockets are instead on the front of the dresses, then your point for comparison would be the differences in the positions of the pockets; If the dress comes with a small purse with a strap, but without any pocket, then what you need to compare is the function and actual use value of the purse to that of the pocket, for example, the capacity: is the purse big enough to put in a cell phone, a wallet and a lipstick? How about the size of the pocket on the side? Maybe it is not deep enough to hold all the items mentioned above.

Cases citation

There is one PT course asking me not to cite cases inside cases, but my favorite tutor said every case has to be cited at least once. This would be your decision about whom to trust. I would prefer citing all cases in order not to lose any points. For the worst scenario, you just waste a little bit more time typing; But if you fail to cite certain cases when you are supposed to, you may receive a low PT score, which is likely to screw up your chance of passing.

Supreme Court cases

Moreover, if you see two or more cases in the library, and one of them is a Supreme Court case, then please remember to give this case more weight when there are conflicting arguments. Furthermore, it is very likely you would forget the Supreme Court case in the middle of the exam. Hence, just make a symbol that you would be able to know its meaning next to that case, then you will be aware that the ruling of this Supreme Court case controls when you type.

Do not waste time playing with the font style

Using bold or underlined or Italic words is good to emphasize the headings or important quotes, but they are only good in doing home assignments, in my opinion, but not in the real bar exam. When the time is so tight, I would not recommend you waste time playing with the font style. That is because for whatever headings you want to change to be bold, you have to highlight the words and then click the bold button. If there are twenty headings, you have to do the same act twenty times. If you accidentally delete the words you typed, you would waste time fixing it. As long as you have clear headings and a clear structure, leaving the words in "regular" fonts or making them "bold" does not really matter. If you do not agree, please ask around to see who would tell you he or she believed he or she passed the bar because of the font style. I believe you would have more failing candidates telling you that they ran out of time because of that!

A PT question in the past exam

Example: Feb 2023 PT

Be clear about what you need to prove in the PT

Any PT questions include many big points and small points. The points mentioned may not necessarily be part of your task. Please first clarify what your task is.

Here, in Feb 2023 PT, you have to show that the statements given by the defendant are voluntary, not to prove if self-defense is a valid defense. The statements about self-defense made by the defendant are part of the context, but that is not the main purpose of the writing.

Carve out the structure and fill out the details

For this PT, there are two big rules to determine whether the statements are voluntary.

What I would do is to complete the analysis of the two elements for Hughes' case, just like a regular IRAC in other essays. Then, I would use the facts from the other cases to strengthen my arguments.

There are similarities between the M case and the P case. You can point out a few points that they are similar, but that is about it. Their differences are far more than the similarities.

This is not a typing exam

Before I start typing or getting dizzy, I have to determine the direction I would go and then categorize the information I have. There is far more information than the amount we are able to type in 1.5 hours in every PT. But it does not matter to miss some points, as long as you hit the big points. Please remember this is not a typing exam but an exam for analysis. Do not expect to finish typing everything, but you have to know how to pick the most important information to type. The suggested answers disclosed on the website of the State Bar might not include all the information either, but they must have included the main rules and hit the main issue.

The last step is just typing

After you have carved out the structure and categorize the facts in the File and in the Library, the remaining time would be typing to the right position. After you have typed the data, numbers and figures, please also try to link them up in a logical manner with conjunctions or connecting sentences. That means you have to give a meaning to the numbers or figures included. For example, the defendant was questioned six hours after his surgery, meaning that he should have enough rest/he did not have enough rest.

Write the conclusion of PT before details are included

Before you fill out the details, you already know your conclusion, so you can simply write the introduction and the conclusion before the details are filled out. If time runs out, at least you will have a piece of writing that looks complete.

Sample Outline

How to use facts from Mincey (M)

Your task is to persuade the judge that the statements made by D in your case should not be deemed involuntary, so you have to find out the big differences in M's case to differentiate your case from M's case.

In the emergency room, tubes were inserted into his throat to help him breathe and through his nose into his stomach to keep him from vomiting. A catheter was inserted into his bladder. He received various drugs, and medical personnel attached a device to his arm so he could be fed intravenously. (Nothing is attached to your D)

The interview was from 8 p.m. to almost midnight, which lasts for about 3 hours. (shorter for your D)

The detective told Mincey he was under arrest for the murder of the police officer. (Your D was not told he was under arrest. Ray: "You understand you're not under arrest, right?")

M could not talk because of the tube in his mouth. He responded to the detective's questions by writing answers on paper. (Your D was able to talk clearly).

M repeatedly asked for the interrogation to cease. M complained to the detective that the pain in his leg was unbearable. (Your D was not in severe pain, and he was eager to talk.) Some of M's written responses were incoherent and he looked confused and unable to think clearly about the events at his apartment or about the interrogation. (Your D's mind was clear.)

The detective ceased the interrogation only during the intervals when M lost consciousness or received medical treatment and, after each such interruption, returned relentlessly to his task. (The detective stopped when he had medical procedures.) The statements at issue were thus the result of virtually continuous questioning of a seriously and painfully wounded man on the edge of consciousness. (Your D was injured, but he was conscious.)

The Supreme Court concluded M's statements were not the product of his free and rational choice. "To the contrary, the undisputed evidence makes clear that Mincey wanted not to answer Detective Just. But Mincey was weakened by pain and shock, isolated from family, friends, and legal counsel, and barely conscious, and his will was simply overborne. Due process of law requires that statements obtained as these were cannot be used in any way against a defendant at his trial."

(Your D was not weakened by pain and shock, and his will was not overborne.)

How to use facts from Perdomo(P)

Your task is to persuade the judge that the statements made by D in your case should not be deemed involuntary, so you have to show that your D's situation was similar to that of P, as P's statements are deemed voluntary.

D argued that the inculpatory statements he made were made to officers who interrogated him in the intensive care unit of the hospital while he was recovering from surgery and heavily sedated with narcotic pain medications. D suffered severe traumatic injuries to his chest area. Several of his ribs were fractured. He underwent emergency surgery to remove his spleen. He also had some bleeding in his brain. (Your D was also injured.)

Four days after thc accident and the surgery, medical personnel in the intensive care unit of the hospital granted permission for the officer to speak to D but directed the officers to keep it brief. (Your D was interviewed two hours after his surgery.)

D was lying flat on his bed. He was in obvious pain. (Your D was sitting upright, not sedated.) D had received his last pain medication 5.5 hours earlier, meaning he might feel pain again when the medication effect was over. He was still connected to intravenous solutions and monitors. (Your D did not have tubes in his mouth and was able to speak freely.)

D's speech was slow and deliberate but not slurred or overly raspy from the intubation.

The Officers' questions were slow, subdued and deliberate.

The interview with numerous pauses, lasted approximately 20 minutes.

D was not interrogated within hours of his injuries and was not interrogated only a few hours after receiving medical treatment.

The officers were not permitted to interview D until four days after D's surgery. Hospital personnel did not permit the conversation to take place until "they determined he was 'alert,' 'oriented,' and could 'obey commands,' as indicated by his medical chart." HIs respirator was removed the day before the interview.

The officers' tone was conversational and not threatening. One of the subjects discussed was how supportive and attentive D's mother had been. D expressed gratitude for his recovery. He asked the officers questions regarding his friends' conditions. The officers wish D good luck and a speedy recovery.

Nothing on the tape shows D's thinking was impaired by the medications. Each of D's answers is appropriate to the question asked. In some instances, his answers were detailed. For example, when asked the name of the security company for which they all worked, D stated the name of the officers, spelled out the company name several times and even recited the company's telephone number. D was even alert enough to attempt to deceive the officers. He initially told the officers the night of the accident that he had been driving his mother's Nissan alone, but later, he acknowledged being with Rodriguez and Quinonez in Quinonez's mother's Honda. D did not express distress or any unwillingness to speak to the officers.

The record is devoid of any suggestion the officers resorted to physical or psychological pressure to elicit statements from D.

Conclusion:

Absent some indication of coercive police activity, an admission or confession cannot be deemed involuntary within the Due Process Clause of the Fourteenth Amendment.

<u>Notes for understanding</u>

<u>Task:</u>

Draft an oral argument in opposition to suppression of the statement, which is claimed to be "not voluntary."

<u>Basic information:</u>

Defendant (D): Sebastian Hughes

Victim (V): Peter Gault (fatally stabbed)

Occasion: During a dispute over a Corvette car engine

Defendant's assertion: he acted in self-defense

Prosecutor's strongest point: a recorded statement the Defendant made to detectives while he was in the hospital recovering from a stab wound inflicted by his uncle.

<u>Big Rule:</u>

Library P.2; the 4th paragraph:

"A statement is involuntary if it is not the product of 'a rational intellect and free will." (Mincey)

"The question posed by the Due Process Clause in cases of claimed psychological coercion is whether the influences brought to bear upon the accused were such as to overbear petitioner's will to resist and bring about confessions not freely self-determined."

<u>Facts matching the rules</u>

Defense counsel stated in the transcript of the pretrial hearing:

"At the time of his questioning, Defendant was not sufficiently lucid, and the coercive surrounding circumstances of the questioning were such that, under the United States Supreme Court's Mincey v. Arizona, his statement was not the result of a rational intellect and free will. The defendant was at the complete mercy of the detectives because he was in physical shock from being stabbed in the lung and in mental shock from being involved in the death of his uncle."

Perdomo:

the D's maturity, education and health, and the details of the interrogation

Perdomo: the D was able to name the company he worked for and recite its telephone number from memory

D- educated, knowledgeable and mature

Here, D-more likely to have been able to understand the nature of the questioning and to govern themselves in a voluntary manner.

-D went to the University of Columbia for two years.

The D here says he feared for his mother's safety, and the V had a short temper and was hot-headed.

He knows that self-defense is his only way out.

Forget to mention the knife.

the facts of the interrogation on August 22, 2022

Mincey: three hours; intense

Perdomo: 20 minutes.

The length of time period: the D was questioned from 7:50 pm to 8:20 pm, including a short break for medical care, which is less than 30 minutes.

Is it a reasonable time?

Mincey- whether the interview was conducted a reasonable time after the D received treatment. The D was being interviewed mere hours after intensive surgery.

Here, D was interviewed two hours after his surgery. He was sitting upright, not sedated.

The physical conditions of D:

Mincey: the D had a tube in his mouth and could not speak at all; he wrote on a piece of paper; his responses were incoherent.

Perdomo: the D suffered from bleeding in his brain and was in "obvious pain" at the time of questioning

Here, D's Health condition - strong

The D did not have tubes in his mouth and was able to speak freely. A medical professional came in to take his blood, which was not akin to the active sedation and treatment of the accused in Mincey.

D's mental condition-good memory

D clearly explained V's unreasonable anger

Background: V wanted to know the whereabouts of a Corvette engine he had been storing in the garage of D's mom's house. D had sold the engine for $800 several months ago and told him about the sale at that time. D reminded V that V had sold the engine to D, and V became angry.

D clearly explained why D went to the house.

What happened on the day of the incident:

"I heard my mom crying in the background. I feared for her safety because Peter had a short temper, and he was hot-headed when it came to her."

What D did to protect himself in case of emergency: (D explained that before the break)

"I stopped at my work locker on my way out and placed an eight-inch wrench in my shirt pocket as protection." (But he did not mention the knife)

D's memory was clear about what happened.

D tried to show that his mom tried to stop the fighting between D and D, and V was aggressive in the fight, and D also tried to claim that he was not armed:

"My mom stood between Peter and me, crying her eyes out, trying to keep us separate. She grabbed the wrench from my pocket. I guess to make sure I didn't use it on Peter."

"Peter knocks me to the ground. He pushed my mom a couple of times grabbed the wrench from my mom and tried to hit me with it. At some point, Peter either dropped the wrench or threw it at me."

D tried to show that he has no choice besides stabbing V in order to protect his own life:

"(Peter) kicked me real hard on the right side of my forehead. I wound up on the ground between the van and the truck. He had the wrench in his hand."

"I thought he was going to grab a knife or tool from the van. So I pulled my knife from my boot."

"He lunged at me, saying 'I'm gonna kill you,' and that's when I stabbed him with my knife."

D explained how he got the knife:

"I placed a big knife in my boot, underneath my pant leg."

D portrayed himself as a victim:

"I realized I had been stabbed only when I saw blood all over myself and could not breathe."

"This was all self-defense, man."

D emphasized that he was telling the truth and tried to persuade the detective to trust him:

"You can give me a lie detector test, or check my phone records, or talk to my family to confirm the truth I'm telling you."

Location

Perdomo: also at the hospital

Location: Here, D- in his hospital bed;

D was injured in the course of murdering Gault.

Coerciveness:

Mincey - D repeatedly asked for the questioning to stop. He invoked his right to counsel several times. The officer kept pushing for three hours. The D actually lost consciousness many times during the interrogation. The statements at issue were found to be the result of relentless interrogation of a painfully and seriously wounded man and were deemed coercive and involuntary.

Here, D said, "I've got tubes in both my lungs, and I'm a little drugged up, but yeah, I can speak."

The D was clearly lucid, and he spoke deliberately. He was able to provide details. He discussed his recollection of how his mother and uncle acted and spoke.

D's possible argument.

D may argue that it was coercive because the police called the hospital about three or four times throughout the day to see if D was well enough to speak with the police. However, the detective asked, and D had no hesitation or reluctance at all.

Moreover, D may also claim that even D did not clearly say no, a patient after surgery definitely needed rest. Detective Ray also described how he was at that moment: "Mr. Hughes is shirtless and lying down kind of in a quasi-seated position with his back kind of at maybe a 45-degree angle in his bed in his room. Mr. Hughes has redness or an abrasion on his forehead and a stab wound on his right side near the right chest area under the armpit." The description matches a typical "patient" in the hospital, and all doctors are likely to say this patient needs rest.

When the hospital staff came into he room to provide medical care, the officers stopped immediately.

Perdomo: the D wanted to talk to the officers, discussing his gratefulness for being OK.

Mincey: The accused had clearly not wanted the interview to take place, requesting many times for the interview to end. Hence, there is a strong likelihood that any statement they made implicating themselves was not voluntary.

Here, D expresses his hope that he wants the detectives to stay - "you guys aren't leaving, are you?" D repeatedly added details and explanations. D did not try to end the interview.

Who dominated the conversation: D

D is speaking clearly, using complete sentences with grammar, and is able to provide follow-up details and further explain the meaning and his intent.

Officers: not aggressive, not threatening; causal in tone; the style of questions are open-ended; did not cut D off; allowed D to answer in a comfortable manner.

Officers did not ask with any assumptions or biases:

Ray: "We need to ask you some questions about what happened. You understand you're not under arrest, right?"

Just part of the police procedures:

Ray: "We need to interview you. Our job is to come in when someone passes away. We weren't there. We don't know what happened."

Asking for permission for tape recording.

"If it's okay, we are going to tape-record our interview." D also agrees.

Considerate and not pushing:

"…but for now, I think we have enough. You've been generous with your time, and we need to let you rest."

Polite: tell him to enjoy the game of the University of Columbia

Compare: Perdomo - the Columbia Supreme Court held the confession to be voluntary.

Mincey: a relentless series of questions posed at an accused

Conclusion:

The interrogation was a brief and reasonable interview for a person who was relaxing after surgery. There is a break in between, and also without coercive questions or behaviors. The situation was akin to the permissible interrogation in Perdomo and distinguishable from Mincey.

Based on the foregoing reasons, I request the Court to deny the defendant's motion to exclude the statement as involuntary.

Sample writing

May it please the court, your honor,

I am opposing the suppression of the recorded statements defendant Sebastian Hughes made to detectives while he was in the hospital. Hughes claimed the statements to be "not voluntary." But Hughes' assertion is contrary to the definition of involuntary statements, which is going to be discussed below.

An involuntary statement

"A statement is involuntary if it is not the product of 'a rational intellect and free will." (Mincey). "The question posed by the Due Process Clause in cases of claimed psychological coercion is whether the influences brought to bear upon the accused were such as to overbear petitioner's will to resist and bring about confessions not freely self-determined."

Here, whether Hughes answered the questions by detective Ray or disclosed any details out of a rational intellect and free will matters.

Two main elements have to be considered, according to Perdomo: (1) the D's maturity, education and health, and (2) the details of the interrogation.

the D's maturity, education and health

Education

Here, Hughes is more likely to have been able to understand the nature of the questioning and to govern themselves in a voluntary manner. In terms of education level, he went to the University of Columbia for two years. He may not have graduated, but two years in college means he has a certain level of ability in comprehension, reading, writing, and listening.

As noted in his conversation with Detective Ray, he speaks in complete sentences. He expressed his thoughts clearly. Hughes clearly explained V's unreasonable anger: V wanted to know the whereabouts of a Corvette engine he had been storing in the garage of Hughes' mom's house. Hughes had sold the engine for $800 several months ago and told him about the sale at that time. Hughes reminded V that V had sold the engine to Hughes, and V became angry.

Thus, Hughes appears to be an educated person with enough ability to express himself and recall what happened.

Maturity

Hughes also considered his mother's safety before the incident happened.

Here, Hughes clearly explained why Hughes went to the house. Hughes says he feared for his mother's safety, and the V had a short temper and was hot-headed. He claims that he acted in self-defense when he fatally stabbed Peter Gault during a dispute over a Corvette car engine, while self-defense could be his only way out.

Thus, Hughes appears to be mature enough.

Health

The physical conditions of D

In Mincey: the defendant had a tube in his mouth and could not speak at all; he wrote on a piece of paper; his responses were incoherent; "At the time of his questioning, Defendant was not sufficiently lucid, and the coercive surrounding circumstances of the questioning were such that, under the United States Supreme Court's Mincey v. Arizona, his statement was not the result of a rational intellect and free will. The defendant was at the complete mercy of the detectives because he was in physical shock from being stabbed in the lung and in mental shock from being involved in the death of his uncle." (Mincey) "In the emergency room, tubes were inserted into his throat to help him breathe, and through his nose into his stomach to keep him from vomiting. A catheter was inserted into his bladder. He received various drugs, and medical personnel attached a device to his arm so he could be fed intravenously." (Id.) Whoever with such a weak condition would like to end the questioning as soon as possible.

In Perdomo: the D suffered from bleeding in his brain and was in "obvious pain" at the time of questioning. D had received his last pain medication 5.5 hours earlier, meaning he might feel pain again when the medication effect was over. He was still connected to intravenous solutions and monitors.

However, Hughes did not have tubes in his mouth and was able to speak freely. He has "redness or an abrasion on his forehead, and a stab wound on his right side near the right chest area under the armpit," but that does not affect his ability to speak. If he felt

uncomfortable answering any questions, he could simply say so, but he chose not to do so. According to Ray, Hughes is "shirtless and lying down kind of in a quasi-seated position with his back kind of at maybe a 45-degree angle in his bed in his room." This appears to be a comfortable posture.

Thus, Hughes' physical condition appears to be strong enough for him to speak.

Hughes' mental condition - good memory

In Mincey, some of the D's written responses were incoherent, and he looked confused and unable to think clearly about the events at his apartment or about the interrogation. When a person is unclear in thinking, it would be unfair to have his statements admitted to be evidence against himself.

However, in Perdomo, the D's thinking does not appear to be impaired by the medications. He was able to name the security company he worked for, able to spell out the company name several times and even able to recite its telephone number from his memory.

Hughes' mental state is similar to that of P. Hughes has a clear mind and a good memory. For example, Hughes explained clearly what he D did to protect himself in case of emergency: "I stopped at my work locker on my way out and placed an eight-inch wrench in my shirt pocket as protection."

Hughes also tried to show that his mom tried to stop the fighting between Hughes and V, and V was aggressive in the fight. And Hughes also tried to claim that he was not armed: "My mom stood between Peter and me, crying her eyes out trying to keep us separate. She grabbed the wrench from my pocket. I guess to make sure I didn't use it on Peter." Also, "Peter knocks me to the ground. He pushed my mom a couple of times and, grabbed the wrench from my mom and tried to hit me with it. At some point, Peter either dropped the wrench or threw it at me."

Hughes also tries to show that he has no choice besides stabbing V in order to protect his own life. Regardless of its truthfulness, he explained that clearly: "(Peter) kicked me real hard on the right side of my forehead. I wound up on the ground between the van and the truck. He had the wrench in his hand."

He failed to explain where the knife comes from, but that is not necessarily related to his ability to recall. "I thought he was going to grab a knife or tool from the van. So I pulled my knife from my boot." He may not want to mention that he hid a knife in his boot to give the detective the wrong impression that he is so innocent.

Hughes tried to portray himself as a victim for the whole time:

"I realized I had been stabbed only when I saw blood all over myself and could not breathe," Hughes said. "This was all self-defense, man." Regardless of the truthfulness of the statements, Hughes was able to make a statement with a consistent standpoint, which is claiming self-defense.

Hughes emphasized that he was telling the truth and tried to persuade the detective to trust him. "You can give me a lie detector test, or check my phone records, or talk to my family to confirm the truth I'm telling you." Regardless of its truthfulness, the message is expressed in an affirmative tone, which indicates a willingness to make the statement. Moreover, he appears to have a clear mind, pointing out a list of what the police can do to confirm if he is telling the truth.

The details of the interrogation

The facts of the interrogation on August 22, 2022, show that the time length is moderate, the timing is appropriate, and he is not coerced to talk to the detectives.

Time length

In terms of the amount of time, Hughes was questioned for less than ——- minutes. Hughes was questioned from 7:50 pm to ——-pm. Including a short break for medical care, so it is less than 30 minutes. Perdomo is interviewed for about 20 minutes, and the interview has numerous pauses. And Mincey was being interviewed for about three hours. Approximately 20 to 30 minutes would be deemed a moderate amount of time, while Mincey's three-hour interrogation is deemed "involuntary" in nature.

Thus, the time length that Hughes was being questioned looks moderate. As such, Hughes is educated, mature, and healthy enough to have answered the questions by detective Ray out of a rational intellect and free will.

All conditions set forth for the interrogation matter to determine the nature of voluntariness of Hughes when he answers the questions or makes the verbal statements.

Is it a reasonable timing?

In Mincey, the D was being interviewed mere hours after intensive surgery. In Perdomo, D had received his last pain medication 5.5 hours earlier, meaning he might feel pain again when the medication effect was over. He was still connected to intravenous solutions and monitors. D's speech was slow and deliberate but not slurred or overly raspy from the intubation. (Perdomo)

But here, Hughes was interviewed two hours after his surgery. He was sitting upright, not sedated. "Hughes is shirtless and lying down kind of in a quasi-seated position with his back kind of at maybe a 45-degree angle in his bed in his room."

Location

In terms of location, the defendants in the instant case and the two other cases are all in the hospital. Here, Hughes was injured in the course of murdering Gault, so he stays in the hospital while Perdomo and Mincey are also in the hospital.

Coerciveness:

In Mincey, D repeatedly asked for the questioning to stop, and he invoked his right to counsel several times. The officer kept pushing for three hours. The D actually lost consciousness many times during the interrogation. The detective did not cease the interrogation until M lost consciousness. The inhumane torture did not stop until it had to be stopped because questioning was impossible for an unconscious person. The lack of care, respect or empathy for a patient is indicative of the nature of coercion and involuntariness.

However, Hughes was clearly lucid and he spoke deliberately. He was able to provide details. He discussed his recollection of how his mother and uncle acted and spoke, even though he had surgery a while ago. "I've got tubes in both my lungs, and I'm a little drugged up, but yeah, I can speak."

Hughes' possible argument

Hughes may argue that it was coercive because the police called the hospital about three or four times throughout the day to see if D was well enough to spcak with the police. However, the detective has asked Hughes if he can speak and Hughes had no hesitation or reluctance at all.

Moreover, Hughes may also claim that even though D did not clearly say no, a patient after surgery definitely needed rest. Detective Ray also described how he was at that moment: "Mr. Hughes is shirtless and lying down kind of in a quasi-seated position with his back kind of at maybe a 45-degree angle in his bed in his room. Mr. Hughes has redness or abrasion on his forehead and a stab wound on his right side near the right chest area under the armpit." The description matches a typical "patient" in the hospital, and all doctors are likely to say this patient needs rest.

During the interview, the police officer also prioritizes Hughes' medical needs on top of completing the interrogation. When the hospital staff came into he room to provide medical care, the officers stopped immediately.

When compared to Mincey, the detectives who interviewed Hughes are more respectful and caring. The Supreme Court concluded M's statements were not the product of his free and rational choice. "To the contrary, the undisputed evidence makes clear that Mincey wanted not to answer Detective Just. But Mincey was weakened by pain and shock, isolated from family, friends, and legal counsel, and barely conscious, and his will was simply overborne. Due process of law requires that statements obtained as these were cannot be used in any way against a defendant at his trial."

In contrast, Hughes was weakened by pain, but his will was not overborne. Hughes, in fact, agreed to talk. After the break of drawing blood, Hughes told Detective Ray that the victim lunged at him on the day of the incident, and the victim told Hughes that "I'm gonna kill you," and then Hughes said: "that is when I stabbed him with my knife." Obviously, Hughes made this statement of confession of killing the victim voluntarily, even though he tried to claim self-defense. As such, Hughes is not coerced into talking.

Eagerness to continue to talk

In Mincey, the accused had clearly not wanted the interview to take place, requesting many times for the interview to end. Hence, there is a strong likelihood that any statement they made implicating themselves was not voluntary.

However, in Perdomo, the D wanted to talk to the officers, discussing his gratefulness at his condition. That means P was not submissive to the detective.

Perdomo's situation is analogical to that of H. Hughes expresses his hope that he wants the detectives to stay for their conversation. "You guys aren't leaving, are you?" Hughes repeatedly added details and explanations. Hughes did not try to end the interview. He appears to be eager to contribute more information.

Hence, Hughes' eagerness to talk does not indicate any involuntariness.

Who dominated the conversation?

In Mincey, a relentless series of questions are posed to the accused. The police officer dominated the conversation in Mincey. The detective told Mincey he was under arrest for the murder of the police officer.

In Perdomo, the officers' tone was conversational and not threatening. The Officers 'questions were slow, subdued and deliberate. One of the subjects discussed was how supportive and attentive D's mother had been. D expressed gratitude for his recovery. That shows a friendly atmosphere. He asked the officers questions regarding his friends' conditions. The officers wish D good luck and a speedy recovery.

Here, Hughes dominated thc conversation between Hughes and Detective Ray. As mentioned above, Hughes is speaking clearly, using complete sentences; he is also able to provide follow-up details and further explain the meaning and his intent. Detective Ray makes sure Hughes realizes that he is not under arrest. " You understand you're not under arrest, right?"

On the other hand, the police detectives are not aggressive and not threatening; they are very causal in tone; the style of their questions is open-ended; they do not cut Hughes off; they allow Hughes to answer in a comfortable manner.

The officers were neutral and non-accusatory in the style of questions. They did not ask Hughes questions with any assumptions or biases. "We need to ask you some questions about what happened. You understand you're not under arrest, right?" Ray also describes the interrogation as merely part of the police procedures. "We need to interview you. Our job is to come in when someone passes away. We weren't there. We don't know what happened."

Moreover, Ray asked for H's permission before the questioning, which shows courtesy; Ray also asked for permission for tape recording, which shows respect. "If it's okay, we are going to tape-record our interview." D also agrees. Ray is being considerate of Hughes. "...but for now, I think we have enough. You've been generous with your time, and we need to let you rest." At the end of the interview, Ray also politely tells him to enjoy the game of the University of Columbia. Even though this statement may not be genuine from the bottom of his heart, the neutrality of the tone of questioning and the polite manner of the officers indicate the lack of coercion.

Furthermore, Hughes also suggested the detective let him take a lie detector test, check his phone records, or talk to his family if the detective does not believe him. Regardless of the truthfulness of what he claimed to be true, he mentioned the above possible ways to test his words on his own initiative without being prompted by the police detective. When compared to making a response to a propounding question or merely a yes or no answer, these suggestions coming from his own mouth appear to be made voluntarily. Moreover, the police detectives never tried to interject one words or interrupt once when Hughcs talked about his suggestions to verify the truthfulness of his words.

Hence, Hughes dominated the conversation instead of the detectives, which also reinforces the nature of voluntariness in the verbal statements made by Hughes.

Conclusion

Although there is something common between Mincey and Perdomo, the commonalities are only limited to a few points: No family members or friends were with the defendant or the accused; tubes were still attached to the body of the defendant or the accused; narcotic pain medications is received by the defendant or the accused; the defendant or the accused appeared to be in pain; the defendant or the accused appeared to still be under the influence of the narcotic pain medication. The only similarity between M and Hughes is probably both of them have no friends or family members around the defendant. According to Perdomo, "no single factor is dispositive," so Hughes cannot claim that his statements are not voluntary just because Hughes was alone, just like M, when he talked to the detectives.

The nature of involuntariness is very apparent in Mincey: The accused is being questioned a few hours before midnight when he is supposed to rest, and he is also told he is under arrest, implying that he had no choice in not answering the question. When he cannot even talk because of the tube, he has to write on paper. He requests stopping the interrogation, but the police officer does not seem to care about his physical condition and only stops when he loses consciousness. The way the detectives handled the questioning was more like promptly getting their job done by urging Mincey to admit his guilt rather than neutrally asking him questions. The whole process of the interrogation for Mincey is inhumane, disrespectful and also unprofessional.

On the contrary, the interrogation of Hughes was a brief and reasonable interview for a person who was relaxing after surgery. There was also a break in between, and there were no coercive questions or behaviors. The situation was akin to the permissible interrogation in Perdomo, whose statements are deemed voluntary, and distinguishable from Mincey, whose statements are deemed involuntary. The relatively strong physical and mental conditions of Hughes, the neutral nature of the questions raised by the detectives and their politeness show that Hughes' answers and statements he made are the product of a rational intellect and free will, and apparently, his free will is not overborne.

Based on the foregoing reasons, I request the Court to deny the defendant's motion to exclude the statement as involuntary.

Let's practice a brand-new PT

Performance Test (PT) practice: Joseph's story

Task Memo

Erica is your client. The school of your client's son Joseph issued a warning letter to him two days ago when about half of the school year was gone. The letter was based on his academic performance, discipline, and other activities. A warning letter is a kind of disciplinary action which could eventually lead to expulsion by the school.

As the attorney of Erica, please write a reply letter to rebut or challenge the accusations.

Here are the bullet points extracted from the warning letter issued by the school:

(In the real exam, you have to extract the useful information by yourself.)

-Joseph always talks loud in the Mathematics class.

-Joseph did not stop playing ping pong immediately, at least once when recess time was over. He also reported to the class late because of that.

-Joseph scores below 60 in the mid-term exam in two subjects in this semester.

-Joseph made many grammatical mistakes in the writing class, and his average score so far is 55, while the passing score is 60.

-Joseph does not practice playing his violin in his music class.

-Joseph was accused of tossing garbage on the ground of the basketball court by Catherine, his classmate. It happened ten days from the day the warning letter was issued.

-Joseph refused to join the singing contest with the rest of the class two months ago.

-Joseph never participates in any contests outside the school on behalf of the school.

File: The story about Joseph

The elementary school that Erica's son Joseph is going to just issued him a warning letter, indicating his bad behaviors at school, lack of discipline, and below-average scores in writing class, science class, and music class. His teacher also claims that he makes noises in the Mathematics class.

This is how one teacher told Erica how bad Joseph is:

“Joseph is naughty, disobedient, and not doing well in academic performances. Other classmates such as Anna, Barbara and Monica are all better than Joseph: Anna has a high score in writing; Barbara won a science contest on behalf of the school at the beginning of this year; Monica plays the violin very well.

Furthermore, Joseph always talks loudly in the Mathematics class.

Last year, another student named Oscar also talked loud in the class. He had no improvement after two warning letters were issued to him by the school. He was expelled from our school eventually when the third warning letter was issued.”

<u>Question: What is the problem here?</u>

<u>Answer: It is unclear what Joseph has done wrong exactly.</u>

What is the standard of the school regarding naughtiness? What rules does Joseph fail to comply with? What is the minimum score Joseph is required to achieve in order to have a good academic standing?

<u>*Instruction 1: You have to discuss the instant case before other cases</u>

What is the point of bringing up Anna, Barbara and Monica by the teacher? Does it mean every student has to win a contest? Every student needs to play a musical instrument. What is the definition of talking loud? Do they have a measurement device? Is the situation of Oscar exactly the same as Joseph’s? As the mother of Joseph, Erica does not know anything about Oscar, who he is it, and what grade he is in. The whole description made Erica puzzled, frustrated and angry. Is Erica's son supposed to be a copy of Anna, Barbara and Monica?

Library: 15 School rules

*Instruction: Find out the rules which are going to help your arguments. (Some rules look "relevant" but they are just "about" the task you are working on, but you do not really need them to complete your writing.)

Here are the rules of the school:

The school starts at 8:15am and ends at 3:15p.m. Students are supposed to come on time.

No unnecessary conversations are allowed in all classes. All class exercises are due at the end of the classes.

Each teacher is assigned to teach no more than two subjects.

Every recess lasts for 15 minutes. When the bell for the end of the recess time rings, all playing activities have to be stopped immediately, and the students have to go back to the classroom to attend the classes scheduled. If students come to the class later than the teacher of that particular class, the students would be deemed "late" to the class, and such tardinesses would be recorded in the school record of the students.

The average scores for all subjects, ten in total, must be over 60 in order to be regarded as completing and passing that school year.

Students with below-average scores or discipline issues would be placed on academic probation.

Joining extra-curricular activities or in-school contests would be a plus for the evaluation of student performances or future applications for scholarships. The school has a singing contest, a modern dance contest, a judo contest, etc.

Every student must learn how to play one musical instrument, which could be piano, violin, or saxophone. The waiting period for any particular instrument cannot exceed six months. If any instrument is unavailable for a student for any reason, the student has to change to learn another one within 6 months, even though that instrument is less preferable to the student.

For students who score below passing scores would be referred to a special tutoring class after school, and participation would be mandatory for students on probation.

The school has five surveillance cameras in total, but there are still many blind spots on campus, and the videos would be retained for seven days only, unless there are special reasons, such as requests by the police officers.

Dishonest behaviors would be penalized, including negative comments on one's school record or receiving a warning letter. Dishonest behaviors include cheating on exams, plagiarism in homework assignments, or lying to teachers, etc.

The lack of discipline, such as tardiness, or failure to comply with the school rules by the students, would also result in receiving warning letters.

A student receiving the first warning letter would be placed on the list of probation, and since then, the school teachers would start closely monitoring him or her. He or she would not be taken out of the list unless great improvement is made. Students with three or more warning letters would be expelled from the school.

Students or their parents who do not agree with the allegations made in the warning letters must submit a responding letter for appeal within 90 days after the letters are issued.

The school values all good conducts of students.

File: Joseph's responses

He always tries to help other students in Mathematics class when they do not know how to answer the questions in the class exercises.

He always stops playing ping pong when the bell for the end of the recess rings, but there was one time his ball was lost. He spent five minutes looking for the ball. When he was found carrying the ping pong and the bat five minutes after the end of the recess, he was accused of "still playing" the ping pong.

He scores below 60 in English writing and Music classes only. His score in Music is low because he does not participate in the performance of musical instrument.

He scores the second highest in class in Science and scores the highest in Mathematics among the whole class.

He chooses to learn saxophone at the beginning of the school year, but the school does not have enough subsidies for the musical instruments, saxophone and piano. If he insists on learning saxophone, he is told that he has to pay for his own saxophone, but he cannot afford it. He is still hoping the subsidies are going to increase soon so he can learn playing the saxophone. He still has two months left in the permitted waiting period.

"Tossing cans" incident:

Joseph was in fact, carrying a big bag of recycled cans to the bin at the entrance of the campus but he dropped some cans on the ground because the bag was too big and it was not tightly closed. He came back to the spot where he dropped the cans ten minutes later, but he did not notice anyone around him when he picked up the cans from the ground.

Non-participation in the singing contest:

He did not join the singing contest because he started having symptoms of Covid.

Tutoring class for English writing

He is also interested in joining the tutoring class for English writing but he never receives any notices from the school. He is eager to join and wants to improve his writing skills.

File: Other supplementary facts

-Joseph has the highest score in Mathematics: not only the highest in his own academic record, but his score is also the highest among all students in the class.

-There are thirty students in a class, but only one teacher. A lot of times, the teacher is unable to answer the questions for most students.

-There are ten subjects in total, including drawing, dancing, music, foreign language, physical education, science, English writing, sociology, Mathematics, sewing or carpentry, etc.

-There are five more months before the end of the school year.

-The student who accused Joseph of tossing garbage is Catherine, who does not get along with Joseph in class well, mainly because of competing for a locker. Catherine does not like her locker positioned at the bottom. One time, she suggested exchanging her locker with Joseph, but Joseph declined her request.

-The school rules do not require mandatory participation in any contests held by the school but encourage participation to strength the sense of unity among the students.

-For contests outside of the school, the school representatives have to be chosen by the principal, and the teachers would make at least two recommendations to the principal.

-Barbara has the highest score in Science among all students.

-Two months ago, Joseph had symptoms of Covid for a week but was found negative in the test of Covid eventually.

-Anna once participated in a tutoring class for writing for about a year.

-Joseph has been studying at this school for two years, and he never comes late.

-Oscar cheated a few times on the school exams and also did plagiarism in his school assignments.

-There are two big and vacant classrooms on campus mainly used for storage.

Outline

*Instruction 2: Categorize the problems of Joseph to make the presentation more organized

Academic performances

Joseph made many grammatical mistakes in the writing class, and his average score so far is 55, five points below the passing score.

Joseph scores below 60 in the mid-term examination of two subjects.

Discipline

Joseph was being accused of "tossing garbage" on the ground of the basketball court by Catherine, another student.

One time, Joseph did not go back to class immediately after recess time was over because he was looking for his lost ball. He also reported to the class late because of that.

Joseph always talks loudly in the Mathematics class because he tries to show other students how to do the in-class exercises in Mathematics.

Musical instruments

Joseph does not practice playing violin in his music class.

Contests (Inside and outside of the school)

Joseph refused to join the singing contest with the rest of the class two months ago.

Joseph never participates in the outside-school contests as a school representative.

Sample Writing

*Instruction 3: When there are missing facts or any unknowns, simply point that out. They are not going to affect your ability to do the analysis.

Academic performances

Writing deficiency

Students whose writing scores are below 60 would be referred to a special tutoring class, and participation is mandatory.

Here, Joseph made many grammatical mistakes in the writing class, and his average score so far is 55, five points below the passing score. Joseph would be glad to be given a chance to join the mandatory tutoring class, but he has never received any notice of the class schedule or information about procedures explaining how to sign up for it. The rule says the students would be "referred to a special tutoring class," but the school fails to do anything to refer Joseph. Apparently, that would be the obligation of the school and not the fault of Joseph.

Moreover, the school is a place for students to learn, and they do not need to be perfect to attend the school. The school cannot just accept smart students to polish its reputation and eliminate the students who fall behind. As long as they do not give up learning, there are opportunities for all students to improve, and that is what education means. Simply expelling or threatening to expel a student by issuing a warning letter violates the goal of promoting education.

Furthermore, a teacher working for the school would not be assigned to teach more than two subjects, showing that the teachers themselves may not be good at all subjects or the school would rather have them be more specialized in some subjects. When the teachers need to focus on two subjects to perform well, how can the school expect a student to be doing well in all subjects?

Joseph vs. Anna

If Joseph is given a chance to attend such a tutoring class, it is also possible that he will attain high scores in his writing in the future. Anna, his classmate, has had high scores in writing recently, but in the past, she also attended a special tutoring class for one year. Given a special training session, Anna has already made great improvements in her writing. Joseph also needs this opportunity, and he has been waiting for it. The school cannot deprive him of the opportunity to improve his writing, and also issue him a warning letter, and merely move him one step closer to being expelled.

Thus, what Joesph really needs is assistance, not disciplinary action or penalty.

Average score

There are ten subjects in total, and the school requires an average of 60 among all subjects.

Here, Joseph scores below 60 in the mid-term examination of two subjects, while he gets high scores in Mathematics and Science. He gets the highest score in Mathematics among the class, and the second highest score in Science. It is unclear about his scores in other subjects, such as dancing or carpentry. But since his scores in the subjects he is good at are the highest and the second highest, respectively in class, his high score appears to be sufficient to offset his low score.

Moreover, there is much time left beforc the end of the school year, and a lot of progress could be made in the coming five months. He is very likely to attain an average of above 60 at the end of the school year based on his hardworking nature of his personality, which is shown on other subjects. It would be too early to worry that Joseph might not be able to get an average of 60 when only half of the semester is gone.

Thus, it would be too early to determine if Joseph would continue to have deficiencies in his academic standing. There is still a good chance for him to achieve 60 or above in his average score.

Discipline

Disruptive behaviors may lead to disciplinary actions, such as issuing a warning letter, and three or more warning letters may lead to expulsion by the school.

Disruptive behaviors

Accusation #1 -Tossing garbage

Tossing garbage on the ground can be deemed a disruptive behavior.

Here, Joseph was being accused of tossing garbage on the ground of the basketball court by another student. But that was not the truth. He was, in fact, carrying a big bag of recycled cans to the bin at the entrance of the campus, but he dropped some cans on the ground because the bag was too big and it was not tightly closed. There is a huge difference between dropping cans and tossing garbage, but his classmate Catherine fails to recognize it and makes a wrong accusation about Joseph.

In fact, Joseph came back to the spot where he dropped the cans ten minutes later. He did not notice anyone around him when he picked up the cans from the ground. Apparently, Catherine, who made the wrong accusation, saw only part of the truth.

Moreover, Catherine does not get along well with Joseph in class, mainly because of competing for a locker at a more convenient position. Catherine does not like her locker placed at the bottom, and she suggests switching her locker with Joseph's, but Joseph declines her request. Joseph believes that is the reason Catherine dislikes him, and hence, she starts having bias towards him. As such, Catherine's accusation is untrustworthy.

Other evidence could be more helpful than the testimony of such a biased "witness." The school can simply review the surveillance videos. It is unclear whether any surveillance cameras are installed on the basketball court or if the angle of the camera is just right to show how the incident happened. Even if the basketball court has the camera installed at the right position, the videos are likely to be deleted because the videos are usually retained for only seven days. If anyone has requested to retain the videos for any reason, I would like to urge the school teachers to review the videos to confirm the truthfulness of Joseph's version of the story.

Even if the videos are unavailable, the likelihood of Joseph tossing the cans is not going to loom large. The school cannot accept an accusation by merely listening to one person.

Thus, no compelling evidence suggests that Joseph has actually tossed the garbage.

Accusation #2- failure to stop playing immediately after the recess is over

All playing activities have to be stopped when the bell rings, and the students have to go back to the classroom immediately.

Here, Joseph is being accused of "not stopping playing ping pong" when recess time is over. But the fact is: He has already stopped playing ping pong when the bell rings, but the ball got lost. He spent five minutes looking for the ball. When he was found carrying the ping pong and the bat five minutes after the end of recess, he was accused of "still playing" the ping pong. The teacher appeared to have difficulty distinguishing the difference between "playing" the ball and "carrying" the ball.

Most importantly, the rule prohibits "all playing activities" when the bell rings, but looking for a lost ball itself is not a playing activity. Playing is something to do for fun or amusement, but looking for something is not fun at all. It could be frustrating or stressful, especially when the acts took place after the bell rang, indicating that Joseph had to look for the ball under time pressure. In other words, Joseph engaged in a stressful task after the bell rang, and did not do any playing activities after the end of the recess.

Also, Joseph simply wanted to retrieve the ball that was missing, and a ball on the ground may be able to strip people over. While complying with school rules is important, preventing other people from getting injured when it is preventable is also important. If Joseph simply went back to the classroom in order to please the teacher but made someone fall over because of the ball, would the teacher think that Joseph was doing right? Joseph had to make a difficult choice at that moment. If he chose to go back to the classroom immediately to avoid getting himself into trouble, he could be deemed obedient at the expense of others 'safety. Would the teacher prefer Joseph to take this choice?

Furthermore, this was just a one-time incident, but not a repetitive habit of Joseph. The teacher should not describe the one-time incident as a frequent problem for Joseph.

Thus, Joseph did not intentionally violate the rule of stopping playing, but he just tried to find the missing ball before he went back to the class.

Accusation #3- Talking loud in Mathematics class

Unnecessary conversations are not allowed in the class.

Here, Joseph never had "unnecessary conversations" in class. There is only one teacher teaching 30 students in the class at the same time. On many occasions, the teacher is unable to answer the questions for every student. Joseph, who has the best scores in Mathematics, always tries to help students who do not know how to handle algebra questions. In other words, he also helps the teacher to show the students how to do the exercises. It would be unfair for him to be accused of "always talking loud in the Mathematics class." In fact, he is teaching other classmates and has to talk in a voice level that others are able to hear, while teaching the students to finish the class exercises is necessary because all exercises are due at the end of the class.

If the teachers do not like the sound created by Joseph, does it mean the teachers would rather have the other classmates sitting in the classroom idle and doing nothing? If teachers are sure that everyone should sit there idle and waste time, Joseph may accommodate that. Or is it possible for the school to arrange a bigger classroom for the class of Joseph to have the mathematics class? Facts show that there are two big and vacant classrooms on campus mainly used for storage. When the sound is spread out, the teachers might not think that it is too loud.

Thus, it is necessary for Joseph to teach his classmates, and no "unnecessary conversations" ever happen in class. As such, Joseph does not violate the school rules.

Joseph vs. Oscar

Three warning letters could lead to an explusion by the school.

Here, the warning letter mentions that Oscar, who has received three warning letters, is expelled by the school. But that would be unfair to compare Joseph to Oscar because Oscar also had other dishonest behaviors, such as cheating in exams and plagiarism in school assignments, while Joseph only had weaknesses in some subjects. While dishonesty means bad morality, falling behind academically has nothing to do with one's moral character.

As such, Joseph should not be placed on the list of probation.

Other activities

The school requires every student to play one musical instrument.

Here, the violin is not the only choice available for the students, but also piano and saxophone. Joseph plans to learn saxophone and the subsidies for saxophone are not available yet. Joseph has to buy a saxophone himself when there are no subsidies, but he cannot afford it. Running out of subsidies is out of the control of Joseph, and he is still hoping to get a saxophone from the school. While he still has two months left in the waiting period, getting a saxophone is still possible.

Moreover, he is never told that he must play the violin before the waiting period is over. Without further communication from the faculty, it would be unfair to accuse Joseph of "not practicing playing his violin for his music class." The school rules allow him to choose one musical instrument he likes, and that is his right. He plans to turn to another instrument if the saxophone is still unavailable when the waiting period is over. Blaming him before the end of the waiting period is unfair.

Thus, Joseph does not violate the rule by refusing to play violin in the music class.

Contests

Inside the school

No contests are mandatory in the school, but it would be a plus to join the contest, inside or outside of the school.

Here, Joseph did not join the singing contest with the rest of the class two months ago because he started having symptoms of Covid, and he did not want others to get infected because of him. Eventually, he found that he was not infected with Covid. It was unclear why Joseph needed one whole week to find out he was not infected, either because the test kit was unavailable or he wanted to be safe by testing multiple times, but it was reasonable for him to decline joining the singing contest when he believes that he could have infected with Covid.

If Joseph ignores the possibility and joins the singing contest, he would have put the health of other students at risk, which would be a selfish act.

Furthermore, even if Joseph chooses not to participate, regardless of his health condition, it is not a mistake or violation since the school rules do not make participation mandatory or to be the basic requirement of the school curriculum. Rules show that participation is encouraged in order to promote a sense of unity among students, but students can still choose what they are interested in to strengthen the sense of unity.

It would be important for the school to acknowledge that the sense of unity is not equivalent to joining something students dislike or have no passion for. In other words, Joseph is free to choose to participate in other contests, such as judo. The original purpose of these activities are to strengthen the sense of unity among students, but eventually, the goals turn out to be tools for attacking students.

Thus, not participating in the singing contest is not a violation of the school rules. Joseph skipped the singing contest due to his safety concern for other students, and that has nothing to do with whether he has a sense of unity.

Outside school

Joseph vs. Barbara

For contests outside of the school, the school representative has to be chosen by the principal, and the teachers would make at least two recommendations to the principal.

Here, Barbara has the highest score in Science, and Joseph has the second highest. It is reasonable for the principal to pick the student scoring the highest to join the contest on behalf of the school. If the principal also appoints Joseph, he would be glad to participate. But it would be unfair to compare Joseph to Barbara who wins the contest, when Joseph is not even given a chance to join or attend the contest. Blaming Joseph for non-participation is equivalent to blaming the choice made by the principal.

Moreover, it is also unclear if Joseph is ever recommended by the teacher to the principal. Even when Joseph's score is the second highest among the class, the principal may not know Joseph's talent without the recommendation of the teachers. If the principal never learns the name Joseph and never considers choosing him to be the school representative, why would Joseph be blamed for non-participation in the contest held outside the school?

Thus, it is not the fault of Joseph for being unable to join the contest on behalf of the school.

Merits

Punctuality

The school starts at 8:15 am and ends at 3:15 pm.

Here, Joseph is a punctual student. Facts show that he never comes late to school, indicating that he takes his learning very seriously, although he does not perform well in every subject.

Thus, Joseph does not have the problem of tardiness, which would subject the student to disciplinary action.

Willingness to help other students

The school values all good conduct of students.

Here, Joseph is willing to help other students who are weak in Mathematics. But, the teacher who issued the warning letter failed to recognize the good conduct of Joseph and simply focused on the sound created by Joseph when he was helping other students.

Thus, the warning letter apparently does not reflect the full picture of reality.

Conclusion: Issuing a warning letter does not make sense

Based on the foregoing discussion, it does not make sense for the school to issue a warning letter to Joseph when he did not have problems with discipline or ethics. He simply falls behind on some subjects, but he is not yet given a tutoring class for him to improve; for the subjects he performs well, he is eager to help other students. It is unclear why the teachers at the school would interpret his merits to be problems. I strongly urge the school to rescind the warning letter issued to Joseph.

Explanations of the sample writing

Rule 1: Taking advantage of uncertainties

Facts for elaboration

When there are uncertainties, vagueness or lack of complete pictures on any points, you might take advantage of them to fulfill your purposes in the discussion.

Example: "If students come to the class later than the teacher of that particular class, the students would be deemed late to the class and would be recorded in the school record of the students."

Here, there is no exact time to distinguish what is punctuality and what is tardiness. The standard is that all students are required to be in the classroom before the teacher shows up. That means even if the teacher was 10 minutes late and the particular student was just 9 minutes late and was able to enter the classroom before the teacher came, the student would be deemed "punctual." Rules like this are very helpful for your analysis.

Rule 2: Paying attention to the keywords

When you handle a rule, do not just apply it and use it in a way the same as the impression left in your mind, but instead, go back to the written rule to digest every keyword.

Example 1: "For students who score below passing scores, they would be referred to a special tutoring class after school and participation would be mandatory for students on probation."

From this rule, we know that students who are not doing well in a class must attend the special tutoring class, and that is not a choice for a student who scores low. However, the students have to be "referred" to the class, meaning their roles are passive. There are no methods for them to sign up for the class, but they have to wait to be referred. That means the school takes control of making this arrangement. For whatever reason students do not receive any notices from the school, the students should not be blamed. Even though common sense tells us students can call the school to ask, the rules do not specify they have to contact the school if they are not referred. In other words, even though students do not call to follow up with the school, they would not be deemed violating any school rules.

Example 2: "No unnecessary conversations are allowed in all classes."

When Joseph has admitted, that he talked to his classmates in the Mathematics class, the only way you can defend him would be to show that the conversations are, in fact, necessary. (Because the existence of conversations is not denied) As long as the conversations are proven to be necessary, Joseph would not be deemed violating the rule.

Rule 3: Find out the unreasonableness of the allegations

Defeat the unreasonable allegations

When someonc has decided to accuse another person, he or she tends to point out all negative things about the accused, which are very likely to include unreasonable descriptions with unfair prejudice. Do not be distracted or misled by that accuser's dominancy. Focus on the nature of the words included in the allegations indicating unreasonableness and the existence of bias; The bias would jeopardize the trustworthiness of the allegations.

Example 1: "For contests outside of the school, the school representative has to be chosen by the principal, and the teacher would make at least two recommendations to the principal."

The principal is the decision-making party

This fact states that the principal is the party to decide who can join contests on behalf of the school, and the teachers would recommend at least two students for the principal to choose from. The teacher pointed out that Barbara won the science contest on behalf of the school. But did Joseph ever have a chance to join any contests outside of the school? If the principal did not pick him from the list, not winning the contest would be outside the control of Joseph; if the teachers never recommended Joseph to the principal, Joseph would have no control either. The foundation of winning a contest is to be given a chance to participate. If a chance is never given to him, never winning a contest on behalf of the school would not be his problem.

The teacher has bias

For something Joseph had no control at all, he should not be blamed. Why did the teacher try to belittle Joseph by emphasizing how good Barbara is? It does not sound fair to Joseph. When you defend Joseph, you have to point that out.

Rule 4: Do not waste time on irrelevant numbers, figures or data.

<u>What are numbers with no real relevancy?</u>

What is irrelevant? That refers to something which has no impact on the analysis of the main issues.

-Example 1: "Every recess lasts for 15 minutes."

No one ever complains about whether there is enough time for one recess. The controversy in the PT was that Joseph failed to go back to the classroom immediately after one recess because he lost his ball.

-Example 2: "Students or their parents who do not agree with the allegations made in the warning letter must submit a responding letter for appeal within 90 days."

Be mindful of "fake relevancy"

The 90-day rule is just indicating a "fake relevancy" because there is no controversy about the expiration date of the appeal, or no facts show that time is tight for the appeal. As such, you do not need to waste time talking about this rule.

To submit a blank paper?

Here, the task is about writing a response letter to appeal for Joseph, so your focus is to write the context of the letter. You would not say "since 90 days is over, or appears to be over, I do not need to write anything." Then, you would turn in a blank PT.

If dates are given and the deadline is over

However, if dates are given in the facts, and 90 days are already over, then at the end of the writing, you may have to say, "despite the 90-day rule, please accept this responding letter for appeal due to……"

It is almost done!

The last hurdle to practice law

You and I have spent a few years in law schools. We all completed many courses, finished many assignments, and took many exams in order to graduate. We also spent much effort reviewing all the doctrines we learned in law school. We also spent time taking MPRE paid for moral character examination, including doing fingerprints. With all of the above completed, the bar exam would be the last hurdle for us to practice law in California.

You already invested a lot

It would be very frustrating to fail the bar over and over again. But if we do not jump over this hurdle, all previous efforts would be wasted. If you are happy to be a paralegal and a legal assistant, you do not need to take the baby bar, or MPRE, or pay for the moral character examination. You spent so much time, effort and money taking all of the above steps, indicating you want to, and you believe you are capable of practicing law in California. Do not let the multiple failures in the bar exam upset the apple cart!

Passing the bar exam would be an important milestone

Passing the bar exam would be an important milestone in one's life. From the day we swear in to be attorneys, we are committed to different obligations, and we are supposed to meet a higher standard of work when we practice laws.

A professional qualification is also a source of dignity and income

It is especially important to pass the bar when we are beyond middle ages or almost reach the senior ages. That is my perception: when I have no more youthfulness and beauty, and my health gets worse, I need a professional license to confirm my own value. In our younger days, we might prioritize other aspects of life over our professional qualifications, including dating, weddings, having children, buying houses, traveling, etc. But when we reach 50, and starting to have hair loss, osteoporosis, and presbyopia, our professional qualifications would be a source of dignity and respect for us, as opposed to unemployed old people with gray hair or hunchback. Professional qualifications are essential for us to find jobs with decent pay. I would not be able to work for fast food shops or stores selling boba milk tea when I reach 50 because my legs would hurt from standing for the whole day. Or if nobody wants to hire me, I would be able to open my own law firm with my attorney's license. If you have other licenses, taking the bar exam would be one of your choices, but if you do not have other licenses, please continue to work hard to pass the bar, in order to guarantee a way to make a living for the rest of your life.

If money is no object to you and you just want to pass the bar to fulfill your dream, then you can relax a little bit and take your time to pass the bar. However, taking the bar exam requires a lot of energy. It is good to do it earlier in your life when you still have enough energy. You would not want to pass out in the exam session with PT lasting for 3.5 hours after reading a great deal of information. The older we get, the more likely we will be bothered by health problems; those health issues would complicate the already complicated exam questions. If you are sure you want to be an attorney, please formulate a systematic and realistic plan to make your dream come true!

My attorney's license refreshes my life

My attorney's license in fact, refreshes my life. I stopped feeling repetitive or bored after I became an attorney in California because there were so many new forms to fill out, new procedures to learn, and new case types to handle. If you want to "click" this "refresh" button, stay focused on passing the bar exam!

Made in United States
Troutdale, OR
11/03/2026

56845409R00259